Communication and Cooperation in the Virtual Workplace

For my husband Bert
Thanks for your love and your input into
this book. Besides this book, we have our
own little common project: the birth of our first child.
Bert, you complete me!

For Geert
Thanks for your cooperation, input and
especially your friendship! Strong Ties!

Communication and Cooperation in the Virtual Workplace

Teamwork in Computer-Mediated-Communication

Gaby Sadowski-Rasters

Regional Urban Coordinator, Municipality of Eindhoven, The Netherlands

Geert Duysters

Professorial Fellow, UNU-MERIT and Professor of Organization Science, Eindhoven University of Technology, The Netherlands

Bert M. Sadowski

Associate Professor, Eindhoven University of Technology, The Netherlands

Edward Elgar

Cheltenham, UK • Northampton, MA, USA

© Gaby Sadowski-Rasters, Geert Duysters and Bert M. Sadowski, 2006

Published by
Edward Elgar Publishing Limited
Glensanda House
Montpellier Parade
Cheltenham
Glos GL50 1UA
UK

Edward Elgar Publishing, Inc.
William Pratt House
9 Dewey Court
Northampton
Massachusetts 01060
USA

A catalogue record for this book
is available from the British Library

Library of Congress Cataloguing-in-Publication Data
Sadowski-Rasters, Gaby, 1975-
    Communication and co- operation in the virtual workplace : teamwork in computer-mediated-communication / Gaby Sadowski-Rasters, Geert Duysters, Bert Sadowski.
        p. cm.
    Includes bibliographical references and index.
    1. Virtual work teams. 2. Telematics–Social aspects. 3. Virtual corporations. 4. Communication–Psychological aspects. 5. Communication in organizations–Case studies. I. Duysters, Geert, 1966- II. Sadowski, Bert. III. Title.
    HD66.S23 2006
    302.3'5–dc22   2006011390

ISBN-10: 1 84542 587 1
ISBN-13: 978 1 84542 587 6

Printed and bound in Great Britain by MPG Books Ltd, Bodmin, Cornwall

Contents

Introduction

Communication is the most important activity of scientists, technicians and managers in terms of working time spent (Ackhoff and Halbert 1958; Frost and Whitley 1971; Allen 1970). Several studies have shown that the amount of communication is positively related to performance (see, e.g., Pelz and Andrews 1976). Today, we can also find researchers working together even though they are not physically in the same room or even in the same building. Even beyond research labs, many other organizations are also attempting to transform their structures and processes through virtual teamwork, global integration and networking. Virtual teamwork has been made possible by electronic networks that support computer-mediated-communication (CMC). Such communication networks are expected to enable organization members to work more flexibly, to span contexts and boundaries, and to collaborate more effectively (Orlikowski and Yates 1994). The problem of distance is no longer an issue: distance has been pronounced dead. 'With the invention of groupware, people expect to communicate easily with each other and accomplish difficult work even though they are remotely located or rarely overlap in time. Major corporations launch global (virtual) teams, expecting that technology will make "virtual collocation" possible' (Olson and Olson 2000: 139).

Key issues

- Improved communication = improved performance
- Electronic networks have enabled virtual teamwork
- Distance is declared dead

Does virtual communication really work? The answer to that question probably is: yes, but not always – just like face-to-face communication does not always work. In spite of all enthusiasm, much uncertainty remains about the prospects of virtual teams and technology that supports collaboration. By now, the examples of grandiose failures are at least as numerous as examples of huge successes (Robey and Boudreau 1999; van den Besselaar et al., 2001). Failures cannot be explained by virtuality alone and neither can the successes. More factors need to be considered. It is highly unlikely that the collocation versus non-collocation dilemma can be solved on the basis of technical arguments, if only because technology is constantly developing. The people who argue that 'distance is dead' may always fall back to the assertion that distance *will be* dead very soon because new technologies will overcome all sorts of constraints.

Despite recent technological development, there still is a large number of researchers and practitioners (see Olson and Olson 2000) who argue that interaction at a distance (using contemporary technologies as well as improved technologies that are expected to be there in the next 50 years) will never be able to replace collocated interaction. None the less, these authors emphasize the need for technological improvements to make effective virtual teams possible. They suggest that advances in technology (e.g. greater bandwidth) in combination with well-designed organizational arrangements and well-prepared virtual team members will suffice to approximate some aspects of face-to-face communication, and they also point out that in the future technical capabilities may arise that are in some way superior to face-to-face options (Olson and Olson 2000: 143). The authors make a distinction between 'behavior that will change for the better when the technology achieves certain qualities' and 'behavior that will never change'. But they keep warning that 'collaborative work at a distance will be difficult to do for a long time, if not forever' (ibid.: 173). And although the technology of the future might be able to support collaborative work better, Olson and Olson remain ultimately skeptical: 'it is our belief that in these future descriptions, distance will continue to matter'.

The position adopted by Olson and Olson can be traced back to an older research tradition. In the media richness theory (MRT) of the 1980s it was argued that the potential richness or leanness of communication is an inherent property of the communication medium. Rich communication was deemed only possible if 'rich' media were being used. The first empirical studies in the field of CMC focused on the choice of the proper medium for cooperation and communication. It was argued that cooperation requiring intensive ('rich') communication would have to be based on the use of 'rich' media, defined as media that allow for the exchange of various kinds of signals between people. Face-to-face communication was ranked as the richest form of communication, because of its capacity to transmit the highest levels of non-verbal cues. Lean media such as e-mail were seen as impersonal, technical and distant (Daft and Lengel 1986).

The view that face-to-face is the preferred communication medium continues to be influential. Weisband (2002: 407) argues that in distributed work, there is considerable uncertainty about others' behaviors: 'Because of delays in remote communication, feedback about others' behaviors is difficult to obtain. With delayed feedback or inaccurate feedback, messages may require several iterations for clarification. Some messages are long, making a response effortful and time consuming.' To reduce this uncertainty, group members need information about the remote work and what other group members are doing. All interdependent work entails uncertainty about others' behaviors. 'Will other group members complete their part of the work in time? Will they do the work they said they would do? Will they pay attention to quality? Will they be available to work this weekend?' Some argue that in face-to-face groups, feedback about what others are doing is immediate and can be acquired passively. Group members are able to observe who attends meetings or participates in hallway conversations (Kraut et al., 2001). It is also possible to glance over another person's shoulder to see if he is working, or you can hear the sound of a particular machine and know what work is being done (Olson et al., 2002; Gutwin et al., 1996). In contrast, in virtual teams there are long periods of silence during which team members will not obtain any information about the team-mates' activities. Virtual team members often have to rely entirely on the messages that appear on the computer screen to figure out what other members of the work group are doing. However, being a virtual team does not per se mean that members cannot pick up the phone and ask for information, therewith supplementing e-mail communication with other forms of communication.

Advantages of face-to-face vis-à-vis virtual communication

- Immediate feedback
- Less uncertainty about others' behavior
- More personal and informal

The MRT approach has been extensively used in analyses of computer-mediated communication (CMC) (Daft and Lengel 1986; Rice 1984; Rice and Love 1987; Spears and Lea 1992). Over time, however, theoretical and practical objections have been raised against this theory, which has led to several alternative approaches that argue that CMC media can (sometimes) be as rich as face-to-face communication (Townsend et al., 1998; Ngwenyama and Lee 1997; Spears and Lea 1992).

The earliest criticism of MRT stuck to the idea that technology can be an obstacle for rich communication, but argued instead that technology would be able to conquer some of the barriers in, say, the next 50 years. The idea that face-to-face communication is the richest, most effective, warm, personal, trust-enabling form of communication has remained dominant in this approach. However, as technology improves, it is argued that it might be able to imitate, substitute, or in some cases even outperform face-to-face communication. Both media richness theory (MRT)-related research and these early critical approaches still tend to focus on the role of technology in communication, thereby excluding many other factors that may enable or constrain (virtual) communication.

This emphasis on the role of technology has been questioned by later studies. Lipnack and Stamps (1997, 2000), for instance, suggest that questions about communication at a distance cannot be answered, or only partly, by referring to technological possibilities. These authors are well aware that technology alone is not enough to make a virtual team work. They state that the success of a virtual team depends 90 percent on the people and 10 percent on the technology. In the present study we will take these remarks as our point of departure, exploring the prospects of an approach in which technology is one among many factors that, in conjunction, shape the communication processes to evolve in virtual teams.

Thus far, the field of CMC has been dominated by questions that tend to juxtapose face-to-face communication and CMC, such as:

1. Do the characteristics of CMC impose strict limitations on the functioning of a virtual team?
2. Under what circumstances (if any) is face-to-face communication necessary for the functioning of a team?
3. What are the characteristics of communication processes when face-to-face communication is replaced by CMC?

The present study will also take up these questions, but in the course of the research its scope has been broadened to reflect the insight that the possibilities of CMC are probably underestimated, if face-to-face communication is considered as the default optimum solution. If we leave the perspective of comparing CMC and face-to-face communication, and start looking at CMC as a communication medium in its own right, increasingly used for the purpose of communication and cooperation in dispersed (non-collocated) teams, questions can be asked that reflect new theoretical views concerning communication and media use (particularly emphasizing the importance of context), or reflect technological or organizational advances in relation to communication and media use:

4. What are the conditions for effective communication in a virtual team? Where do they differ for effective communication in a non-virtual team?
5. Are there any special problems and risks involved in the management and organization of teams that mix virtual and face-to-face modes of communication?

We will explore these questions through a critical review of the literature as well as through detailed studies of the communication patterns developing in three different virtual teams. Reading the literature, it is difficult to come to firm conclusions because so much emphasis is put on the technology that constrains or enables communication, while little attention is paid to other constraining or enabling factors such as the organizational and institutional context of the cooperation and communication. The MRT has influenced the nature of the discussion with an emphasis on the technical characteristics of communication. In addition to that, the lack of attention to non-technical factors probably also originates from the fact that much of the previous research was very experimental, creating virtual teams for study purposes but ignoring real-life situations. In our study a broader point of view will be taken through examining real-life teams in different organizational and institutional contexts. We will not systematically compare different forms of CMC – which is why we did not include this subject in our list of questions – as we are primarily interested in communication and collaboration processes as evolving in such real-life virtual teams.

In sum, we will explore in this study how social, organizational and institutional factors complement technological factors in the development of computer-mediated communication in teams. We seek to identify the conditions that enable or constrain the (virtual) collaboration process.

Throughout our qualitative analysis (chapters 3, 4 and 5), we were extensively relying on comments provided by interviewees. In order to protect their anonymity, we decided not to specify in detail which member of the Delta team (chapter 3), Advance group (chapter 4) and Debian community (chapter 5) have been the source of the comments. In some cases (e.g. if secondary data sources were consulted), we provided the source for the quote.

This book consists of three parts: theory, case studies (method) and reflection. Chapter 1 provides a theoretical overview of the literature in the field of CMC. The first part of this theoretical chapter is general but becomes more refined in relation to the specific case studies conducted. The first part of the literature overview focuses mainly on the media richness tradition and the 'substitution hypothesis' (Nohria and Eccles 1992), i.e. the view that CMC may replace face-to-face communication. We will systematically compare the different approaches in the CMC field. The second part will show that the questions about substitution were not as important as we thought. Chapter 2 will present the methodological approach(es) used in this study, including the research questions and methodology. Chapter 3 (Delta case), 4 (Advance case) and 5 (Debian case) are the real-life case studies. These studies were chosen in a cumulative way and each provided input and questions for the next study. The final part of this study consists of a comparison of the three cases (Chapter 6) and our conclusions and suggestions for future research (Chapter 7).

1. The prospects of virtual teamwork: a theoretical discussion

Differences in local physical context, time zones, culture and language all persist despite the use of distance technologies. Some distance work is possible today, but some aspects of it will remain difficult if not impossible to support even in the future. (Olson and Olson 2000: 141)

Versus:

When we think of team building, we often conjure up images of three-legged relay races at company picnics or long afternoons spent in dreary conference rooms. In other words, activities we do together, face-to-face. It's time to let go of such archaic thinking because today's virtual times call for virtual action. Waning are the days of building business relationships on a handshake across a conference table, replaced by sometimes unseen business associates clicking a mouse. Technology has expanded our scope of team building efforts. Teams are not dependent upon physical location, but upon common goals.

(Lipnack and Stamps 1997: 34)

1.1 INTRODUCTION

In this chapter we will discuss theories in which the eventual 'death of distance' is defended as well as theories positing that distance matters and will continue to do so. The discussion between proponents of both theories provides us with many factors, conditions and process descriptions that need to be examined in detail, and in real-life settings, before we are able to accept one of the positions defended. Moreover, considering the arguments given and examining actual processes of virtual communication in teams will allow us to make suggestions to researchers and practitioners in the realm of communication and collaboration in virtual teams.

1.2 THE STANDARD APPROACH TO CMC: IMPERSONAL, TECHNICAL AND DISTANT

Researchers in the field viewed computer-mediated communication (CMC) as impersonal (unsociable, cold and insensitive), technical and distant (Lea and Spears 1995: 214). It was assumed that the 'inherent characteristics' of the CMC context reduce the amount of non-verbal and contextual communicative cues and thus diminish the level of intimacy between interactants (Soukup 2000: 411). Therefore, CMC should only be used in simple task-related interaction. Perhaps the most widely used theory in research on virtual communication is media richness theory (MRT) (Daft and Lengel 1984, 1986; Daft et al., 1987) – sometimes referred to as information richness theory (Ngwenyama and Lee 1997) or channel richness theory (Blecherman 1999) – which states that CMC will never allow rich interaction since CMC does not allow for non-verbal cues.

Media richness is defined as 'the ability of information to change understanding within a time interval' (Daft and Lengel 1986: 560). Meeting face to face is seen as the richest communication medium. Electronic mail is considered as a 'lean' medium as it does not offer many cues, while memos and voice mail are often viewed as 'lean' because these media provide slow feedback (Fulk et al., 1990; Duxbury and Neufeld 1999). Some authors, however, consider voice mail a rich medium, on the basis of its capacity to convey vocal information (El-Shinnawy and Markus 1997: 447). The point is important since media choice seems to depend considerably upon designations such as 'rich' and 'lean'. MRT suggests that a rich medium enables users to communicate quickly and to better understand ambiguous or equivocal messages, and thus is to be preferred for equivocal tasks, while leaner media can be preferred for low equivocality tasks because in that case rich media provide users with too much information and superfluous messages (Dennis et al., 1999).

MRT assumes that a 'rich medium' is a necessary condition for 'rich communication'. The latter is defined as communication that reduces equivocality. Weick's (1979) view is accepted that cooperation requires that equivocality is reduced. That is, in order to work with others, one must be able to make causal inferences: 'The problem of equivocality for a recipient is that, given an output, the receiver can't decide what input generated it'. Rephrasing equivocality as 'the lack of shared knowledge about a given task' (Weick 1979: 180), Kock (1998: 297) notes that this lack prohibits reduction of uncertainty, which he describes as 'the lack of information in carrying out a given task, and therefore as being reduced by access to information relevant to the task'. In other words, when cooperating, people must be able to understand, if only approximately, what others do and why they do it. Only when tasks are simple and predictable (i.e. uncertainty is low) is coordination possible on the basis of rules, standards and procedures. However, when tasks are complicated, direct communication is considered necessary between those whose activities need to be coordinated (Fulk and Collins-Jarvis 2001). According to MRT, this is why organizational communication takes place (Kock 1998). Note that 'lack of shared knowledge' must not be read as 'lack of shared goals'. In fact, at least in Weick's theory of the formation of cooperative structures (or groups) the sharing of ideas about means will precede the sharing of ideas about goals or ends: 'Partners in a collective structure share space, time, and energy, but they need not share visions, aspirations, or intentions. That sharing comes later, if it ever comes at all' (Weick 1979: 91).

While developed to support decision-making on traditional means of intra-organizational communication such as face-to-face meetings, telephone conversations and memos, MRT was soon to be extended to new communication media, such as electronic mail and video conferencing (Trevino et al., 1987; Yu 1999; El-Shinnawy and Markus 1997; Baron 1998). In this extended domain, MRT argues that CMC cannot substitute for face-to-face communication in complex situations and, by implication, that electronically mediated exchange is only adequate for routine communication. Virtual teams cannot be expected to perform well if issues are complex or ambiguous. However, it is assumed that particularly virtual teams perform tasks that are rarely routine: 'The social dimension of an organization is especially crucial in the network organization, because the type of coordinated action that is required is rarely routine' (Nohria and Eccles 1992: 292). This social dimension depends heavily on face-to-face interaction to support the coordinated action. Following MRT, Nohria and Eccles state that ' "Rich" media – those that transmit higher levels of non-verbal cues – are more appropriate in ambiguous or relational communication situations, "lean" media are more appropriate in less ambiguous, routine situations' (ibid.: 295).

We summarize the alleged limitations of lean communication as opposed to face-to-face communication:

1. Lean media reduce the social context cues and the social presence is weakened. As a result team members have little real-time knowledge about each other.
2. Lean media prevent the sharing of complex and ambiguous messages. Thus they preclude the transmission of equivocal messages.
3. Lean media make it difficult to discuss human and social topics and build personal relationships.
4. As a specific form of lean communication, e-mail communication increases the amount of flaming within conversations. 'Flaming is regarded as a form of uninhibited behaviour and is typically defined as language that includes swearing, insults and name-calling (Siegel et al., 1986) or profanity, negative affect and "typographic energy", i.e. capitalizations and exclamation points (Sproull & Kiesler 1986)' (Lea et al., 1992: 95).

5. E-mail communication is expected to be formal and cannot initiate or sustain informal communication.

In short, these limitations, if they applied, would make it nearly impossible to build good (working) relationships using e-mail. That is not, however, the outcome reported by various recent studies of the use of e-mail in actual work settings, as indicated. In the next section, we will reconsider the above-mentioned points, and discuss arguments that have been put forward to refute them.

Key issues

- Computer-mediated communication is argued to be impersonal (unsociable, cold and insensitive), technical and distant.
- Traditional theory argues that CMC cannot substitute for face-to-face communication in complex situations and, by implication, that electronically mediated exchange is only adequate for routine communication.

Before discussing the refinements added to the MRT, and the theories arguing that CMC can be warm and personal, this section will provide a general overview of the objections raised against the MRT.

Strictly speaking, the claims of MRT have already been refuted by some examples of complex or ambiguous issues that were successfully dealt with using CMC and cooperation. So far, the theory has largely been used in studies that compared face-to-face and computer-mediated communication. The findings from these studies are mixed, or even conflicting (Sudweeks and Allbritton 1996).

While there is a solid body of research supporting the MRT, an equally large body of studies does not. The studies presenting confounding evidence (thus tending to refute MRT) are more recent:

> It is no surprise that research giving conflicting evidence tends to be of more recent origin. With the incorporation of more modern communication technologies in the research design, studies are only recently in a position to expose the predisposition of the media richness theory towards traditional communication media. The increased prevalence of technology usage in organisations in general may provide another explanation. (Yu 1997: 2.4.1.1)

1.3   TOWARDS AN EXPLANATION OF SUCCESS IN VIRTUAL TEAMS

Not only social psychology, behavioral studies and collective-level theories have shed new light on the discussions within the field of communication media; organization sciences (e.g. Markus 1994) have also produced interesting new insights in explaining the working of virtual teams. Many organization theorists (e.g. Gallivan 2001) have predicted the emergence of the networked or virtual firm as a model for the design of future organizations. This cannot be taken to suggest that only a single form of non-collocation work exists: we may distinguish, for instance, networked organizations, virtual teams, global alliances, dispersed new product development (NPD) teams, communities of practice. Next, it has become clear that the circumstances or the context in which virtual communication is required, possible or desirable can vary enormously. In addition, different circumstances may require different forms of communication and different communication media. The alternative media choice theories (collective-level theories) as discussed in the previous section have already provided evidence that the context of the organization is important for the way new technologies are incorporated and used within the organization.

The open source software (OSS) movement has often been taken as an example of a successful virtual organization/community, but only recently have researchers developed an interest in what organizations can learn from the OSS world, e.g. Markus et al. (2000); Tuomi (2000); Dafermos (2001); Hertel et al. (2001); von Hippel and von Krogh (2003); Reinhardt (2003).

Some of these lessons remain to be learned. Little rigorous research has been done on how traditional organizations can implement and benefit from OSS practices (Sharma et al., 2002), and despite the success of the OSS model, commercial organizations find it difficult to build a business model that complies with the open source paradigm.

Although the OSS community might be an extreme example of a virtual organization in which most of the accepted organizational circumstances and factors (e.g. working according to a contract) are not of any influence, other factors *do* apply to the more commercial organizations.

Susman and Majchrzak (2003) argue that despite the attention to virtual collaboration, there is much not yet understood about effective virtual collaboration to support new product design. They have focused on answering questions such as: do people learn differently, interact differently, manage knowledge differently, and share perspectives differently in a virtual environment, as compared to collated team effort? Do the features of today's collaborative tools sufficiently address the needs of virtual collaborators?

Markus (1994) found that there could be drastic variations of the usage and acceptance of CMC between units within the same organization. These variations, which stem from norms, values and standards engendered by the institutional environment, in turn reshape these norms, values and standards. It is likely that the differences between *different* organizations will be even larger.

The key issue is this: why it is difficult for 'traditional organizations' to copy or to learn from OSS communities? The above description of circumstances and contexts that vary according to different projects may already provide the beginnings of an answer. In this study we will examine three different virtual projects, one being an OSS project. We are highly interested in the contextual differences between these projects, and how these contextual differences influence the virtual cooperation.

1.4 CONCLUSIONS

Research on cooperation and communication via CMC has drawn many (conflicting) conclusions with respect to working in virtual teams.

One of the early views of CMC was that it was both liberating and limiting. It made communication across time and space possible, but in a 'cold' and 'computerized' manner (Walther 1996: 33). It has been suggested that CMC cannot substitute for face-to-face communication on complex or ambiguous issues (Nohria and Eccles 1992), nor would CMC be able to build trust within a team (Handy 1995). It was argued that, due to the relative anonymity that filters out social and contextual cues, CMC is very lean compared to face-to-face communication. Some researchers thought of ways to overcome this leanness by stating that future technological improvement will ensure richer communication technologies. Others have shifted away from this technical view on communication and used psychological and behavioral arguments to contradict the statements of the MRT. For instance the argument of anonymity was reversed in a positive, 'rich' way: 'However, this anonymity provided by CMC has also been heralded as a way to avoid common dysfunctions found in groups such as social loafing and groupthink (e.g. Stroebe & Diehl 1994) and to equalize participants in terms of gender and status (e.g. Siegel et al., 1986)' (Rogers 2002: 35). And 'it has become clear over the years, as research has accumulated, that CMC is not always as fixed and stark as early research indicated' (Walther 1996: 3).

What has become obvious from this chapter's review of the literature is that face-to-face communication is too often seen as an ideal for cooperation. Due to processes of idealization, 'face-to-face interactions have become social artifacts that seem necessarily and universally rich' (Rice and Gattiker 2001: 554). Whether researchers were optimistic or pessimistic about CMC, their judgment has (too) often been based upon expectations about the (improved) technology, as derived from the MRT paradigm.

In reality, face-to-face communication and CMC are seldom mutually exclusive. People in collocated teams send each other e-mail to confirm meetings, and people in CMC settings sometimes meet in a face-to-face setting. In both cases the comparison between face-to-face communication and communication technologies is becoming less relevant, since these forms of communication are intertwined. Moreover, it is important to note that there are forms of cooperation that would not exist without CMC, and cannot be compared with face-to-face settings.

Every organization has different features and characteristics that influence the way a virtual team is working, and it is necessary to understand the underlying organizational principles of virtual organizations. We expect that while using adequate (adjusted to the specific project and context) communication media, having agreements and norms about the way of communicating, and taking into account many more contextual aspects (yet to be identified in the case studies within this study), effective communication may occur in the absence of face-to-face communication.

This study will explore the communication patterns developed in three different geographically dispersed (or virtual) teams or communities. Analysis of each group's communication processes – patterns and developments in the use of electronic mail, the switching between electronic and face-to-face communication, seamless in many respects – will allow us to address the question whether and how electronic *communication* (*not* the medium) can be 'rich'. When putting less emphasis on the technology and its alleged richness or leanness, it will appear that topics other than technology need our attention. Chapter 2 will explain how the three different teams will be explored.

Key issues

- Face-to-face communication and CMC are seldom mutually exclusive.
- Face-to-face interactions have increasingly been seen as social artifacts that seem necessarily and universally rich.
- There are many conflicting views on the role of CMC in the communication process.

2. How to study virtual communication

2.1 CASE STUDY APPROACH

Although classical studies of CMC and MRT have been criticized on many different grounds, there is still a vast and growing body of literature that adheres to this tradition. In an attempt to overcome the main criticisms of the classic theories we aim to provide a more balanced and less biased view on the use of text-based communication. In this study we try to overcome most of the critiques as presented, as mentioned above. We conclude that a longitudinal case study approach in a real-life setting will provide us with practical and scientific findings that are more insightful than the outcomes of the experimental studies that were criticized in our previous chapter. In order to be able to provide a longitudinal real-life description of the case, we decided to monitor closely a specific virtual team, all the way from its initial start-up phase towards the end of the project. This provides a unique perspective which makes it possible to observe whether the team will gradually adapt to the usage of CMC once the team has been granted sufficient time to develop its own processes.

For our research we have chosen to follow a longitudinal case study approach which aims to gain insight into a (social) system or empirical problem within its real-life context (Yin 1994). Case studies are particularly effective when a large amount of variables that cannot be manipulated have to be dealt with, and when little information about a number of these variables is available. Given our research questions as described below and given the considerations above, the case study approach seems to be an appropriate method:

1. Do the characteristics of CMC impose strict limitations on the functioning of a virtual team?
2. Under what circumstances (if any) is face-to-face communication necessary for the functioning of a team?
3. What are the characteristics of communication processes when face-to-face communication is replaced by CMC?

4. What are the conditions for effective communication in a virtual team? Where do they differ from effective communication in a non-virtual team?
5. Are there any special problems and risks involved in the management and organization of teams that mix virtual and face-to-face modes of communication?

2.2 CHOICE OF THE CASE STUDIES

The case studies were chosen in a cumulative way. We expected differences in the use of communication media, acceptance of CMC, and different constraining and enabling factors for communication and cooperation, because of the different organizational and institutional contexts of the three cases. From the descriptions of the different organizations/teams (and the contexts connected with these) this will become more apparent.

The cases chosen for this study represent three different forms of collaboration. Two of them were R&D projects in an EU context. The first case was a European project involving seven university researchers, which was fully paid for by the European Commission. There are many examples of academics working together on research papers while being located at different places in the world, which will be discussed in case study 1 (Chapter 3).

The other EU project was only partly funded by the EU, and was situated in an aerospace engineering context, with 53 partners involved. The European Commission is interested in stimulating European-wide cooperation, especially when the project partners are using information technology to communicate. Moreover, the EU wants to stimulate cooperation within the EU in order to stay competitive with the rest of the world. The aerospace industry wants to use information technologies to stimulate cooperation and to stay competitive, which will be examined in case study 2 (Chapter 4).

The EU projects both had a three-year duration, their project management relied on structures provided by the European Commission, and they both made use of the Internet for cooperation next to face-to-face meetings. Debian, the third case study, is an ongoing project, that is, a project that has no duration limit. Debian is an open source community, thus an instance of what is considered to be the earliest form of Internet-based collaboration (see von Hippel and von Krogh 2003 for an overview).

Studying three specific organizations introduces differences in organizational culture and structure as a possible (partial) explanation of communication differences. If background conditions vary, while the communication tools used are largely the same, communication differences should be attributed to variation in the background conditions, rather than to the usage of rich or lean communication media.

As explained earlier, it is unsatisfactory to study distant communication without examining and discussing the context in which the communication takes place. In order to test our idea that the organizational context defines the communication needs and influences the way communication and cooperation is enabled or constrained by CMC, we will study three cases. The first case (Delta) tests whether or not the medium permitted all forms of (rich) communication. The second case (Advance) will examine context-related reasons for a lack of communication and cooperation. The third case (Debian) will show a community that fully utilizes the possibilities of the new communication media, and, in doing so, has developed new organizational forms.

2.3   DATA COLLECTION AND ANALYSIS

Each of the three case study descriptions is based on a variety of data sources. Internal documents are the first source. This includes documents concerning the content and the process of the project being studied, as well as documents pertaining to the context of the projects.

Semi-structured interviews (both face to face and by telephone) were used as the second source of information in all three case studies. Dafermos (2001) argues that semi-structured interviews provide rich detailed data of greater value than straight question-and-answer sessions, especially when the research is explorative. These semi-structured interviews were also useful in developing an ongoing conversation with the interviewees. The face-to-face interviews were taped and transcribed verbatim. As a check, the interviews were sent to the interviewees. The interviews that were undertaken by telephone were written down on paper as accurately as possible. Again, we sent out these texts to the interviewees in order to check whether they were accurate. In our case studies, we frequently used interview fragments. We have not referred to interviewees by name (for reasons of confidentiality), but by function or role in the project.

In our second case study we also used an online survey to gather additional data. In the next sections the data collection will be described in more depth. We will show that, for the first case, there was an involvement from one of the authors as a member of the Delta team. In the second case study, as well as data gathering, interviews and the survey, a project meeting was also attended.

In addition to documents and interviews, for the third case we attended several conferences, and 'lurked around' on the Debian mailing lists. The manuscript of this third case study was shown to several of the Debian members, who made some (additional) comments and adjustments.

As mentioned, two of the case studies – Delta and Advance – concerned projects of limited duration. In both studies, the attempt has been made to describe how communication evolved in the course of the project. For that reason, we present the processes and events that we observed in more or less chronological order. If possible, these processes and events are depicted as 'facts'. We are, of course, aware that the phenomena underlying these 'facts' are subject to different views and opinions. For the sake of presenting a coherent analysis, however, we have only taken such differences into account if they were obvious enough to have an observable impact on the behaviors of the actors involved. In those cases, we have tried to describe the reasons for these differences, which, especially in the Advance case study, soon revealed a variety of organizational and 'context' factors that influenced those who were engaged in communication and collaboration.

The Debian case is different in many respects, as will be seen from the next section. Debian is not a project in the traditional sense, that is, if limited duration is taken as a criterion. In the Debian project, communication processes evolve, but not in a way related to time pressure, as in the cases of Delta and Advance. Moreover, differences of view or opinion are less striking in the Debian project. Rather than focusing on project or organizational processes and how these may influence actual communication and collaboration, we have used this case study to sketch a picture of circumstances that, apparently, encourage virtual communication.

2.4   INTRODUCTION TO THE CASE STUDIES

Delta

The three cases were approached in different ways. The study on the Delta project was longitudinal and participatory. The description of Delta will show the development of mailing list and e-mail communication among team members of an emerging team, and the link between communication patterns and cooperation within the team. This description of developments over time complies with the suggestion made by Williams et al. (1979: 56) to engage in longitudinal research in computer-mediated communication: 'researchers studying new media (should) use theories, designs, and methods that take change over time into account in order to improve the meaningfulness of their results and to capture the social dynamics of new media'.

The description of Delta will rely in large part on two years of direct observation by one of the authors as a member of the team. In this respect, the case study presented here contrasts with many other field studies of virtual team communication, as researchers of virtual teams usually do not have direct access to the communication as it unfolds in such teams. However, the method used was not conventional participant observation (Atkinson and Hammersley 1994). Only after a prolonged period of 'real participation', was it realized that the history of Delta allowed a description of virtual and face-to-face communication processes that could usefully contribute to a discussion of the media richness theory. By implication, some typical problems of participant observation – getting access, role finding, balancing the roles of participant and observer – did not occur. However, two further issues, concerning 'control effect' and 'biased-viewpoint effect' (Riley 1963), need to be considered. 'Control effect' refers to changes in the process being studied that are brought about by the researcher's presence. Effects of this type did not occur, we contend, because the actions by one of the authors were only made in the context of an evolving virtual team's membership. More serious is the possibility of a 'biased-viewpoint effect'. In Riley's formulation, 'The observer, by virtue of the fact that he plays a role in the group, tends thereby to impose certain restrictions upon his own understanding of the situation' (Riley 1963: 71). Various forms of 'biased viewpoint' are listed: perceiving only those aspects of the system that are apparent from the researcher's own role, cutting oneself off from some channels of information by alliances with some, and not with other, members, and taking certain phenomena for granted as a result of increased familiarity with the group, with acceptance of prevailing stereotypes and of too neat an image of the action under study as possible consequences. To reduce such biased viewpoint, *ex post facto* interviews with several team members were added to the direct observations. These interviews were not structured; they focused on the evolution of the project as perceived by individual members (start-up, first 'virtual phase', face-to-face meeting, second 'virtual phase'), and on perceptions of the way trust, communication and cooperation evolved in the course of the project. In addition, the description could also be based on virtual documents; that is, nearly all textual communication (mailing list, e-mails) has been preserved, which means that information can easily be retrieved. An exception must be made for private e-mail, that is, e-mail communication between two team members. A considerable share of private e-mails could be consulted, however, as some team members granted access to their personal archive.

Advance

In the Advance case study, we collected general information from the project website and more detailed information from internal documents.

We gained access to personal e-mail archives, as well as to the Advance internal database in which we could see all the documents of the project. Apart from interviews, we carried out an online survey to gather additional data. The survey instrument was used as a source of complementary information to support the interview questions and the document analysis. While the interviews were mainly conducted with the higher-ranked members (TOP team members, team leaders), the survey would provide us insights in the way ordinary team members had experienced the project. The interviews were taken in a non-structured way. We had different interviews in a face-to-face setting, as well as through phone calls. Our first interview was with one of the EU reviewers of the project, who helped us to gain access to the consortium. A project proposal was written for the project management in order to get the management's approval for the study. The EU reviewer introduced us to one of the key figures in the Advance project: a member of the management team. This member granted several interviews, and helped us to retrieve documents and other sources of information that were needed. Since the project was nearly at the end when we started our research, only the rehearsal meeting for the public forum was attended. This offered the opportunity to talk informally to project members.

We identified key figures who served as informants during the research. When sending out the survey, some members reacted by e-mail, asking for the outcome of the study. This sometimes started as an e-mail conversation about the goal and subject of the research. Occasionally, members would suggest other members who could offer interesting information about the project. Because most Advance members were not located in the Netherlands, most of the interviews went through e-mail communication or phone calls. The companies in the Netherlands that were involved in the project were visited in person for interviews. We conducted nine interviews, and with some of the interviewees we had more than one session. The interviews were transcribed verbatim and were checked by the interviewees. Apart from these interviews, we had several informal e-mail conversations that helped in our case study.

The survey complemented the interviews by providing more detailed information from different members of the project. We wanted to understand the group processes in the project, the media choice preferences of participants, and their ideas about the richness of the communication. Given the myriad of issues and questions related to our study, it appeared most efficient to gather the information through a survey, since this allowed us to compare many characteristics of media usage and their influence on cooperation. Being an observation at a specific moment in time, the survey alone is not enough to identify the reasons and factors that impact on the relation between the usage of communication media and cooperation. The document analysis and the interviews have to be analyzed in connection with the survey.

Since online surveys have been noted to be more cost-effective, easier to use, have quicker response times and higher response rates than paper surveys (Bowers 1999; Kumari 1999; Jones 1999), we chose to conduct an online survey instead of a traditional (paper-based) one. To be able to answer the questionnaire the respondents had to have access to the web. Through a special link to the homepage of our study, respondents could get access. For those respondents who did not have access to the Internet, we developed a Word version of the survey and sent it by e-mail, as well as a printed version. We expected that most respondents would have access to the Internet, since the project they were involved in required an Internet connection. However, this was not always the case and we had several requests for printed versions of the survey.

The questionnaire was sent, together with an introductory e-mail, in which the purpose of the study was explained. Also enclosed were the instructions, and a password for the questionnaire was provided. On the website of the online questionnaire the same explanation was given. The input from earlier interviews, together with the findings from the Delta case study, provided a list of topics that needed further exploration, or that we wanted to test in a larger environment. The questionnaire was divided into different sections, in such a way that these sections would not be obvious to the respondents (in order to prevent them from giving deliberately consistent answers). The subjects of the sections were:

Part 1:   General questions about the respondent's involvement and role in the project and questions related to the project management.
Part 2:   Specific questions about the usage pattern and attitude towards technology or communication media.
Part 3:   Determination of subject's media choice for different tasks and different variations of the tasks. Three different communication media were discussed: face-to-face communication, e-mail communication and phone calls.
Part 4:   Determination of the complexity of the task, the clearness of the project and the different roles (leadership, new members, part-time members) in relation to the cooperation.
Part 5:   The degree that team members had to work together (task interdependence) and the influence on the communication/cooperation.
Part 6:   The degree of trust and commitment in relation to the communication and cooperation.
Part 7:   Demographic information.

We used the initial contact list (1999) to retrieve the e-mail addresses of Advance members. It listed 289 names, but there were 33 without e-mail addresses. We sent out 256 e-mails with an accompanying note. This first mailing failed to the extent that 93 were returned with the delivery notification: 'delivery has failed, your message cannot be delivered to the following recipients', or: 'the recipient name is not recognized, or no longer valid'. The reasons varied from people no longer being employed by a certain company, through e-mail address changes, to addresses in the list that were simply wrong. There were also many automatic out-of-office replies. There were a few responses of people who asked if the survey could be sent in a printed format. Of course we responded positively to these requests. Obviously, the original contact list was outdated. The contact list had to be updated very frequently because of the coming and going of the team members. The communication manager was supposed to take care of this contact list. Some of the names on the original list should not have been on that list; people responded by asking: 'Please, take me off your mailing list, since I have never really worked on Advance.' In a second attempt, 272 e-mails were sent out, but the response rate was also very low, and delivery failures were still high, so we tried to find a more up-to-date contact list. Finally, the communication manager was able to produce such a list, and he was willing to write to the Advance consortium members a supporting note to urge them to fill in the survey. He sent out 301 e-mails, but we do not know how many delivery failures occurred.

Debian

To find an open source project that would best suit our purposes, various such projects were examined. The open source project to be selected would have to be representative for the whole open source community, and have a considerable number of members. Moreover, the project needed to exist for a longer period time, and thus to have had enough time to develop; we were interested in its ongoing development. After several discussions with different participants in the open source community, the Debian project was chosen since it was one of the most structured projects in relation to communication and organization.

Our primary means of conducting this case study was by mailing list observations and interviews. We could see the past and the present of the Debian project because everything about the project could simply be found on the Internet (through the mailing lists, websites, IRC – Internet relay chat – channels, etc.). We followed the Debian project in its ongoing development and activities and asked for help from this community when the processes were difficult to understand. We identified the

Debian-devel(opment) mailing list as our focus of study, as it is the most important (the 'head' mailing list) of the project, and we analyzed a few threads of messages on the Debian-devel mailing list. Interviews were used to gain insight into the Debian community. Some of the interviews were face to face, others by e-mail. All face-to-face interviews were taped, transcribed verbatim and sent back to the interviewees for a check. In some cases, the interviews were conducted jointly with another researcher who was involved in a similar research project. After the interviews, we could discuss our observations and compare notes. This approach also was used so as not to overload the Debian developers with interview requests. Remarkable is the enormous willingness to contribute to this research, e.g. by interviews and e-mail interaction. Especially in the Netherlands the Debian developers were very supportive and helpful, and always willing to travel for an interview meeting. Even developers from other places in the world said that they would help; however, as one of them remarked: 'Of course, I'm willing to contribute, but when I detect "cluelessness" from the side of the researcher, I will invest my time in something else.'

After having established our first contacts, a kind of network developed. Members of the community pointed out: 'You could ask this member about that', or, 'I know someone who can help you with that'. In that way we were introduced to most informants and important contributors to the Debian project. Several pages on the Debian homepage also pointed out the key figures in the Debian project. Via this network approach, we met diverse programmers, from the inner circle to newcomers on the project, which made our range quite broad. In addition, we posted an overview of this case study on one of the Debian mailing lists and asked people for comments; this also brought us in touch with members of the community.

An intensive literature search and study was done in order to be able to understand the open source software (OSS) movement in general and the Debian project in particular. We read about software development projects in order to understand the specific type of work that programming is supposed to be (e.g. Kraut and Streeter 1995). For the Debian project, we have used articles on Slashdot.org, members' biographical writings and diaries, previous interviews with key members and descriptions of the group written by other researchers and key figures. We also subscribed to diverse mailing lists where we discussed research issues related to OSS communities. We also attended several OSS-related conferences and even organized one. In the next chapters we will discuss the various case studies.

3. The Delta case study

There is a world of difference between making a decision alone and making a group decision. The unique chemistry of social interaction can distil the best each member has to offer, creating a resonance of ideas and a synthesis of viewpoints. A different chemistry can stop the reaction and contaminate the product. The catalyst for such social chemistry is communication. It is the medium for the coordination and control of group activities, member socialization, group integration, and conflict management, among other functions.

(Poole and Hirokawa 1996: 3)

3.1 INTRODUCTION

This part of the book explores the communication patterns developing in a geographically dispersed (or virtual) team. The team being studied here evolved as an international group of researchers who sought to submit a European Union research proposal. For their communication, the members of this group used electronic communication (personal e-mail, mailing list), but they met face to face when important decisions had to be made.

A description of the group's communication processes – patterns and developments in the use of electronic mail; the changeover between electronic and face-to-face communication, seamless in many respects – will allow us to address the question whether and how electronic communication can be 'rich', and how this relates to media richness (see Rasters et al., 2002).

We will describe the history (mainly the start-up phase) of a virtual team consisting of researchers from several European countries who engaged in the process of writing a joint research proposal, first virtually (e-mail and mailing list communication), then in a face-to-face meeting, then virtually again, in the attempt to submit the proposal to the European Union. A description of communication patterns and events in these 'stages' will disclose media-related differences as well as similarities that are relevant for a discussion of media richness theory.

The emphasis will be on the communication patterns developing as a result of the interplay of communication medium used and (organizational) context. These patterns can be described in terms of team culture, the formation and further development of the team, the tasks of the team and the style of interaction within the team.

We will concentrate on how team members actually cooperate and communicate, instead of starting from assumptions concerning the richness or leanness of the communication media being used. Observations concerning the way communication actually unfolds will eventually allow us to review the claim of the media richness theory that teams need face-to-face communication or another allegedly rich communication medium for effective communication about complex problems or equivocal tasks.

3.2   DELTA CASE STUDY: A EUROPEAN RESEARCH PROJECT

Delta is a research project in which researchers from several different European countries combine forces to study the impact of new information and communication technologies on organizational communication and coordination. The idea to create Delta first emerged in July 1999. One researcher, who later became the project leader, started to approach researchers from all over Europe, trying to recruit them to the project. From this early stage in 1999 until August 2000, the project was little more than a loose collection of ideas that had to be transformed into a real project, and of course the researchers had to develop into a real team – not a normal project team, but a virtual one, since team members would operate from their own country with occasional face-to-face meetings.

We will divide our description of the Delta history into four periods or 'stages'. The first stage includes the start and earliest developments of Delta, from July 1999 until spring 2000. The second stage, from spring to early September 2000, is the period during which the team composition was completed. A characteristic of this period is the attempt to engage in joint virtual cooperation. The third stage is a face-to-face meeting in September 2000, arranged to settle practical issues as well as to reach agreement concerning the direction and contents of the proposal to be made. The fourth stage is the 'virtual' period that followed the face-to-face meeting, a brief description of which will cover the period from October until December 2000.

3.3   ISSUES

Teams Do Not 'Just' Exist: The Early Days of Delta

The Delta team was largely formed by Mario, the later project leader. The idea for Delta was born at a congress from discussions he had with several researchers. E-mail addresses were exchanged, and after the congress

(8 August) the first of a series of personal and content-related e-mails was sent. In this first e-mail, Mario made an early attempt to involve Karin in a project to be funded by the European Union, saying that he had contacted two young researchers who were studying the impact of informal communication on group interactions. He had also approached Yannis, 'an expert on CMC', who later appeared to be a friend and colleague with whom Mario had already worked on other projects.

Yannis joined the project, and soon took the initiative to create a website, which included a mailing list. The website could be accessed by every visitor to read about the project. Team members could post links and articles. This website had both a pragmatic and a symbolic function (Sanderson 1994: 50). It could be used for storing and retrieving project proposals, documents, links and the mailing list archive. But the presence of a shared working space, protected by a password, also might give team members the feeling of a common endeavor, and a shared frame of reference.

In his very first e-mail, Mario made clear that the project was still undefined and that he still had to look for some other partners since European Union research proposals are more likely to be funded when they include researchers from at least five or six countries.

In previous projects, Mario had met several researchers whom he now, from August 1999 on, started to contact via e-mail. Note that these contacts were based on earlier face-to-face communication. Already in one of his first e-mails Mario mentioned Jan, a researcher he and Yannis had already worked with on other projects. Mario followed a network approach, apparently, to find researchers to join the project (or 'partners', as team members in European Union-funded research projects are called). For instance, he asked Jan to look for other possible partners.

Only one researcher – James – was approached without Mario having met him before, either face to face or by any other medium (Mario was impressed by James's publications, and now contacted him using e-mail). Another researcher – Sophia – took the initiative to contact Mario after being told about Delta by her supervisor, who had been approached as he was part of Mario's personal network. Thus it may be possible to form a team purely based on e-mail communication, but in the case of Delta this was not what happened. Generally speaking, if an area of research is rather small, many researchers will know each other from conferences, and purely virtual contact is unlikely. Delta was concerned with such a small area of research.

Let us have a closer look at the stage of team formation. In retrospect, it appears that several researchers did contact the mailing list but withdrew after exchanging only a few mails. We contacted some of these researchers in an attempt to discover the reasons for leaving (or for not entering) the project, but obtained few replies. After consulting the mailing list, some researchers did join the consortium. But what does 'joining' mean?

Preparing a research proposal that is to be submitted to the European Union is a rather complex endeavor, if only because research tasks must be distributed between the partners and decisions about the allocation of (limited) budgets need to be made. The geographical distance between team members, time pressure (submission deadline), and uncertainty about the project's being approved may well make (potential) team members reluctant to invest much time and money in the project. In one of his earliest mails, Mario announced that he would write a draft proposal and that before submitting a final proposal he wanted to have a meeting, in September 2000, to discuss and modify the draft. Soon he started to invite the team to meet face to face in Rome to discuss the project. Mario's faith in computer-mediated communication as a medium for group discussion was not very high, perhaps, but a face-to-face meeting would also serve another goal. For Mario, a face-to-face meeting also seemed a test of commitment. Attending it in an early stage of the project would show that people were willing to invest time and money in a still risky project (and attending such a meeting would make it more difficult to quit the project; at least one would waste time, money and effort). Precisely for this reason, presumably, it took quite some time before team members were prepared to accept such a face-to-face meeting. As a result, for a lengthy period the Delta project developed through e-mail and mailing list communication.

Thus 'joining the project as a mailing list team member' does not imply the willingness to travel in person. Membership may develop by overcoming a series of barriers, in much the same way as the development of participation in a social movement (Klandermans and Oegema 1987).

During its start-up stage, Delta developed slowly and iteratively. Since the project was hardly defined, initially, finding researchers and defining the project's contents were related problems. The team was formed step by step, and so was the research proposal, in spite of the fact that Mario assumed or even appropriated the task of writing the proposal.

The Delta team, as it was finally shaped, was heterogeneous in many ways. Each source of heterogeneity contributed to different views on the content and the process of the project. First, there was heterogeneity in disciplinary background; some participants were social scientists, others more technically oriented. Second, team members differed considerably in age and experience. Third, four different countries were involved, which produced cultural differences. Fourth, communication preferences were different; some team members liked computer-mediated communication while others favored face-to-face meetings. Fifth, members' experiences with working in an EU-funded project varied; some had been working in previous EU projects and knew what would be expected. As an extra dimension, universities appeared to differ in legal restrictions regarding EU projects. (For example, one of the universities involved was highly dependent on project funding instead of government financing.) In short, the Delta team was heterogeneous in terms of disciplinary backgrounds, attitudes, knowledge, experience and expectations regarding the media used.

Research teams in European projects

- are often formed in a very unstructured way;
- are often heterogeneous in terms of backgrounds, attitudes, knowledge and experience;
- are often hesitant about the use of virtual media.

Teams Do Not 'Just' Communicate: The Months Before the Meeting

With Sophia joining the team, in February 2000, the project team became more cohesive. Still, it would take several months before a suitable 'framework' for the proposal was found. From August 2000 onwards, this framework would provide the team with two incentives. It was clear now what specific guidelines would have to be complied with, which gave direction to discussions concerning the proposal. In addition, it meant that the deadline for proposal submission was known. This deadline was very close: 25 November 2000. A new mailing list was created, this time a private one. Old e-mail messages were removed from the open area webspace, and the private mailing list allowed for confidential discussions between team members.

A date was set for a face-to-face meeting. Such a meeting was considered necessary. Mario had almost completed a draft proposal that would have to be discussed, and matters regarding the budget needed to be solved. It was felt that these subjects were best dealt with when communicating face to face.

On the mailing list team members started to write comments and make suggestions, especially after receiving the draft proposal. Somewhat surprisingly, this proposal emphasized the distribution of tasks and budgets rather than adding content details to an earlier 'working document'. Whereas the mailing list in the first year had hardly been used for serious discussion – there were even long silences, and the communication never became impassioned – now the amount and the tone of communication changed drastically. Decisions had to be made about the division of budgets and tasks, which caused conflicts between team members. For the first time it was clear that team members had different motives and interests in joining the team. At this point, the partners' personalities came to the surface, more than they did on the mailing list. Communication became intense, mails were direct and sometimes personal. Some team members adopted a very emotional way of writing.

Sometimes mails would be pushy: 'If you will not do this, please quit the team.' Several times the project leader repeated that committing yourself meant committing yourself fully ('for the whole 100 percent'). In response, the use of private (one-to-one) e-mail increased. Within the team, members started to group together, forming small sub-teams that might provide support if necessary.

When examining the private mailing list closely, we find that problems arose over finding dates and fixing budgets, that is, over issues other than the project's contents. We will sketch the kind of communication in this period, presenting a fragment of the exchange of e-mails concerning the budget issue.

The part we examine started with a message sent by Mario, with the subject header 'General framework for proposal'. In this message, Mario discussed managerial aspects of the project, arguing that these could be considered as a general framework. In particular, he delineated a budget division scheme. This scheme would become the subject of a heated discussion, particularly so because Mario presented it as a decision rather than a proposal.

Jan was the first to reply, making clear that a face-to-face meeting was needed to resolve the issue. James agreed with Jan, stating that the personnel budget had to be worked out to ensure that each team member would have sufficient resources to carry out the work. James too referred to the forthcoming face-to-face meeting as necessary to reach a common understanding within the team. Franco, in turn, was very concerned about this budget discussion, writing that he had never seen such a discussion before. Franco joined Delta as a member of the personal network of Mario. He had not been active on the mailing list in the period preceding the face-to-face meeting, but joined Mario making budget proposals. He supported the project leader: 'As we have trusted Mario in the first part of the proposal I would suggest to continue to do it.'

In his message, Franco implied that he had helped Mario to write the proposal. He now used it as an argument: 'I would like to know if some of you have written or coordinated a proposal in 5 days and if yes if you have been able to get the project approved from the EU.' In other words: you are not in a position to make any complaints. He proceeded to make a clear statement: team members should decide if they were still interested in joining the project. 'Take it or leave it', he seems to say. However, Franco ended his message in a positive way, stressing that good decisions would be made and that an agreement to satisfy everyone was likely to be found.

Jan replied, still arguing that the budget had to be divided more equally.

Sixteen mailing list messages followed in just one day and the atmosphere was rather tense, even though everyone tried to stay polite. But not only the mailing list was used for communication; personal e-mails were sent as well, and even telephone calls were made. Team members probed other members' opinions, and tried to find (or organize) support.

The budget issue escalated when Yannis, on the mailing list, made clear that the budget problem might preclude his attending the forthcoming face-to-face meeting. His Delta membership was under the supervision of his research institute, but Yannis was also frustrated by the fact that Mario wrote the budget proposal on his own instead of making it a subject of negotiation in the face-to-face meeting. In his mail, Yannis referred to successful collaborations with Mario in the past, but also to their friendship. It is not clear whether these remarks were meant to indicate that Yannis's comments were just work-related, therefore not jeopardizing this friendship, or rather were made to say that there are things you cannot do to friends. Yet the message was quite formal – Yannis even signed in a formal way – probably because his message was not only sent to the mailing list but also to the supervisor of his institute.

All in all, the budget discussion produced a hectic situation within Delta, more than some members were able to take: 'I feel like quitting all this shit with projects, funding, collaborations . . .' The discussion ended without the problem being solved. It was passed on to the face-to-face meeting.

Would it have been possible to solve the budget issue merely through e-mail? Would Jan, James and Yannis have insisted on a face-to-face meeting if this meeting had not already been planned? And, would the conflict have arisen as it did now if the team members had met earlier, and not after a long period of mailing list communication? Comparing the computer-mediated discussion with the discussion as it evolved in the subsequent face-to-face meeting may offer a first answer. In the meeting, many 'deals' were made. A conspicuous example was the exchange of Italian conversations between the Italian partners in front of the whole team. Metaphorically, this can be seen as similar to the exchange of private e-mails. By exchanging 'private information' through using their own language, the Italians were deliberately excluding the team. If they did not hesitate to do so in a face-to-face meeting, what would have happened if the discussion had taken place only through e-mail? Probably there would have been e-mails shared through the mailing list, and an equal (if not larger) number of private exchanges. In fact, that was happening already in the pre-meeting discussion, but then the discussion was soon to be suspended. Had that not been the case, it might well have become impossible to oversee these private e-mails. In the face-to-face meeting, though, the private conversations in the non-English language were constantly called to an end.

This comparison, however, is not fully adequate. If a team is close to a deadline, as was the case in the face-to-face meeting, individual team members have only two options: accepting some agreement or leaving the team. Of course, there is time for negotiation tactics – waiting, getting angry, building a coalition, fabricating a compromise – but at the end of the day one has to decide whether or not to accept. In the preceding mailing list negotiation, there was a third option – suspending a decision – and precisely that was the option chosen.

Had not a face-to-face meeting been scheduled (or had it been impossible to do so), no such third option could have been chosen. In that case, the same choice between accepting and declining would have had to be made, but now on the basis of electronic communication. Then, the process might have taken longer (no flight departure times would apply). And as the negotiation process would have been different – tactics in electronic communication are not necessarily like face-to-face tactics, and not everyone masters both – a different outcome is quite conceivable.

Returning to the 'electronic negotiation' as it actually went, it is striking to see how quickly the 'suspend' option was brought to the fore. This may simply reflect the team members' inclination to discuss 'difficult issues' face to face, but we suggest two further reasons as well. One is that the team members who did not accept Mario's budget proposal preferred a more balanced negotiation setting (considering the mailing list a disadvantageous setting, one that favored Mario's initiatives). The other is that Mario could not refuse, as he had already often stressed the need of a face-to-face meeting. The first reason (untested so far) is interesting, implying that the increase of readily available communication media, like e-mail, may provide the 'weaker' parties in a negotiation process with escapes that were previously unavailable. The members in the team were not all used to negotiating by CMC, and therefore some of them 'naturally' preferred to negotiate in a face-to-face setting. But because of the usage of e-mail, team members could now:

1.   refer in the face-to-face meeting to the next e-mail discussion; or
2.   postpone the discussion within the e-mail conversation to the next face-to-face meeting.

In both communication settings, it is possible to postpone the decision by referring to the next decision-making possibility (either by mail or in a face-to-face setting). The escape for the weaker party thus involves the attempt to postpone a decision to a more suitable moment.

But would the budget conflict have appeared in the first place if the team had met face to face earlier? The question is hypothetical, as the team had long been little more than a permanently changing collection of people – which simply means that now was the first time that a reliable group of people could be invited for a meeting. Still, some remarks can be made on the issue. Hollingshead et al., (1993) report that groups negotiating face to face outperform groups that only use electronic communication media. Generally speaking, then, it is plausible that an early face-to-face meeting will be helpful in an electronic negotiation process. However, it is questionable if such a previous meeting would have helped in the case of Delta. In the face-to-face meeting that was soon to be held, Jan, Mario and Yannis, precisely those who knew each other well from previous projects, got involved in a heated debate about the budget. Therefore, it seems highly unlikely that an earlier face-to-face meeting would have sufficed to prevent the electronic discussion about the budget.

In summary, the sharing of the budget and the setting of a date for a face-to-face meeting were the issues that stirred emotions and caused conflicts in the team. It can be questioned if the budget issue could have been resolved through e-mail communication: not because of the leanness of the medium, but because team members would use private e-mails for discussion, negotiation and coalition-building without the rest of the team knowing. However, the team members did not give the mailing list a fair chance. When confronted with problems concerning the budget they immediately passed this issue on to the face-to-face meeting.

Key issues

- The use of e-mail gave team members the opportunity to postpone important decisions.
- Because of some hesitation in using computer-mediated communication, it is often not considered as a viable option for reaching agreement.

Looking in Each Other's Eyes: The Face-to-Face Meeting

In this section, we will look at the face-to-face meeting, and we will try to find the same patterns (or different ones) as have surfaced in the mailing list discussion.

To recapitulate, before the face-to-face meeting there was limited cooperation between team members, and the project was still open. Team members did comment on a draft proposal and made suggestions, and the team leader put these comments and suggestions together in a new draft. As we have seen, the difficult part was the division of the budget between the partners. On 30 August, the team leader presented a draft proposal that included scientific content as well as issues of project organization, in particular a budget division scheme and a distribution of tasks. As indicated, he denied the other team members the right to make changes, at least regarding the budget scheme.

After 30 August, things went very fast. It appeared that not all team members approved the division of the budget, and a budget discussion started that was soon to be passed on to the face-to-face meeting. A place and date for this meeting had already been set: Rome, 3–4 September 2000. Meanwhile, Mario sent many e-mails requesting documents, signs of commitment, documents signed by university administrations, etc. Some team members had problems producing all requested documents at short notice, and Mario kept urging them to hurry.

What follows is a brief description of the face-to-face meeting. An agenda was set that included discussions about the budget scheme, about the contents of the draft proposal (which included the allocation of members to specific research subjects, and the appointment of work package leaders), and about a timetable.

After arriving in Rome, all team members came together for an informal meeting on the night of 2 September. No one touched the subject of budgets.

The next day, the team was to meet at Mario's university. Due to the traffic, Karin, Sophia, Yannis and James were late. When they arrived, they got a frosty reception. Mario, assuming the chairman role, started to say that he did not want to waste any time discussing the budget. He went on to relate briefly how Delta had been formed. Then he said that he had, in cooperation with Franco and Adriana (Mario's personal assistant), made two new budget proposals, A and B, and he urged the team to choose between these two. Again, he made clear that he did not want to lose any time on this. What happened was that everyone started calculating and discussing the two proposals. It soon became clear that neither proposal was able to satisfy all team members. 'Camps' were formed, more clearly than earlier on the mailing list. The only team member trying not to get involved in a process of camp formation was James. He made attempts to keep the team together, and was even prepared to give away a part of his budget if that would be necessary to keep other partners on board.

A complex negotiation process followed. First, the discussion became hostile between Mario and Jan. After a short break, a new conflict arose as Mario and Franco continued to talk in their own language. While James and Sophia tried to calm things down, Adriana lost her temper. Several times Mario might have acted as a mediator, but he failed to do so, letting Adriana do the talking instead.

At some point, a choice had to be made between two new proposals. One was overtly supported by Jan, the other by the South European partners.

Yannis pointed out that he could not live with the proposal that Jan was heading for. A ballot followed, and Jan's proposal won. Yannis got angry, blaming Mario for not having done enough to prevent this outcome. Those who were not involved in the conflict left the room. When they returned the problem had been solved: Mario had agreed to give Yannis more money.

Now that the budget problem had been solved, the communication became more relaxed. However, not too much time was left for discussing the division of work packages and further issues that needed to be addressed. During the rest of the first day, the team was able to discuss the contents of the project without being disturbed. The next day negotiations on work packages continued. Franco had to leave early. Mario was unhappy with that: you cannot walk away from a team meeting. Franco responded by saying he trusted Mario enough to let him take decisions for him. The second day went without heated discussion and in the evening, at dinner, the team members were almost euphoric that all had been settled. The only item left was making a proposal and sending it to the proper European Union department. This, all agreed, could be accomplished using the mailing list.

Key issues

- A face-to-face meeting was set up to discuss complex issues.
- Seemingly more straightforward issues were dealt with using the mailing list.

The Return to the Virtual Communication

After the meeting, the mailing list was used heavily again. The team members had to adjust and complete the proposal quickly since the deadline was very close. This was not, however, the original (25 November) deadline. During the meeting in Rome, Mario had announced an additional face-to-face meeting with European Union representatives, to be held in Luxembourg on 18 September. Here, the proposal would have to be defended, which required a full proposal. The reason may have been that Mario regarded it necessary to involve EU representatives at as early a stage as possible, because of the large funding that was applied for. But what considerations Mario may have had, he did not share them with the rest of the team. He would only drop an occasional hint that he was pretty well informed about the European Union's funding limits.

Making a proposal, the work package leaders (that is, nearly all team members) had to communicate intensively to fine-tune the project: different work packages had to link up well, but overlaps should be avoided. Numerous messages were posted concerning the planning and coordination of the project. Within two weeks, some 132 mails concerning the adjustment of the proposal were sent to the mailing list.

Mario, trying to accelerate the process, kept sending alarming e-mails every now and then (headed 'Urgent') in which he stressed that the deadline was close and that partners should hurry. He also sent a message in which he invited the team members to meet one day before the meeting with the EU representatives to discuss some final details and to foster team spirit. Some members replied that they would not be able to attend this preparatory meeting because of flight problems. Mario stuck to his position, repeating how important the meeting was. And indeed, on 17 September all team members met again face to face to prepare for the next day's meeting. Views were adjusted, some formal issues solved, and budgets checked.

The meeting with the European Union representatives went off well. Questions were asked about the Delta team's motives and goals, and some comments and suggestions were made that called for further adjustment of the proposal. In the following weeks these adjustments were made without any problems occurring. Members would make changes or come up with suggestions, ending their messages asking: 'What do the rest of you think?' The others would most of the time reply by just saying 'I agree.' And if team members already had different views on a subject, this was solved in only one or two mails. One member would come up with a suggestion, and the other would reply: 'This sounds good to me, go ahead.'

The question of when to use particular research methods was important, as work packages' time schedules had to be adjusted. The work package leaders responsible for the issue at hand would discuss the subject, however, without any interference from other team members. This is why the mailing list contains many threads of messages invoking only two members.

In the end, the team managed to meet the deadline. What followed was a prolonged period in which the team received confusing messages concerning the project's approval, and then, after the project had been accepted, confusing messages concerning the formal arrangements that needed to be made, especially the signing of contracts.

3.4   DISCUSSION

E-mail is believed to be the communication medium that is more than any other medium likely to produce 'flames', that is, 'messages that are precipitate, often personally derogatory, ad hominem attacks directed toward someone due to a position taken in a message distributed (posted) to the group' (Mabry 1997). And indeed, there have been such 'flames' on the

Delta mailing list. However, similar flames did occur in the face-to-face meeting we described, and definitely these 'face-to-face flames' were as intense as their electronic counterparts.

This is the general picture to be gathered from the account we have given: different communication media – e-mail/mailing list communication and face-to-face communication – did not produce large differences in the way Delta team members communicated. Rather, it was the actual stage in the group formation process that shaped if not determined the way team members would communicate.

The 'group formation stages' we described can be linked to Gersick's (1988) model of 'punctuated equilibria' rather than with the often-quoted sequence of 'forming, storming, norming, performing' (Tuckman 1965; Tuckman and Jensen 1977). That is, instead of gradually progressing, the Delta team went through a long period of alternating composition, lack of clues for the direction to take, and even uncertainty about its very existence. Rather suddenly, this period was closed and a highly condensed period followed in which forming, storming, norming and performing took place more or less simultaneously.

However, the Delta team differs in at least two important respects from the organizational task groups analyzed by Gersick (1988). First, the Delta team was formed in the absence of a clear initial structure (e.g. an organization), and second, it took a very long time before members could rely on time schedules and deadlines, simply because these had not been decided. This implies that Gersick's (1988: 32) prediction did not apply that a (project) group will stay through the first half of its life within the framework of behavioral patterns and assumptions that emerged in its first meeting. It was not known in advance what the group's life span would be. Gersick (1988) has argued that, for a project team of which the length of the project is known in advance and for which the goal of the project is known, the team will spend the first half of its life cycle in reviewing this goal – if this goal is clear and useful, and if there are any alternatives – and then all of a sudden, when the second half of the project is about to start, the team will realize that there is a task to perform. At first glance it looks as if Delta resembles Gersick's model. However, at the beginning of the Delta project (in the start-up phase) there was no clear initial goal/assignment and no restricted time period for this project.

This particular process of group composition alternation – members come and go in unpredictable ways – was, at least in part, a result of electronic communication: it was easy to come, and it was just as easy to go. Computer-mediated communication seems to lower the threshold in both directions, with the result that group composition may become a lengthy process, and an uncertain process for those who intend to stay. Moreover, this uncertainty may well reduce members' willingness to make substantial contributions to the task. Of course the threshold may be raised, as was done in the Delta case, but this is not an easy decision to take – for as long as the threshold is low there is a chance that highly promising researchers will join the team.

At some point, the final team composition had been reached, a 'submission target' found, and a deadline determined. Only then did the Delta members started to work as a team. Probably Gersick's prediction (to a lesser extent) becomes visible here. With the start of the project, 'a new project life' started, but this cannot be compared with the stages described by Gersick (1988). In the start-up phase the Delta members had already been through the questioning stage (is the goal reachable, and are there any alternatives?). From the contractual start of the project, the project members realized that they had to start working immediately in order to meet the deadlines.

The collaboration went without problems as far as the contents of the proposal were involved. This seems to disprove some basic predictions of media richness theory, since creating a research proposal is a task likely to involve high degrees of uncertainty and equivocality (Markus et al., 2002).

Problems did occur, however, but mainly about the issues of budget allocation and setting of a date for a face-to-face meeting. The latter is not surprising considering the close date for a meeting that was suggested. Nevertheless, the budget issue is puzzling since in comparable projects we know of, the division of budgets proceeded rather smoothly. Why not in the Delta case? In the context of this chapter, this question is only relevant to the extent that 'virtual communication' is part of the answer. A tentative answer, then, may refer to the availability of e-mail and mailing list communication that allows a 'quick fix' team formation. Mario made significant investments. He devoted much time to writing a series of draft proposals, and he exploited his personal network to create a team. This team was necessary because of European Union requirements. He may well have considered team membership a gift to his friends that would provide them with a sizable research budget – not as large as Mario's own budget, of course, but generous anyway. What he asked from his friends in return was grateful acceptance, compliance with suggestions he made, and every now and then a small contribution to the proposal's contents. But he failed to recognize that other team members might not accept such a secondary position and, moreover, that some team members were prepared to 'abuse' their team membership by starting to make demands as soon as Mario was left to the mercy of the team as it was. Thus Mario's initial conception of a 'passive virtual team' did not work, and even worse, in the end he would be called (but not directly!) a dictator and a Machiavellian.

Apart from the reasons why the budget distribution appeared as an issue, the process of dealing with it is revealing. First, the mailing list provided the team with everything that is needed to have a good fight. Second, the conflict was easily transferred from computer-mediated to face-to-face communication, without significant transformations in terms of tone, involvement or solution types. Third, it was remarkable how soon the 'suspend' option was chosen on the mailing list. This may reflect habit ('if problems occur, you should talk face to face'), or tactics ('better to move to another negotiation setting'). Fourth, the very presence of e-mail, mailing list and many other forms of computer-mediated communication currently being developed may greatly increase the prospects of 'suspending and moving' a discussion or a problem.

All in all, our account suggests that different communication media are likely to give rise to different group formation processes, and to communication processes that may be rich, poor or something in between. It does not, however, support the assertion that media richness determines, or is 'only' related to, communication richness.

Key issues

- Communication patterns are rather similar if one compares CMC and face-to-face meetings.
- Flaming is not a typical CMC issue.
- Computer-mediated communication seems to lower the threshold for entering and exiting groups.
- Media richness does not determine communication richness.

3.5 SOME ADDITIONAL OBSERVATIONS

At the time of writing the Delta members have finished their work on the Delta project, apart from some technicalities such as filling out management reports.

Some readers might be curious to know how the Delta members proceeded in their work. Therefore, and for other reasons, the Delta case study will have an epilogue. An important question that can be answered in this epilogue will be whether time is enough to overcome the (possible) constraints of virtual teams. After the start-up phase of the Delta project, the official project started in May 2001 and was finalized at the end of October 2003. For more than three years (taking into account the start-up phase) the team members could communicate with each other (in various modes, virtual or in the several face-to-face meetings) in order to improve the cooperation which took place mainly at a distance. Various authors (see the overview in Chapter 2) have stated that given enough time, a virtual team will develop effective ways to work together (or, for instance, develop trust and friendly relationships). In observing the start-up phase of the project, it was concluded that there were no major differences in richness between face-to-face communication and virtual communication. We wonder whether the cooperative climate would change, given enough time to develop. Alternatively, would it have been impossible to change the atmosphere in a team when the start-up phase was troublesome? Would it have been possible to overcome the conflicts about the budget; or to turn the distrust into trust through more communication?

From the discussion of the start-up phase, we can summarize the following observations:

- There was often a lack of communication on the part of the leader.
- Although communication was often lacking, all of a sudden the leader came up with alarming e-mails: 'hurry for the deadline' and other 'warnings'.
- The meetings were seen as stressful, especially colored by budgetary problems.
- While writing the proposal and using the mailing list for discussion, it was seen that this discussion was merely about approving each other's ideas, or coming up with some adjustments, which were easily accepted. The work took place in isolation.
- The suspend option was chosen frequently: preferring face-to-face meetings over e-mail discussion.
- We saw flaming in e-mail, and shouting in face-to-face meetings.

After the contract was signed, a clear structure was provided – not only by the team itself, but also by the framework provided by the EU and by signing the contract, the members were committed to the research design and deadlines. In sum, a few aspects are different in the 'official phase':

- Team members can cooperate in a clear structure (project management, deadlines, etc.).
- Team members are committed by a contract.
- Members (e.g. institutions) cannot join and leave the project as easily as in the start-up phase.
- Time was on their side: three years to develop a cooperative climate.

We now wonder whether there was indeed an increase in communication and improved collaboration, because the team got to spend more time with each other as a real team and there were opportunities to get to know each other. We will not discuss what was going on within this team to a full extent, but we will focus on one event that was a colorful example of what the overall project looked like.

3.6   THE DELTA TEAM AT WORK

In one of the face-to-face meetings the Delta team had to resolve one of the many management issues that the team has been facing from the start-up phase onwards. To put this in the context of time, we are talking about one of the meetings held in the beginning of 2002. Members were faced with the discussion about redistributing some of the money from each partner's budget to pay an external contributor to the Delta project. This contributor would provide the team with some services for which the Delta members felt they had no time or resources to provide for themselves. The climate of the discussion was rather tense, and agreement had to be reached quickly since the meeting was almost at its end. The proposal was for each partner to pay an equal amount of money for the services of this external partner. There was a discussion about the costs of this service, which some of the partners found quite large. This also raised the discussion about the fairness of the equal redistribution of the money, since for some of the members this amount was seen as just 'pocket money' while for others it was rather high. The difficult situation about whether the Delta team was willing to subcontract this other partner for some services was solved through voting. The members agreed that there was no other option than to subcontract this task. This did not solve the issue of the amount of money that needed to be paid for it. The conflict actually increased when one of the partners (Franco) made a claim for extra money because of the services he was providing to the team. The situation got very hectic and Mario forced a decision. A round of votes followed, during which all of the partners, besides Sophia and Karin, agreed on the division of money. Sophia claimed that she could not give a final 'yes' to the division of money until she had spoken with the administration of her university. Karin said 'yes' on the same condition. The rest of the meeting was chaotic and it was not clear on which subjects they had come to an agreement.

In the numerous (heated) mailing list discussions afterwards, it became clear that the situation about the subcontracting was not really solved in the face-to-face meeting.

A few months later, in the May meeting in 2003, solutions were sought to resolve problems concerning the budget and subcontracting issues. We will not go into further detail, since new problems arose during this meeting and several meetings and e-mails after that. We take a jump in time to arrive at the end of the project. While in October 2003 the project was officially closed, Mario still is waiting for the work from a few partners. In an e-mail sent in November 2003 he reminds Franco, Jan and James that the fourth and final payment is subordinate to the acceptance of these final works. At the final meetings held in October this was also the subject of discussion, Mario claiming work from other partners before any payment could be done. The other partners did not agree with his claims.

3.7   INTRA-TEAM COMMUNICATION PROCESSES

So far not much attention has been paid to the communication processes stimulated by CMC. In this section we will briefly discuss what impact the communication media had on the communication and cooperation processes. We think the impact of CMC was only modest and other factors, such as the division of the budget, cultural differences and the impact of leadership, were more important in understanding the communication processes. The use of CMC was briefly examined by the Delta members at the close of the project, and these data, complemented with e-mails from the mailing list during the Delta period, will be used in describing communication processes.

When the Delta team agreed to form a consortium, means of communication had to be found in order to bridge the time between face-to-face meetings. In the start-up phase the team was using e-mail to communicate. At first e-mails were sent to one person and all the other members were 'cc-ed' (carbon-copied) in that mail. One of the Delta members initiated and maintained the Delta mailing list. All the mails from this list were archived and could be used as a log of all the communication.

In the start-up phase only this mailing list was used to communicate. After the official start of the project it was decided to start another mailing list as well, the so-called management mailing list. Only the management members had access to this list.

As the Delta project evolved, more rules appeared on how to use both mailing lists, for instance the rule to use a new subject line when raising a new subject. At the beginning of the project misunderstandings arose when some of the members were very silent on the mailing list, which made others wonder if they were still working on the project. Over time, it became (for most members) a habit to inform others about their work in progress (or illness, etc.). Once in a while the mailing list did not work properly, and some members did not receive all the general messages or could not send e-mails to the list. Using private mail, they informed other members on what was going on and asked them to send a message to the list to avoid misunderstandings.

The experience with CMC grew as time passed, and new rules and norms were formed in order to structure the communication. At one point, a member raised the discussion on 'subject lines': 'We use this mailing list and when we write about a specific matter we use the subject line for this. It is a good way to keep track of subjects of messages. However, sometimes we reply on a message with a completely different subject/content. My proposal is: please use e-mail in a more structured way and when you are not replying to a certain message, use a new subject line.'

At face-to-face meetings, the members discussed how to use different tools to improve their virtual communication. Some of the Delta members were acquainted with a chat tool named Messenger (MSN). It was decided to try to use this chat system for online discussions. After various attempts the chat sessions were not satisfying enough for some of the members, especially since it appeared to be difficult to arrange a virtual meeting at a particular date and time that suited all members.

The members decided that MSN could be used for sub-group meetings, but not for the whole team. After the first try-out of the chat sessions, two members of the team (who used MSN for private purposes, and were the most experienced users) formulated some guidelines for using MSN:

- *Be online!!* When we have agreed on having a meeting, be online, or else be polite and give notice that you will not be there, i.e. in an e-mail through the mailing list. In this way we make the virtual meeting a bit more formal, a kind of an obligation.
- *Appoint a chair for each meeting.* The chairperson will circulate an agenda a few days before the virtual meeting. He or she will also send mails to remind the team of the upcoming meeting. The chairperson will also send a short overview of the meeting's objectives, and will also set date and time for the next meeting and remind the next chair it is his/her turn.
- *Address the sentence to the person you are talking to.* For instance if you have a remark to the whole group, type: to all. If you want to respond to Mario, type: to Mario. This makes the chat session more clear and structured.
- *Always save your chat meeting in a file.* That way it can be used as a storage file for data.

Despite the guidelines for the chat sessions, the difficulties with finding appropriate times and dates for a chat session remained, just as it was difficult for the team to find appropriate dates for face-to-face meetings.

The problem with MSN was more an organizational problem than a technical one. Another problem was the lack of expertise of some of the members in using MSN, in spite of the guidelines that were provided. The project leader explained his absence from the scheduled chat meeting as follows: 'Sorry, I'm late and don't know how to use MSN. After installing MSN, what should I do?' This partly explains why some of the members did not show up at the prearranged chat meeting.

Another tool was introduced in order to structure their work: the Blackboard tool. While Blackboard has many features, the tool has been mostly used as a repository of documents. All members could upload documents to specific areas structured according to the Delta project itself. While Blackboard has features to stimulate cooperation and communication, for instance chat sessions, the members did not use those features. In an evaluation session at the end of the Delta project, some of the Delta members expressed regret at having worked in relative isolation on their tasks, without consulting their Delta colleagues. Blackboard as a repository tool was needed as a coordination mechanism: to store large documents, which were difficult to send through e-mail. Furthermore, the tool was also used for dissemination purposes: EU reviewers had access to the documents stored in Blackboard.

3.8   CLOSING THE PROJECT AND SOME REMARKS

At this point, December 2003, it was not possible to close the Delta project entirely. The last messages from Mario had not yet received any answer from the other partners, at least not through the mailing list. The preceding pages have made clear that the team processes within the Delta project did not change over time, or after the contract was signed. Probably one could argue that what starts off wrong will never turn into something right. The conflicts remained and were unresolved even after the project. A few observations can be made:

- There were still no differences in the team communication style with respect to virtual and face-to-face communication.
- The mailing list was used for sending messages to the list, but private e-mails were used when matters got difficult, or when support from other members was needed. In the face-to-face meetings, the coffee breaks served the same purpose. It seemed that at the end of the project more coffee breaks were needed!
- The leadership style, especially the 'blackmailing style', colored the team processes. Mario himself wrote that due to the fact he had

control of the money he could force some of the decisions. This power obstructed the collaboration.

- The power games, as mentioned by Sophia, had to do with status differences and gender issues. At least this was felt by Sophia and Karin, who were the youngest female researchers within the management team. Neither e-mail nor face-to-face communication could solve these differences. Different e-mails sent by Mario to Sophia and Karin, as well as personal gatherings, made very clear that he saw them only as junior researchers.

- Another factor in these power games was the issue of Mario denying the other team members the right to communicate with the EU officer. Mario was the only one who could speak to the EU officer and was the only one who provided the Delta team with information from this officer. Some of the team members felt disadvantaged by this situation, since they felt that Mario sometimes abused this situation by providing the wrong kind of information or not providing them with information in a timely manner. Probably Mario wanted to prevent team members from complaining to the EU officer about certain issues or conflicts concerning the project.

- The suspend option was often preferred while discussing conflicts. E-mail was only utilized for the initial discussion, while face-to-face meetings were used to resolve matters. However, at some of the management meetings, face-to-face meetings were not sufficient to force people to take decisions. Sometimes members had to catch a flight and the meeting could not be extended because of that. While agreeing on taking the discussion back to the mailing list level, this in practice never happened (and some of the issues remained unresolved).

- There were different degrees of bureaucracy and institutional rules from each home university. The cultural differences gave the Southern universities more room and flexibility to make budget changes, while the case of Sophia showed that her university, situated in the UK, had more problems with managerial changes.

- The bureaucratic style imposed by the EU, stipulating that every single piece of paper has to be signed by the responsible financial administrator within each university, slowed team processes.

In sum, we would like to argue that the Delta project failed in many ways, at least in dealing with the management issues of the project. Because of all the conflicts, the team climate was not 'healthy' and this prevented the team members from collaborating in a stimulating way.

Most of the work was carried out in a relatively isolated manner, waiting for the work package leader to put it together. In the closing session of the last meeting, there was a round table discussion about what everyone thought or learned from the project. The conclusions were that it was doubtful whether the team members had read each other's work at all. The junior researchers, who did not deal with management issues, could sense conflict situations in the management team and pointed this out as an obstructing factor for knowledge sharing. Because of these conflicts, the commitment to work on the project declined to the level that could be described as 'we must do what is stated in the contract and nothing extra'. Because of all the management issues, less time and energy were left for scientific discussions. Not only were the institutional and cultural differences a problem for the team while working in a virtual mode; they also caused problems that could not be resolved in a face-to-face setting. We therefore hold to our initial conclusions drawn from the start-up phase: this study does not support the assertion that media richness determines whether a team succeeds in its collaboration.

Key issues for management

- Create a warm team climate.
- Be prepared to deal with institutional and cultural differences.
- CMC environments are similar in many respects to face-to-face environments. They have to be managed in a similar way.

4. The Advance case study

4.1 INTRODUCTION

Many studies have addressed the differences between face-to-face and computer-mediated communication (CMC), often informed by media richness theory (MRT)'s claim that face-to-face communication is necessary if tasks are complex and information is equivocal. And even today, the widespread conviction is that CMC, viewed as (a collection of) lean communication media, may be adequate if and only if tasks are simple and information is unambiguous.

The Delta study, presented in the previous chapter, examined the reliability of the MRT claim in the real-life setting of a geographically dispersed group of scientists who prepared a joint research proposal. The Delta study as such is one of the first studies to compare face-to-face communication in a real-life setting; most previous studies tended to rely on experiments only.

In that setting, the claim was implausible. Allegedly poor communication media such as e-mail and mailing lists were found to enable rich communication, including exchanging ambiguous information, defining and allocating fairly complex tasks and expressing a range of emotions. In all these respects, the difference between virtual and face-to-face communication was less obvious than predicted by MRT. Thus, it was argued, 'inherent characteristics' of the communication media used cannot account for the way communication between non-collocated individuals or groups unfolds, which once again directs attention to the conditions and circumstances that may contribute to smooth, efficient and satisfactory communication at a distance.

The case study presented in this chapter will highlight the impact of organizational factors, including the initial set-up, the division of tasks, leadership and guidance issues, process monitoring and deadlines, and organizational identity. An international research project will be described – called Advance – that was aimed at developing concurrent engineering-compatible instruments for interfirm cooperation on equipment design in the aerospace industry. Advance is a fictitious name and, for reasons of confidentiality, no details of the project will be given that could be used to identify persons, project groups or companies. The emphasis in the Advance case study is on the circumstances of cooperation in an aerospace engineering research project and how these influenced, and were influenced by, both face-to-face and electronic communication.

Studying Collaboration in the Aerospace Industry

The aerospace industry is a suitable domain for studying the way in which various modes of communication may facilitate cooperation at a distance. Various studies stress the importance of electronic communication in aerospace engineering activities (Black 1990; Beuschel and Kling 1992; Bishop 1994). According to Bishop (1994: 697) the aerospace industry is an appropriate environment for the implementation of electronic networks: it is a high-tech, highly computerized industry, it involves a significant amount of R&D (which is a communication-intensive activity), and its end products are highly complex, requiring extensive work task coordination and integration of information from various sources. Hall (1990) suggests that aerospace companies may use advanced communication technology to improve productivity, to contribute to a competitive edge, to reduce timescales and to accomplish close collaboration, efficient management, common standards across sites, operational flexibility and enhanced workforce skill levels. Of these uses, O'Sullivan (2003) stresses collaboration, arguing that firms in the aircraft building sector (as well as firms in telecommunications or in software systems) are developing products characterized by large-scale, diverse technologies and long duration. Therefore, these firms must engage in multi-organization product development, for the scale, complexity and duration of these technologies impose requirements that cannot even be met by very large firms. As will be explained in the next section, these arguments – especially those concerning collaboration and standard setting – are pertinent to the European aerospace industry.

Whereas the above studies observe that aerospace companies actually use electronic means for various communication and cooperation activities, they also point out that the very presence of high-quality electronic networks does not make cooperation between aerospace firms an easy task. Häusler et al., (1995) offer a general argument, stating that scientists and engineers perform boundary-spanning roles in interorganizational R&D collaboration. They act as 'organizational gatekeepers', and negotiate on behalf of their respective organizations, but in doing so they assume a dual responsibility: they represent their 'home organization' in the negotiating setting, but also represent the negotiation setting when defending the negotiation results in their 'home organization'. The consequence may be that the organizations involved in the collaboration view each other with a certain degree of distrust, seeing the other companies as potential free riders.

In the aerospace industry, characterized by intense competition, perhaps the situation is even more complicated. For proprietary and security reasons, companies tend to implement their own private networks, used only by their own employees, and firewalls limit the communication outside these networks. Only occasionally, employees outside the organization are granted controlled access to information, which is sometimes referred to as 'bounded trust':

> An example . . . is the joint venture between Boeing and the Japanese in building the Boeing 777. In this joint venture engineers worked together by sharing significant amounts of technical and proprietary information. However, Boeing consciously protected itself against Japanese spying by limiting the access of Japanese engineers to 'secure' areas within Boeing. (Lewicki et al., 1998: 447)

As a final source of complexity, 'local contingencies' have to be taken into account. Interfirm collaboration may be difficult in general; it certainly is in the European context. Thacker-Kumar and Campbell (1999: 105), in a study addressing the 'technology gap' between Europe and the US/Japan, note that in Europe 'collaborative efforts must overcome historical rivalries and traditional forms of cooperation among scientists, businessmen and officials. Barriers in language, geography, legal provisions, accounting standards and working practices multiply these problems.'

The European Aerospace Industry

The Advance project is best considered as part of a trend towards cooperation and consolidation in the European aerospace industry. In the past 40 years, national governments, later followed by the European Commission, have persistently tried to achieve aerospace industry consolidation on a national scale, and they have also encouraged international cooperation within the European context. Consolidation and cooperation were considered necessary if the European aerospace industry were to stay in competition with the large American companies (Weber and Hallerberg 2001).

Regarding cooperation, much progress has been made over the years, that is, if the number of organizations concerned with European aerospace R&D cooperation is taken as a measure. Some examples are AECMA (European Aerospace Companies and Institutions, founded in 1950), GARTEUR (Group for Aeronautical Research and Technology in Europe, founded in 1973), CEAS (Association of European Aeronautical Research Establishments, founded in 1992), EREA (also referred to as AEREA, Association of European Aeronautical Research Establishments, founded in 1994), EASO (European Aviation Suppliers' Association, founded in 1996), and ACARE (Advisory Council for Aeronautics Research in Europe, founded in 2002). However, if cooperation had been successful, there would have been few incentives to keep adding associations and councils that seek to foster European R&D cooperation.

With regard to industrial consolidation, Thacker-Kumar and Campbell (1999: 105) referred to Flysky as one of the few examples (across industries) of successful 'pan-European' cooperation. Later, in 2000, two of the largest European companies (Aerospatiale Matra and Dasa) merged, soon to be joined by a Spanish company (CASA). The resulting company, EADS, is one of the world's largest aerospace companies (Hertrich 2000).

In spite of all these cooperation and consolidation efforts, the European aerospace industry is still fragmented, compared to the American industry. In addition, the European aerospace industry as a whole is smaller than its American counterpart. A recent estimate (Rose 2000: 5) is that the US aerospace industry is roughly twice as large as the European, in terms of employment and turnover. But that is not all. Rose (ibid.) also notes that

> in relative terms, the European aerospace industry invests more of its own resources in research and development than the US industry, which receives greater support. The need to strengthen R&D efforts at a European level and to coordinate with national programmes is, quite simply, essential.

As indicated, however, collaboration between European aerospace companies is not simple. The Advance project, launched in 1999 and partly funded by the European Commission, was a significant attempt to improve the conditions for collaboration in the industry. Concurrent engineering was seen as a suitable instrument. It would foster

> the integration of people, technologies and processes after a company merge; the development of very large product projects that require even more resources and a clear organization; a tighter integration between customers, partners and suppliers which requires a simple way to exchange data, and more than ever, the need to improve operational efficiency while reducing costs. (Cavarero and Schroter, 2002)

Next to promoting concurrent engineering, the Advance project would have to make European aeronautical product development more efficient by shortening time to market and reducing the costs of data management, conversion and transmission. For this, a set of common references had to be created that, supposedly, would drastically improve understanding and collaboration between people. These common references (in a variety of domains) would allow engineers to use similar concepts and software, thus increasing compatibility within the European aerospace industry. The software to be used was created and already used by the company coordinating Advance. Domains in which such 'common references' were viewed to be particularly useful were project engineering, life cycle management, and technology and methodology for the 'extended enterprise'. The last concept is a term to express the idea that companies not only include internal groups such as employees and executives, but also business partners, suppliers and customers. Kinder (2003: 504) uses the term 'extended enterprise' instead of 'networked organization' because it better captures the purposiveness of commercially oriented networks, and may avoid undue emphasis on the architecture of the electronic communication environment.

Companies were willing to join the project. Apparently they saw the need to combine knowledge and to integrate activities from various stages of the innovation process, throughout the whole supply chain. Thus they complied with the project's basic view that the success of combined activities heavily depends on the early and wide diffusion of the 'new common ways of working' – which meant the use of concurrent engineering methods, combined with standard setting and IT solutions for working at a distance. This view entailed that as many firms as possible, from the whole aircraft building supply chain, had to be involved: 'Since Advance is aimed at creating standards, everybody had to be in it. We had all the large companies in the aeronautical sector (more than 20) from the very beginning. We had them very early – with lots of political discussions.'

The presence of a large number of otherwise competing companies required the Advance project to be carefully organized, the more so because these companies represented various levels in the supply chain – which introduced a range of different interests and a variety of working relationships. It also introduced very practical differences: distinct areas of work deal in different ways with new communication technologies and organize their cooperation accordingly.

The Early History of the Advance Project

It took a couple of years before the Advance consortium was established. A first attempt was made soon after 1994, when the European Commission's fourth Framework Programme (FP4) was launched. In this framework, research project proposals could be submitted in response to many regular 'calls for proposals'. But FP4 also included €700 million of additional funds – the so-called 'supplementary funds' as defined in Article 130K of a regulation by the EC. In 1995, the sectors of car manufacturing, aeronautics and train manufacturing persuaded the Commission to use these additional funds for 'large industrial projects'. Five 'task forces' were installed to prepare proposals for these large industrial projects. This was when the mission of the Aeronautical Task Force (ATF) began. ATF had to write 'enough' large proposals to spend its share of the €700 million of funding, i.e. €140 million (roughly €300 million of overall budget, 50 percent funded).

The aerospace sector was the only sector to answer the request from the European Commission. Competition among car manufacturers and among train manufacturers prevented these sectors from preparing sufficiently detailed proposals.

When the decision to launch the ATF was taken, in April 1995, three international management groups (IMGs) were created, representing each of the then 12 European aircraft manufacturers. EIMG (Engine IMG) assembled the engine suppliers, and EQIMG (Equipment IMG) the equipment suppliers. IMG3 embraced these, including representatives of both EIMG and EQIMG. The IMGs' role was to organize the preparation of proposals in response to the FP4 call, so that one and only one proposal would be made for each of the call's topics. According to one of the participants involved, this organization worked quite well.

The IMGs first tried to identify promising subjects. By the end of 1995 they had defined three projects, one concerning concurrent engineering, a second concerning engines of the future, and a third 'about almost everything':

> At that level, the project proposals were written by a small group (6 to 10 people) from the IMGs. There were contributions from experts of each company but the people that actually wrote the documents in meetings, gave the key ideas and validated the final versions were the IMGs/ATF members.

When the three proposals were finally handed over to the European Commission, it was assumed that all projects would be funded, at least partially. However, in early 1996 'mad cow' disease struck Europe, creating an urgent need for cremation systems, and the European Commission decided to use the 'supplementary funds' for this purpose. The ATF managed to secure 'a bit of money', thanks to intensive lobbying, but proposals had to be rewritten since only half of the initial funding would be available. This is why, in the summer of 1996, 'the IMGs decided, after a long and terrible fight, to keep only one of the three "potential projects". Advance (of course, it was not called Advance at that time) won and was then considered as "the official ATF project".'

While the ATF/IMGs waited for the European Commission to issue a 'dedicated call for proposals', the available budget began to shrink. By the end of 1997, after more than a year, the 'dedicated call' was issued: 'Concurrent Engineering in Aeronautics', a joint call of the Brite Euram

(DG XII) and the Esprit (then DG III) programs. The call had to be answered before April 1998. From the viewpoint of the ATF/IMGs, the call was disappointing. It reduced the overall budget to €40 million (€20 million of funding) and, in addition, it was not to be answered by one large proposal; the call contained many sub-tasks that had to be dealt with by separate, small projects (€2–3 million). The ATF/IMGs decided to ignore the latter requirement and submit only one large €40 million project, 'with everybody and his brother in it', to be coordinated by Flysky France.

Forming the Consortium and Writing a Proposal

Between the end of 1997 and the end of March 1998, the Advance consortium was formed and a draft of the proposal written:

> The ATF members formed the core of the now called Advance consortium and we worked our fingers to the bone to gather the partners (the political talks alone took us months – we had competing companies on board), and to write the proposal that was submitted in due time.

Thus a first group of Advance partners (now 14) included the companies and the research institute that had already been part of the Task Force and IMGs. A second group of partners (around 20) was formed either on the basis of existing contacts (companies well known to members of the first group), or because they added competence in specialized fields. Almost all the companies that were contacted to join the consortium accepted and became partners immediately. The first group, however, remained the core of Advance; the members of this group would receive over 80 percent of the budget, and they would be responsible for most of the technical work.

Not the easiest part of preparing an EU proposal is the allocation of tasks to accomplish and, in relation to that, the distribution of months to be paid for. In the case of Advance, the definition and allocation of tasks and the distribution of 'man-months' were discussed throughout all the phases of proposal preparation. Negotiations about these issues took place in a collocated setting, and were attended by the 14 contractors (that is, the 'core group' partners). It took several rounds of rephrasing before the proposal was ready for submission.

The proposal was accepted in May 1998, but the European Commission asked the Advance consortium to rewrite entirely, and in greater detail, the technical contents. The scope of some tasks needed to be adjusted, although the project ideas were not really modified. The Commission also requested more information about the exploitation strategy. Rewriting was done in November 1998, soon to be followed by the signing of a contract (a contract had to be signed before the end of the year, as FP4 ended on 31 December 1998). The rewriting process was organized so that the main partners (some working together with associated partners) provided new descriptions of the task assigned to them, and also a new version of their exploitation strategy, and four (collocated) members of the management team integrated these texts, sent to them by e-mail.

4.2   ORGANIZATION OF THE ADVANCE PROJECT

The Advance consortium, as it was shaped by the time of signing the contract, was large and heterogeneous. It involved more than 300 people (approximately 3000 man-months), from 52 partners (14 contractors, 38 associated contractors), from ten countries of the European Union. Partners originated from the aerospace industry (both end product manufacturers and suppliers) and from the software industry (both vendors and engineering companies), but research institutes and universities were present as well. These partners had to engage in multidisciplinary collaboration, as required by the nature of the work. Thus geographical distance had to be bridged, as well as organizational, linguistic, cultural and disciplinary distance. The work was divided over 33 tasks.

The large number of partners was, in part, a result of the request by the EU Commission to include as many EU member states as possible. This request made it difficult for the consortium to maintain high standards while trying to find additional partners. As a consequence, the consortium was unable to set rules to sanction lack of cooperative behavior. There were hardly any instruments available that could be used if a partner proved to be unwilling to cooperate, or even failed to make the agreed-upon contributions.

Advance was aiming at research collaboration, but it can be viewed as a political arena as well. The project brought together very different actors, each with their own (hidden) agenda and set of interests. The aerospace companies hoped to generate knowledge, experience and working models (and perhaps to retrieve knowledge from other companies), thus improving their competitive capabilities. The European Commission sought to improve collaboration between European aerospace companies, so that the European industry would be able to compete with the rest of the world. The research centers and universities were aiming at the acquisition of knowledge, were in need of funding, and perhaps hoped to develop working relationships with aerospace companies. Finally, software vendors/developers were eager to learn about the needs of the aerospace industry, and to promote their own products. In short, political games were likely, both between the Advance project and the 'customer' (the European Commission), and between the different partners within the project.

Project Management Structure

Airplanes are very complex systems, and the systems to produce them reflect that complexity. Nearly all the core partners in Advance were in the airplane production business, and therefore used to complexity. The core partners designed the Advance project, and they made it complex, both in terms of project organization and in terms of task decomposition. We will describe the management structure of the project, the arrangements made to decompose the general Advance task into sub-tasks, and 'events' and other coordination mechanisms to keep the project on target.

The management structure of the Advance project

The Advance management structure reflected the project's history, revealing a clear distinction between 'contractors' (mainly including the first group of partners) and 'associated companies'. From the first group of partners, one large company assumed the role of 'coordinator', which meant a great deal of authority. The Advance project was supposed to require a high degree of flexibility, as well as adequate control over all the partners. Because these requirements are not easily reconciled, a 'heavy' management team was installed, the members of which all belonged to the coordinator company.

Management team   The members of this team were: a project manager, a technical manager, a project controller and a communication manager. As all these officials belonged to the coordinator company, the team was located in Frencité, the city of the coordinator company's headquarters. The management team was in charge of the project as a whole, directing the work package leaders and being responsible for the general project coordination. In addition, the team acted as *the* liaison between the project and the world outside (which included, first of all, the European Commission, but also other European projects, the aerospace industry, and user groups), monitored and evaluated the work as it progressed with work packages and tasks, and if necessary intervened when technical or other problems arose between partners. The project manager was leading the management team; he was the only Advance member authorized to represent the Advance consortium in its contacts with the European Commission, and he chaired the Advance project's executive committee (see below).

Work package leaders   The research to be conducted in Advance was separated into work packages, each of which was separated again into tasks. These work packages and tasks will be described in the next section. Each work package was supervised (or coordinated) by a work package leader, who had to belong to a contractor company. Leaders of different work packages discussed 'interface issues', they had to report about the progress of work within their work package to the management team (usually to the project technical manager), and they were members of the technical operations team (TOP team).

Task leaders   Each of the tasks within a work package was coordinated by a task leader, who would organize and administer the work of that particular task, report to the work package leader about performance and progress made, and report to the project controller if financial or administrative issues were concerned.

Thus the Advance project had a clear hierarchical decision-making structure, even if the project description's vocabulary reveals a preference for the word 'recommendation' rather than 'command'. Complementary to this decision-making structure was an internal consultation structure consisting of committees and teams for discussing, preparing, coordinating and performing the research tasks. In the Advance project, actual task performance was to be found in the task teams, coordinated primarily within the work packages. Wider coordination, and the other activities mentioned, took place within the confinements of the Advance executive committee and the TOP team.

The executive committee   The executive committee was composed of the project manager (chair), technical manager, project controller and a representative of each contractor company. The committee met regularly (as a rule, on the basis of a six-week interval, in a face-to-face setting) to review the project progress (relying on information provided by the TOP team), to ensure that agreements made within the Advance consortium complied with the European Commission contract, to deal with issues raised by associated contractors, and to resolve issues that need to be refereed.

The TOP team   The TOP (Technical Operations) team included the technical manager (chair), the project controller, the nine work package leaders and the WP5 deputy leader (because WP5 was very large, here a deputy leader was appointed). The TOP team dealt with the project's technical and operational management issues, which included monitoring and control of technical progress and of the quality of delivered work, resolving 'critical' technical problems and coordinating the work packages.

The work package teams The Advance project involved nine work packages, each headed by a work package team that was responsible for the technical and operational work within the work package. The members of this team were the work package leader (chair) and the leaders of the tasks within the work package. A work package team monitored and controlled the technical progress of the work package (including the quality of inputs and deliveries), dealt with technical problems and coordinated the tasks.

Task teams Each work package contained several tasks (the number of tasks varied between work packages; the total number was 33). Each task was led by a task leader, responsible for the technical and operational work within the task. The members of a task team were the task leader (chair) and what was referred to as the 'company resources' allocated to the task. The task team controlled the technical progress of the task (including the quality of inputs and deliveries) and dealt with technical problems.

The division of tasks in the Advance project

The Advance project, thus, was broken down into nine work packages (WP0 to WP8), these being divided into tasks. WP0 was the management work package, while WP1 to WP3 were the COMMONs work packages, developing procedures and methods defining 'the common ways of working' that aimed at electronic product modeling for short- and long-term product evolution. Each of the three COMMONs work packages covered one engineering domain.

WP1, the work package on product engineering, addressed issues such as products configuration management, aircraft support activities, the interoperability of calculation algorithms, certification processes and a component electronic catalog. The work package enclosed five tasks: (1.1) develop 'digital product master models' to enable a common view on product-related data within the European aeronautical sector; (1.2) define an electronic catalog as a common repository of standard parts that may encourage the use of standard parts in product development; (1.3) create common standards in calculation to foster extended enterprise-compatible engineering; (1.4) focus on certification process changes brought about by concurrent engineering design methodologies; and (1.5) explore the 'ability to be easily supported' as a principle of integrated aircraft design.

WP2, the work package on life cycle models and business management, started from the observation that different aircraft life cycle models and different business management tools were being used in the industry, which might hamper the exchange of information and impede collaboration. The work package enclosed four tasks: (2.1) to develop a generic aircraft development life cycle model that could be used throughout the European aeronautics supply chain; (2.2) to aim at a common understanding on program management in European aeronautical engineering, and to turn the prevailing variety of practices into a common way to manage (concurrent engineering) aircraft development programs; (2.3) to bridge the gap between (old) contractual conditions and (new) communication and information-sharing technologies, which included new approaches to knowledge management and to property rights management; and (2.4) to adjust administrative processes of support organizations, to ensure that airline companies receive appropriate information from aircraft builders where the latter, as a result of concurrent engineering design methodology, are no longer a single company.

WP3, the work package on technology and methodology for the extended enterprise, defined work methods that would enable aeronautical engineers to collaborate if they were not collocated. These methods, which were geared towards the aeronautical industry but were relying on state-of-the-art information technology, included standards, principles, rules, methods, tools and IT infrastructures. The work package enclosed four tasks: (3.1) to improve the capability for distant cooperation of European aerospace companies by creating a CSCW (Computer Supported Cooperative Work) environment referred to as 'common multi-site collaborative environment for concurrent engineering'; (3.2) to facilitate data exchange by developing common principles for exchanging technical information, to be adopted by all aeronautical companies; (3.3) to address the fact that aerospace companies used different IT environments that would have to be standardized and integrated to become one common, open IT architecture that could support concurrent engineering; (3.4) to increase awareness of concurrent engineering techniques and processes, and to teach companies (and individuals within them) to use the methods and tools developed for that purpose.

WP4, on concurrent engineering integration and experiments, integrated the results of the three 'COMMONs' work packages and of WP6, the work package on information technology. This work package, in addition, aimed at 'validation through experiments'. In Task 4.1, the first of two tasks, the results of the COMMONs work packages were 'harmonized' to make them amenable to experimentation. The Advance project was very keen to verify the different findings from the WPs, and therefore created a 'validation and integration logic' based on a classical V-type development life cycle model.

This V-cycle development (see Figure 4.1) shows how the three levels of analysis in Advance – (1) business level, (2) concurrent engineering level, and (3) information technology level – were connected and organized.

Concerning the first level, at the beginning of the project several business case studies (BCSs) were defined as being important to the Advance scope and project aims. These BCSs had to identify generic sets of needs that the

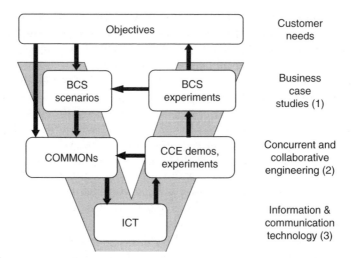

Figure 4.1 V-cycle model

Advance tools and methods would have to meet. At the end of the V cycle, the BCSs were supposed to be used for dissemination of the project results and demonstration of the functional achievements in the business environment. Concerning the second level, concurrent engineering-derived needs were used to refine the definition and deliverables of the COMMONs work packages. Concerning the third level, information technology-related needs were analyzed in order to provide the project with the tools to support the integration and demonstration tasks of the other levels.

Next to offering an integration methodology and implementation plan using the V-cycle model, Task 4.1 also included the creation of the Advance laboratory (A-lab), meant to bring together all the necessary means for integration and experimentation in a single location. This A-lab had to operate an IT platform for deliverables and demonstrators integration, support the demonstration of interoperability of outputs provided by the COMMONs work packages, provide the IT environment needed for concurrent engineering experiments, support business case studies experiments, ensure the operation of dissemination tools and operate the Advance website. As to the first phase of the V cycle, Task 4.2 identified the concurrent engineering experiments to be conducted, by analyzing the functionalities that would be required for BCSs' operations. In the second phase of the V cycle, this task contributed to the validation process in a collaborative process in which the COMMONs would receive feedback to improve their deliverables.

WP5 was the work package containing the business case studies (BCSs).

Advance aimed at the introduction of a new, common way of working in the European aerospace industry, and compliance with real business needs was considered essential for a favorable reception of the common references to be proposed. Accordingly, eight tasks were defined to explore the prospects of integrated development: (5.1) a new rotorcraft concept; (5.2) the design of new large aircraft; (5.3) the avionics systems; (5.4) the engines systems; (5.5) the aircraft mechanical systems; (5.6) the airplane customization; (5.7) the analysis and use of in-service data; and (5.8) product improvement. These BCSs had to provide the COMMONs and the supporting work packages (WP4, WP6) with business-oriented requirements to substantiate (on the basis of experiments) the value of the COMMONs' results for real business processes, and to convince companies of the benefits of using Advance's methods and tools, which also included the production of dissemination materials.

WP6 was the work package devoted to information technology. It was felt that the aerospace industry had not taken proper advantage of available information technologies thus far, and that concurrent engineering-based collaboration would only increase the need to exploit these technologies' potential. Task 6.1 identified IT innovations and future trends that had to connect state-of-the-art IT research with requirements from the COMMONs or BCSs, thus enabling collaborative development processes in the aerospace industry to be improved. Task 6.2 had to add an IT point of view to the concurrent engineering experiments, including the selection of relevant hardware and software tools to support these experiments. Task 6.3 provided IT support and guidelines to ensure the consistency of the overall IT environment within Advance, thus preventing redundant work and divergent views on information technology between tasks.

WP7 and WP8, finally, were assisting work packages. WP7, called 'Support', included tasks related to concurrent engineering and human factors, and WP8, 'Dissemination and Exploitation', had to 'broadcast' the outcomes of Advance to the project members, to the European aerospace industry at large (especially SMEs), and to related manufacturing and engineering European industries.

Thus the tasks in Advance were numerous, and highly interrelated. In a later section we will return to this in some detail. In the present section we will present a picture showing the main sequence of work to be accomplished by the major Advance work packages, a sequence that derives from the V cycle's 'validation and integration logic' (see Figure 4.2).

Events and other coordination mechanisms in the Advance project
To keep the project on track, and to evaluate the progress made, five internal reviews and four external reviews had been scheduled before the start

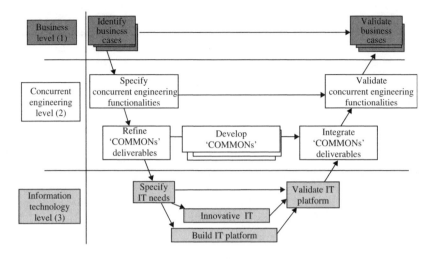

Figure 4.2   V-cycle model's validation and integration logic

of the project. In addition, parts of the management structure (executive committee, TOP team) and of the task structure (WP4, especially the V-cycle model) were supposed to contribute to integration and technical progress, as well as the decision to consider some COMMONs' tasks as 'flagship tasks'. We will briefly introduce these events and mechanisms.

Internal reviews   The internal reviews were associated to milestones that had been defined to structure the course of the project. Each milestone (except the first) completed a particular phase of the work (see Table 4.1). These internal reviews all had the same structure. The project manager, assisted by the project controller, assessed the project progress mainly against 'key control' items (such as workshop, reviews, documents). Relevant materials were provided by the work package and task leaders.

External reviews   A further instrument to assess the Advance project per-formance were the four EU review meetings. Present at these meetings were representatives of the European Commission (accompanied by experts), the project manager, the technical manager, the project controller and the work package leaders. Advance project technical experts had to be available on request. In the meetings, presentations were given, and progress was assessed against deliverables, progress reports and cost statements (which had to be presented to the European Commission every six months). Each deliverable – an official document presented to the EU

Table 4.1   Structure for internal reviews

Milestones	Date	Phases
M0: Project kick-off	T0	
		1: Requirement
M1: Start of preliminary definition	T0+4	
		2: Preliminary definition
M2: Start of detailed definition	T0+11	
		3: Detailed definition
M3: Start of industrial validation	T0+22	
		4: Industrial validation
M4: Start of finalization	T0+33	
		5: Finalization
M5: Final review	T0+36	

Commission – corresponded to a specific activity within the project. The review committee could, based on a review meeting, make recommendations that had to be complied with by the consortium.

Forums   For each year an 'Advance forum' was scheduled (each time in a different country, to encourage attendance by members of the project's supply chain user groups), organized by WP8 and the communication manager. These forums had to serve several purposes. They were a 'dissemination' activity (a compulsory part of EU-sponsored research), but also a setting in which users, particularly from the supply chain user groups, could comment on the utility and quality of results presented, and they were a further instrument to accomplish integration between work packages and between tasks. Three forums were held. Forum 1 (2000, UK) was a general one, meant to inform the outside world about Advance and what the project was going to deliver. Forum 2 (2001, Belgium) presented the first results of the project. Forum 3 (2002, France) had to show the end results to the aeronautical engineering world. To prepare a forum, several internal workshops would be organized.

Decision-making   Another integration mechanism was decision-making by the TOP team and the executive committee. As the members of these groups could rely on scheduled meetings, their need for other communication modes, including virtual communication, was limited. In these meetings, decisions were made (on management issues) according to the rules in the so-called Quality Assurance Plan. All main partners had to conform to these rules. During a meeting, decisions were taken based on voting and then noted down. In many cases consensus was reached, and the decision was accepted in a 'raise hands' kind of vote. If no consensus was reached, or if the subject was very important (for instance the decision to postpone the end of the project), a more formalized procedure was followed. In such cases, all TOP team members had to sign. At the end of each meeting decisions were reiterated, to make sure that everything was clear to all. Decisions not considered 'crucial' could be made using e-mail. In such cases, the rule applied that 'if you do not object to this in 15 opening days (3 weeks) it is considered as approved.' A member of the executive committee points out that there were only minor problems in taking decisions. The reason was, according to this member, that interpersonal problems were largely absent (with the exception of a conflict between the technical manager and the TOP team; see further below). As an explanation for the lack of conflict, he puts forward that the members of the core of the project (i.e. the main partners) were used to working with each other. Together they had prepared the project proposal.

Division of tasks With respect to the mechanisms to integrate the work packages, the pattern of output exchange can be mentioned, but also the division of tasks. As described, the COMMONs (work packages WP1 to WP3) had to develop procedures and methods defining the new 'common ways of working', to be integrated by WP4 and to be used by the business case studies (WP5). The COMMONs themselves were also highly interrelated, according to the project plan. Each of the COMMONs' work packages addressed one particular engineering domain, which split the project into different disciplinary domains. Therefore, internal workshops were planned as a means to secure interdependence and the exchange of knowledge between the COMMONs.

The COMMONs work packages were subdivided into different tasks. In each work package, one task was viewed as the 'flagship'. As stated in the detailed task description of (2.1), '(2.1) together with (1.1) and (3.1) is one of the three main flag-ship COMMONs which will have a major influence on the design and operation of most of the other COMMONs and Business Case Studies within the Advance project'. Thus the proper execution of these tasks could be used as a key marker for both structuring and evaluating the work process in Advance.

Integration work package This work package (WP4) had to validate and integrate the COMMONs results into a consistent action plan, and to validate its operability through generic (concurrent collaborative engineering) experiments. For this purpose, WP4 created the A-lab (Advance concurrent engineering laboratory). The lab consisted of a main site (even having a showroom), two secondary sites and an auxiliary site. Another secondary site was intended, but never got ready for operation. Each site had the facilities and the expertise for carrying out BCSs' concurrent engineering experiments and validation tests.

4.3   HOW THE ADVANCE PROJECT EVOLVED

So much for the 'hard facts' about the Advance project, as found in the 1998 Project Programme. The question is whether this initial structure enabled the processes of distant research collaboration that were necessary to achieve the project's aims. Here we must be careful. The Advance project was meant to serve several objectives, some of which were difficult to assess in the absence of plain criteria. From the interviews conducted it appears that those involved in the project tend to weight these objectives differently, and even differ in their judgment of project performance on a given criterion. Moreover, it is clear that a 'structure on paper' is not the only factor to determine actual processes. It has to be implemented, refined, perhaps adapted to specific circumstances, and its functioning depends on conditions that may be beyond the control of those who designed the initial structure, e.g. the type of leadership exercised by work package and task leaders, or a participating company's attitude towards the project. This being said, the striking fact remains that in the Advance project's final meeting most task teams had to resort to presenting slides, unable as they were to give real demonstrations.

In the present section we will, first, describe the codes of conduct that were added to the 'paper structure' in an attempt to encourage the kind of communication deemed necessary for the project to thrive. Second, we will explicate that these codes (and the structure they were to support) did not suffice, and present evidence of poor communication (or even lack of communication) between research groups that had to communicate well to complete their work. Third, we will propose a list of factors that may account for the communication problems that plagued the Advance project. We will show that the quality of media for distant communication is only one, not very important, factor among many others to explain the (lack of) communication between people who are supposed to collaborate at a distance in an Advance-like environment.

Codes of Conduct for Communication in Advance

Kick-off meetings
The official kick-off meeting for the Advance project took place in February 1999. The meeting was guided by the management team, and attended by

the executive committee, the WP leaders and the task leaders. The WP leaders presented the planning of their work package, as each work package team was allowed to decide on its own work rules. In the meeting the project organization was discussed, including planning and timetables, and the technical contents of the project. Some quality assurance aspects were considered as well, such as templates to be used for documents, review procedures, and standard tools to be used, such as Word and Excel.

Some WP leaders organized kick-off meetings for their own task teams. It depended on an individual WP leader whether such a kick-off meeting was organized and how it was shaped. Not all task members attended 'their' meeting. As a task member remarked: 'One day before the task kick-off meeting, I was notified to attend this meeting, in order to replace a colleague. It appeared that half of the task members present were notified at such short notice.' At some of these kick-off meetings, guidelines for the organizational part of the specific work package were issued (e.g. 'respect the project schedule', 'anticipate on actions, issues, deadlines and milestones', 'check and monitor progress regularly'), as well as 'hard' and 'soft' communication rules. One of the internal documents presents a list of soft rules:

- Ensure that all members of your sub-team have clear objectives.
- Communicate with and mobilize your sub-team members.
- Ask for help if necessary.
- Accelerate information exchange (use e-mail, website, video-conferences).
- Confirm the receipt of information instantly.

The hard rules were defined as follows:

- It is essential that all sub-task leaders have Internet access,
- It is essential that all sub-task leaders have a functioning e-mail address,
- It is mandatory that all team members have Internet access.
- Use the software tools as adopted.

Furthermore, the leader of the work package from which the document originated provided a list that specified exact role definitions for task leader and task team members, apparently in an attempt to make sure that all members would have a clear and common understanding of the various responsibilities within the task. For example, the role of the task leader was to:

- Behave as the general manager of your task – you are the boss.
- Take care that your sub-task is up and running on time.

- Establish communication.
- Know your sub-task team members (by name!).
- Check if that information is distributed the way it should be.

After these kick-off meetings, the consortium started working. Not all tasks could start at the same time, as some needed input from other tasks first. Some tasks only lasted a few months, or started early in the project, to fade away in the middle and reappear at the end. According to the interviewees, this was one of the flaws in the project organization: members who are only involved at the beginning, or just for a small period of time, did not stay informed or committed to the project.

Ground rules
In the first year of the project, a management crisis developed. As indicated, the management team was located in Frencité, which is where the management team gathered every six weeks with the TOP team. In these meetings, a conflict between the TOP team and the technical manager soon produced an unworkable situation. As one interviewee remarked: 'At this point, we were even thinking to end the whole project.' Many blamed the technical manager, who was seen as an individualist, not a team player. Another interviewee added that there were also problems within the TOP team itself, concerning the division of the budgets and man-months. A lack of mutual trust also caused some cooperation problems in the TOP team.

The management team decided to organize a team-building event in October 1999, the 'syndicate meeting'. At this event, ways were discussed to improve working relationships and to create a more social and friendly atmosphere. In particular, the attempt was made to construct a set of ground rules for communication and cooperation. For this purpose, those attending the meeting were divided in small teams called 'syndicates'. Each syndicate had to submit a few ground rules. Listed here are some important rules that came out of the event:

- Use any convenient medium (telephone, e-mail, etc.) for communication.
- Use simple, unambiguous language.
- Share information and problems with people who are affected by these.
- Use face-to-face interaction, telephone, or e-mail to confirm receipt of information.
- Check that you have grasped the meaning of information conveyed by rephrasing or reformulating your understanding of the information.

- Structure written communication by providing recipients with the subject, title, importance and relevance of your message. Be concise.

The syndicate meeting helped the TOP team members to improve their communication. In addition, cooperation improved after the technical manager eventually left the project, to be replaced by one of the other management team members. An EU review document would later state that the TOP team 'appears to be cohesive and motivated' and that 'regular informal contact and meetings have ensured a good and pro-active team spirit, with open communication channels and evident commitment'.

Evidence of Poor Communication

As mentioned, many tasks were unable to demonstrate the results of their work in the final meeting, even though the project duration had been prolonged by four months. Such a failure to deliver on time is not necessarily a sign of communication problems, but in the case of the Advance project it was. To validate this claim we can rely on various sources of information, including EU review findings, a 'lessons learned' report, and interviews and e-mail exchanges with various Advance members. These sources clearly indicate that collaboration in Advance did not always go smoothly (including communication in a narrow sense), though descriptions of the problem vary, as well as explanations proposed. Moreover, they suggest that the communication problems were inextricably linked to the way the Advance project was structured, and to circumstances of its operation – such as the type of involvement of several partners in the consortium.

Review
Every EU project includes regular meetings (one or two days) in which the project is reviewed by a committee consisting of EU representatives and external reviewers. Such meetings are compulsory. If the review is positive, the EU will continue to fund the project. As the stakes are high, usually such review meetings are carefully prepared by those involved in the project being reviewed. Presentations must be engaging, provide a credible statement of the project's strengths and weaknesses, and convey the impression that the project as a whole is internally consistent.

The first Advance review meeting took place in Frencité in March 2000; gathered were officials from the EU Commission and the members of the TOP team and the executive committee. Despite the many efforts that had been made to make the project look attuned and coherent, the review committee found that the various WPs and tasks were lacking integration.

In this respect extra attention would be necessary, according to the review report:

> Some interesting activities have been performed . . . However, these activities seem to be performed in an independent mode and can only be valuable if they are done in close collaboration with the activities of other work packages as the results to be integrated and validated are being produced elsewhere. (EU review report: 4)

Accordingly, the review committee considered it necessary that communication and cooperation within the project be encouraged, especially between representatives of the different firms involved in the consortium: '[there is] much evidence that the project partners may be working in relative isolation within their own companies' (EU review report: 10). Furthermore, it was recommended to use collaborative work tools to support distributed teamwork, and to appoint an 'integrator' who would be able to strengthen the integration of the WPs.

After a review meeting, the review committee would present a report to the management team, whose responsibility it was to convey results to all consortium members. Interestingly, the Advance management team communicated the main review findings, but did not circulate a full version of the review report.

Lessons learned report

After the final forum, the Advance communication manager and a work package leader wrote a 'lessons learned' report in which they presented a number of rules to be complied with. The problems that would have been prevented or solved by following these rules were hinted at, rather than described. Still, the report makes it quite clear that in Advance there was 'granularity of tasks', meaning that the number of tasks was too large. It also indicates that communication was hampered by cultural and language barriers, that commitment and team spirit were insufficient, that some partners did not perform as they should ('sleeping partners' or 'defaulting partners'), that people (or even task leaders) did not always know what to do, that the project faced too many changes (e.g. in companies' status), that the management team lacked the instruments required to lead the project properly, that many in the project had to deal with 'far too much information and far too little useful documents or messages', and that soon into the project the amount of information became too large to handle. Thus the report tends to take knowledge of actual problems for granted, and mainly confines itself to offering (possible) elements of an explanation. These problems, or deficiencies, are also mentioned (often in considerable detail) in the interviews conducted and in subsequent e-mail exchanges with interviewees.

Interviews and e-mail exchange

Interviews were conducted with several TOP team members and task team leaders (see Chapter 2); occasionally, the interview was followed by e-mail exchange in which additional questions were asked. Typically, a question about communication processes within Advance would elicit the observation that lack of communication was a major problem, a remark that was sometimes followed by illustrations and often by an explanation. The observations most frequently made were that the COMMONs and BCSs hardly communicated, and that tasks (and jobs within tasks) were specialized to the extent that task-related communication was effectively pre-empted. These observations are part of a larger 'syndrome' of communication difficulties in Advance:

1.   It was not an accident that a demonstration could not be presented in the final meeting. In Advance it was the rule, not the exception, that deadlines were not met. One of the interviewees even claims not to know of a single task that was *not* delayed. Another interviewee observes that in meetings people showed up late (or not at all), and that expected results were not presented. In addition to such delays, the quality of deliverables varied highly. While some reports were excellent, others seemed to have required only minor efforts. Since there were no instruments to maintain quality standards (e.g. sanctions to apply if reports were poorly written), the issue of quality was a disturbing one throughout the Advance project. Such instruments could not be made available in the absence of performance indicators or 'metrics'. The Advance project never managed to define such metrics, even though the European Commission strongly emphasized their use.

Workshops and other Advance meetings also suffered from lack of preparation on the part of attendants. Several interviewees suggest that the Advance project was not important enough in the eyes of many participating companies, and that it was not rare that a company would appoint someone with some spare time to join an Advance meeting, and to appoint very late. Thus meetings were attended by people who were unprepared, hardly knew the others, and who were therefore unable to make a meaningful contribution. This may explain why the meetings did not become significant social events (added to the fact that many task team members were only briefly involved in the project). Rather than becoming integrative experiences, meetings continued to be occasions where people from the same company looked out for each other.

Their floating population made meetings and workshops an unsuited situation for making arrangements (and engagements that were made were often broken). This does not apply to partners with few man-months, as they were absent from most meetings and workshops. Being present there would have squandered most of their budget.

2.   The V-cycle model, meant to structure the internal supply of products and services in Advance, did not work properly. Those who set up Advance as a systems engineering project were not involved in its implementation. The people who were performing actual tasks within the project had a poor understanding of the V-cycle model and the systems engineering approach. Moreover, knowledge of and experience with concurrent engineering were inadequate. As a result, it never became clear what requirements should be formulated to tailor the information technology to be developed, and Advance ended as a project in which such technology was developed without being guided by empirical studies and experimental findings geared towards the aerospace industry.

3.   Task teams and individual task team members could not compensate for this. Task team members had little knowledge of Advance work outside their own task. The meetings did not serve that purpose, as indicated, and within their own task they had mainly e-mail contact with their task leader, for the most part about details concerning their own part of the deliverable to be produced. Horizontal communication between task team members was rather unusual. There was little need for that, as the teams' tasks were divided into small sub-tasks (thus, 'others in your task team do not depend on you').

It is also important that many task teams did not develop as true social units. Membership turnover was often high and team commitment was low. Many team members had not been involved from the start of the project, or were only task team members for the period it took to complete a particular piece of work. Moreover, task team membership tended to be only a part-time job. And whole task teams could start late, or disband early, or were part of a work package that had contributions to make only at the very beginning and at the very end of Advance. Finally, the task teams comprised members from various companies, and they often worked 'in relative isolation' within their own company.

4.   The Advance project was highly complex, and not well understood by many participants, but complexity was increased by halfway changes in the allocation of resources or even in the program organization. Some tasks were withdrawn or combined, other tasks were added. While such changes

were confusing to 'the workers' in the project, they were welcomed by the management team:

> There was freedom which we negotiated with the EU. We reduced the number of deliverable 'versions', we re-arranged the budget several times in line with recovery plans and moved review dates. A task was also suppressed and one was added. The rule is: You can reorganize yourself if you stay within the budget that was defined.

5. Collaboration between the BCSs and the COMMONs should have been intense, but it was nearly absent. The BCS task team had to supply requirements derived from the literature (for instance on concurrent engineering), and indeed they produced large state-of-the-art literature reviews. The COMMONs, however, did not read these reviews, did not respond to them, and did not use them. An important reason, it seems, has been that the BCS reports (written by researchers from universities and research centers) were theoretically oriented, not acknowledging the COMMONs' need for practical guidelines. In addition, many reviews were meticulous and large, and therefore not delivered on time. Since theoretically oriented and more practically oriented researchers were assigned to different work packages, scant reading could hardly be compensated by other ways to convey BCS findings. Before blaming the BCS task team for self-indulgent writing, it must be added that the business case objectives were quite unclear (as admitted by many interviewees) and that the COMMONs were unable to articulate their needs, at least initially. Later, the situation had settled that COMMONs and BCSs did not care to communicate. The management team decided to organize workshops and forums (in which the teams presented results to a broad and partially external audience), but these events did not suffice to make collaboration happen; COMMONs presenting their work would not receive responses from the BCSs. This pattern of non-communication was reinforced by the fact that BCS work was situated in the earliest stage of Advance (definition of requirements) and in a much later stage (validation). In the two years in between, other work replaced Advance as a focus of BCS members' attention. Many 'early' BCS members did not even return to perform validation tasks. As a result, interaction between COMMONs and BCSs was limited, and thorough validation of the requirements once formulated by the BCSs did not take place.

6. Apart from such collaboration problems, some BCSs performed poorly. One reason seemed to be that the companies involved were not always willing to provide the BCSs with the materials needed. As remarked by someone participating in several COMMONs tasks and BCS tasks, part

of the problem between the analysis developed by the COMMONs and the BCSs ('But these problems are normal whatever the subject') was that for the BCSs it was hard to find cases consistent enough to test the COMMONs' proposals: 'It is normal that each company did not want to provide their most recent studies or the results of R&D they had.' Therefore, the BCSs had a difficult start.

As a further point, some BCSs did not see a 'market' for what they were supposed to deliver, and lost motivation (especially when the COMMONs rejected the work by the BCSs) until others (visiting external members at the forum meetings) showed them that their products were answering to an external demand.

7.   ADR, the Advance Data Repository, was insufficiently used. ADR was a database system for working documents, designed to mirror the structure of work packages and tasks. The system suffered from technical and organizational problems. If ADR was used at all, information was not kept up to date, and ADR failed to become a commonly used tool for information sharing. The poor use of ADR was not only, and perhaps not even primarily, a result of the system's design. It was also a consequence of access restrictions (firewalls) applied by companies for the sake of data protection. In any case, ADR was seen as a means for control, rather than a tool to facilitate collaboration: 'ADR didn't work for collaboration. It was just a vault manager used to publish official data, something like a common repository for sharing deliverables. It did not at all support collaboration, nor concurrent activities.' Therefore, not ADR but e-mail and telephone were the main media for distant communication within Advance.

8.   Given the way Advance was structured, the TOP team was the obvious agency to distinguish the shortcomings in the Advance project, and to make corrections if necessary. Coordination was largely in the hands of the TOP team, and separate work package teams had few instruments to foster integration if the TOP team failed. The TOP team, however, did not function well. First, there was distrust. Some work package leaders were suspected of organizing their work package in a way beneficial for their own company. It was also believed that some TOP team members hoped to work their way into the main contracting company: members accused each other of trying to make secret deals with Flysky and, as an interviewee puts it, 'The Flysky total company was being formed so the Brits, French, Germans and Spanish in the parts of Flysky were always exchanging views on the movements and organizational changes and looking for new jobs in Flysky. The rest of us were discussing the aircraft business in general.' And second, the TOP team faced cultural differences. Members representing

North European companies acted more autonomously and were more politically capable than members from South European countries – who had to consult their companies' headquarters before being able to make a commitment.

Explaining Poor Communication in Advance

In the above-mentioned observations, causes and effects are not clearly distinguished. Thus it is not obvious whether the absence of good working relationships between BCSs and the COMMONs, for instance, should be viewed as evidence of poor communication, or as a partial explanation of the failure to deliver quality products and presentations in a timely manner. However, a clear distinction between cause and effect can only be made if a single objective (or a single hierarchy of objectives) is present, which is a requirement not met in this case. A very concise description of work packages and tasks (as in section 4.2) shows the high aspiration level of Advance. The project was, first of all, an attempt to develop a new way of organizing product development (in a broad sense), integrating state-of-the-art knowledge from a variety of domains, including project management, concurrent engineering, supply chain management and information technology. Tools and techniques had to be developed, and their practical use demonstrated. But the project had other objectives as well. It sought to set standards, for example for the size of parts to be used for calculation methods, in a hitherto deeply divided industry. And both the development of a new way to organize product development and the setting of standards had to be accomplished largely through distant collaboration, as that was considered the only way to bring such a large collection of companies together in a single project. This was a final objective: to escort companies to the point that they would find themselves actually cooperating, as a first, necessary step towards further consolidation of the European aerospace industry.

   In terms of the first objective, the lack of cooperation between BCSs and the COMMONs should be taken as an explanation of the failure to deliver, but in terms of the third objective this lack of cooperation is evidence in itself. The lack of cooperation does not have to be proven, since this was obviously the case. If the single goal of the Advance project was cooperation between European aerospace companies, then the lack of cooperation (already evident) is not the explanation for some underlying principle but a fact on its own.

   From the project documents and the interviews, not a single 'chief objective' can be distilled. Concluding from various interviews, it was obvious that Advance had to answer to different goals from different members and organizations. Because of this we are not sure what to conclude from the obvious lack of cooperation: was the Advance project a total failure (because cooperation as a whole failed) or was the Advance project a project that, for various reasons, including troublesome cooperation, had problems with dealing with the deadlines of the deliverables?

In the context of a general evaluation of the Advance project, the issue of objectives' compatibility might be considered. As it was, the people in Advance had to collaborate at a distance in order to develop tools and methods that would enable future collaboration at a distance. No wonder if this was difficult. In the present context, the communication processes in a non-collocated setting are being studied, and no general evaluation is aimed at. A first step in the analysis was to establish that, within the Advance project, communication processes were very difficult. Now, a second step is to explicate why this was so. Again EU review findings, the 'lessons learned' report, and the interviews with Advance members will be relied on, but we will not present these sources separately, as we seek to make an inventory of exogenous factors (factors not shaped by internal processes within Advance) that, in conjunction, produced the state of poor communication in Advance as described above.

Various factors can be deduced from the most noticeable characteristic of the Advance project: its complexity. The project, we suggest, was very complex first of all because of the large number of participants. This large number, in turn, resulted mainly from the European Commission's request to involve as many partners as possible. The Commission had good reasons for its request. It was widely acknowledged that the European aerospace industry was fragmented, consisting of companies that were not inclined or geared towards European collaboration. For that reason, the industry was hardly able to keep in competition with large American companies. Thus collaboration had to be encouraged, through developing instruments and standards that would facilitate the exchange of plans, information and products (the 'nuts and bolts'), and through involving companies in actual communication and collaboration processes. The latter tactic implied that as many companies as possible had to be enrolled, from many EU countries. This introduced national and cultural differences as a likely source of communication problems. Less predictable, perhaps, it also enabled companies that were less than fully dedicated to enter the project. And finally, the large number of partners made it necessary to have a large project task domain, as shown by the number of work packages and tasks.

However, large project size does not necessarily mean that the project structure is complex. Arrangements can be made to keep the structure simple: create autonomous teams, define fairly independent task modules, encourage a 'flat structure'. In the Advance project, such simplifying arrangements were absent. Before going into the reasons for that, we will briefly examine the concept of 'complexity' itself, which refers to such different notions as 'cognitively complex' and 'wicked' problems (Barlow 2001). Cognitive complexity relates to processing information that is not well defined and possibly not even internally consistent. Approaches to solve cognitively complex problems involve the development and use of algorithms, and problem decomposition. Very different are wicked problems, also called messy problems. These terms are used to describe 'situations in which there are large differences of opinion on the problem or even on the question of whether there is a problem' (Vennix 1999: 380). Barlow (2001) suggests that wicked problems can be reduced but not solved. He mentions two reduction techniques: relating decisions to ultimate goals on which different parties agree, or inventing concrete solutions that leave the parties involved equally dissatisfied. Vennix (1999) recommends problem structuring and the creation of consensus and commitment with a group decision. Thus cognitive complexity can be dealt with by a single individual while wicked problems cannot. The latter require interaction, deliberation, negotiation and often tact. In Advance, both forms of complexity did occur, but not always as distinctly as the above descriptions suggest. It can be very complex, in the cognitive sense, to organize a project (allocating tasks and responsibilities, making arrangements to ensure the efficient exchange of information), but since the 'parts of the puzzle' are largely social in nature, 'wickedness' may easily develop.

Cognitive complexity stemmed, first of all, from the way tasks were structured. As indicated, many partners were involved, working on a large number of tasks in a variety of domains. The names of the work packages offer a fine summary of domains being covered: 'product engineering', 'life cycle models and business management', 'technology and methodology for the extended enterprise', 'concurrent engineering', 'information technology'. Each of these domains had to inform all the others, which created a need for collaboration across (work package and task) boundaries. To ensure this collaboration, a bewildering number of task interrelations were scheduled. A table in the Overall Project Description (a section of the project program's annex) shows that nearly all the tasks in WP1 to WP5, and several in the other work packages, had a 'medium' or 'strong' contribution to make to almost any other task. Two factors may have contributed to the decision to schedule collaboration in such detail. One is the European Union's demand that research projects to be funded must be carefully planned. Proof is needed, and detailed schedules provided for that. The second is the Advance project's hierarchical structure, explicated above. This structure may reflect project management routines in the aerospace industry, or only the way Flysky (the coordinating partner, in whose headquarters the proposal was written) used to organize its projects, but it also may reflect this company's aspiration to control the project. Standard setting was a main objective and Flysky hoped to have future European standards modeled after its own, internal standards.

Whatever the reasons, the schedule produced cognitive complexity for collaborators involved in Advance. It created a dense pattern of compulsory 'give and receive' – risky because this made it almost inevitable that a given task had to wait for contributions from other tasks, in a situation moreover where delay generates further delay. Those in a position to oversee the whole project had to intervene when deliverables jammed – an example of cognitive complexity. Those who were not able to oversee the project, i.e. the majority of members, had to contribute to 'collaborative' products without knowing exactly why and for whom, and often without being familiar with quality specifications – which makes it a complicated job to deliver something useful. Thus the conditions were present that must have hampered processes of intensive 'give and receive', and as soon as such processes cease to go smoothly, 'wicked' problems may well arise.

Part of the hierarchical structure was that task team members communicated almost exclusively with their task leader. In many cases, this communication was strictly task-related. The task leader would receive pieces of work produced by individual team members, integrate these, and send the resulting deliverable to the WP leader. As a result of thorough decomposition of tasks into sub-tasks (and so on), there was hardly any need for task team members to contact one another. This seems to hold in particular for the theoretical tasks. Thus, paradoxically, collaboration was made unnecessary by the very system that was meant to secure it.

Another source of cognitive complexity was the project composition. Advance was heterogeneous in many respects. Between partners responsibilities differed, as well as the nature and size of contributions to be made, in a way that reflected the Advance project's history. Partners originated from various branches of industry, and they were different in size. Partners originating from the aerospace industry proper had been (and still were) involved in fierce competition. Different nationalities were present, which entailed cultural differences as well as different languages, ways of conduct, management styles, and relations with home companies. Different disciplines were involved, ranging from aircraft engineering specialties to psychology, and from information systems design to life cycle management. Besides the 'usual' communication problems that disciplinary differences tend to produce, in combination with task division they generated a knowledge discrepancy: the specialists who 'implemented' systems engineering and concurrent engineering, the basic approaches in Advance, did not stay in the project, leaving the others with approaches they did not master.

A final source of heterogeneity listed here were the status differences between tasks in Advance. As indicated, three task team members were considered the project's 'flagships', which seems to have left the other tasks somewhat puzzled about their own role and importance, and about priorities in handling deliverables. All these differences did not foster communication, nor did they contribute to mutual trust. Rather they made it difficult for someone in Advance to anticipate someone else's actions, or be tolerant if others failed to produce their deliverables adequately. Here again, wicked problems were a latent threat.

A third source of complexity, finally, was membership fluctuations in Advance. These fluctuations have been described already; we will only recapitulate the categories that have been observed. A first was that not all task members attended meetings on a regular basis: some companies sent employees who just happened to be available; these were companies not too deeply involved in Advance. Either they were skeptical about collaboration between European aerospace companies or they did not trust such collaboration under Flysky supervision (and therefore just wanted to be present to see what happened, or to absorb whatever useful product would come out of the endeavor), or their situation did not allow them to give priority to work in the context of Advance, or they were reluctant to disclose anything that might help their partners/competitors (as shown above: companies were reluctant to disclose their recent R&D results). A second fluctuation category was that many task members were only involved in the project for a very short period. A third was task asynchronies: not all tasks worked concurrently. A fourth was that some task teams did not function well (on occasion, a task was even withdrawn or a partner replaced), and that new tasks or individual employees were added. Such changes make collaboration more complicated. Exchanging views, finding information, discussing conflicting solutions, making agreements, checking priorities: these and other communication issues become difficult to handle if there is no social network to rely on (not to mention a social network's community-building capacity). Due to membership changes, such a network could hardly develop in Advance.

From the above discussion, we can derive the following exogenous factors that have, most likely, influenced the collaboration processes evolving in Advance:

1. Fragmentation and competition in the European aerospace industry (discouraged collaborative tools and practices, contributed to inability or reluctance of several partners to give priority to the Advance project).
2. The general EU requirement to plan research projects thoroughly (supported task decomposition and vertical project organization), and the

general EU preference to have research conducted by commercial partners and universities jointly (introduced different professional perspectives).

3. The specific EU requirement to involve as many partners as possible, and as many countries as possible (contributed to national and cultural heterogeneity, introduced uncaring partners, obstructed meetings and agreements, hampered development of a communication network).
4. The Advance proposal history (encouraged partner withdrawal, increased inequality among partners, diminished motivation, hampered development of a communication network).
5. The high ambitions of the Advance proposal consortium (introduced many disciplines, various branches of industry, allowed various objectives).
6. Flysky's desire to control the standard-setting process (supported vertical project organization and centralized decision-making).

The list does not claim to be complete. It summarizes the line of reasoning according to which several exogenous factors have contributed to communication and collaboration practices in the project – and, as stated above, these practices were not satisfactory. The combination of factors shaped a project context that was cognitively complex and often 'wicked', a context moreover that made people work on very detailed sub-tasks instead of providing them with real incentives to collaborate, that relied heavily on an almost unworkable schedule, and that did not motivate individual action that might have compensated for flaws in the project design. It would have made little sense to study communication processes in Advance without taking into account the project's exogenous factors and the context they helped to create.

Thus the Advance case shows that the 'context' cannot be ignored in a study of real-life virtual communication processes. The relationships between communication partners, the way tasks were structured, the relationship between the project and participating organizations, and the role of project initiators are examples of factors co-determining the communication patterns evolving, including form, direction and contents. Part of this combination of factors in the communication media used (that did not function very well). We have already mentioned that ADR (the Advance project's database system for working documents) was poorly used, in part as a consequence of the firewalls used by companies to protect their data. E-mail was the main communication medium, not ADR. Despite the lack of horizontal communication, and despite the fact that many e-mails were announcements from the management team or from WP leaders (which did not have to be answered), there was a huge amount of e-mail traffic in

Advance. Some project members developed a sense of e-mail overload. A WP leader recollects: 'I received 40 to 50 e-mails per day, so I could speak of e-mail overload.' Not only the sheer number, but also the size of messages could be a problem: 'There were people who sent e-mails with ten attachments. This caused trouble for the firewalls and slows down your PC.' But a distinction can be made here. Those who did not occupy a 'high' position in Advance did not need to bother about a large number of e-mail messages: they simply did not read them. Some Advance members even created a special folder to which the Advance e-mails were immediately redirected, so that they were not shown in the 'inbox'. For TOP team members the feeling of e-mail overload must have been more intense. They had to communicate with many others, thus received larger volumes of e-mail, and they could not afford to ignore them.

In addition to the sheer number of e-mail messages, the length and poor structure of these messages could be inconvenient. Some Advance members would write long e-mails without indicating what the message was all about until the last sentence. No instrument was available to deal with this type of problem; there were no guidelines concerning the number, the size, or the structuring of e-mail messages, let alone rules to be complied with. Ground rules for communication had been set in the syndicate meeting, but these rules were too general, not addressing typically e-mail-related issues, and they were only a recommended code of conduct that had been created by (and was best known to) the members of the management team and the TOP team.

In sum, 'technical problems' may be added to the list of factors that influenced the communication and collaboration processes in Advance: firewalls hindered e-mail communication, and so did the fact that many in Advance only had access to a company's intranet, not to the Internet. (There is good reason to take the latter as an organizational, rather than a technical, issue.) Thus technical issues can be added, but they do not detract from the general conclusion that the (lack of) communication in Advance was largely shaped by contextual – institutional, organizational, cultural, political – factors.

This conclusion itself needs to be put in context. Within the borders of a study that seeks to account for actual communicative behavior, it makes sense to show that communication is shaped by context. However, if the question is what communication processes will evolve as a result of the introduction of media for virtual communication, the interplay of context and new media has to be considered instead of 'only' the way context influences communication. Giving attention to this interplay – and accepting that 'context' may change as a result of introducing new media for communication – allows us to observe that the perception of CMC being available changes the whole scene. As a first point, it was this perception that made actors initiate the Advance project. Collaboration among European aerospace companies had long been considered necessary, but the geographical distance between companies had largely prevented it. Now that CMC had broadly been adopted, the distance argument seemed no longer valid, but it was felt that tools (and standards) geared towards the aerospace industry would improve the prospects of collaboration. Second, and more important, the Advance project tended to rely on traditional methods of project organization. The case study we conducted reveals few signs of recognition that non-collocated teamwork might have to be organized in a different way than collocated teamwork, which will be discussed further in Chapter 6.

True, the availability of CMC eliminates distance as an inhibiting factor, and it enables the undertaking of very large projects, but it also creates a new setting in which established ways of getting to know each other do not apply, in which traditional team-development processes do not work, and in which meaning of terms such as 'commitment' and 'group identity' can be radically different from face-to-face settings. Those administering the Advance project did not recognize – or not fully recognize – that the rules of the game of communication are changed by the introduction of CMC. These new rules require that old certainties be abandoned: accepted ways to organize and facilitate communication need to be rethought, and new approaches explored. The Advance project had its share of rethinking and exploration, but it was limited to communication among higher-level actors (who did not need it most), and discussed in face-to-face meetings.

Such was the case before the 'integrator', recommended by the EU reviewers, started his work. The next section will describe the attempt made by him and his colleagues to improve communication and collaboration in Advance, and the results achieved. As we will see, it is not easy to change a situation of discouraged communication.

4.4 SOME ATTEMPTS TO CHANGE THE COURSE

The observations made as a part of a larger communication 'syndrome' within Advance had the following characteristics. We have seen that the evolution of Advance became rather troublesome. Both the EU reviewers and the Advance management identified the lack of cooperation between BCSs and the COMMONs as a problem that endangered the project. As the EU reviewers observed, some activities seemed to be performed in an independent mode, not in close collaboration with other work packages, they suggested appointing an 'integrator' whose function it would be to improve the integration of tasks.

The recommendation to appoint an integrator was made in the EU review report of April 2000, but such an integrator would not be appointed until November 2001, which was fairly close to the end of the project. As to the reasons for this delay, in some of the interviews it was suggested that various companies involved in the Advance project tried to push a candidate of their own. Some candidates were rejected, interviewees presumed, because the management team did not want any party – candidate or company – to become too influential. Clearly the new job was at the heart of the organization, and it might provide the opportunity to influence the shape of future collaborations.

Once an integrator was appointed, his work was announced as follows:

> a major Advance consortium partner has enabled [company name left blank] senior consultant Dearmark to join the project coordination team in Frencité from November 2001. In the role of Advance System Architect he is supporting integration of this complex project, building on his knowledge of systems engineering and his experience in coordinating multi-national aircraft engineering teams.

Under Dearmark's leadership, the advance global architecture team (AGA) was created. In accordance with the EU review recommendations, the consortium gave an important role to the AGA team, which had to ensure close integration between tasks and members within the project. The team tried to develop a new way to handle the project breakdown structure. Dearmark explains: 'You can imagine that different tasks within Advance dealt with the same product, but most of the members were not aware of that. It was our job to make this more visible and, more than that, to ensure integration between the tasks.' Another AGA member adds: 'The introduction of AGA team was an attempt to improve Advance (something like a mission impossible) in a moment where different tasks were working without synergy.'

It was difficult to make the integration idea spread throughout Advance, the more so since the AGA team started working when the project was in its final stage. First of all, the problem between COMMONs and BCSs had to be addressed: 'The lack of communication and cooperation became obvious after Forum 1 when tasks had to face to the realization of experiments. As long as you are working on paper this is not a big problem, but as soon as you have to realize a prototype based on paper that nobody knows and shared . . .'

The AGA team started from the assumption (or the observation) that the Advance project suffered from lack of coherence and poor accessibility of results. As an AGA team member recalls, one of the team's presentations was titled 'Ensuring Coherent and Accessible Advance Results to highlight two major challenges facing the Advance project for which the AGA task was asked to provide solutions.' According to the team, an approach to solve these problems had to involve:

1. *processes* derived from systems engineering principles;
2. *methods* to define and utilize multiple views on project data and the relationships between these views; and
3. a computer *tool* (ANS) to define, manage and navigate the views and the relationships between them *and* to support the Advance concurrent, multi-site, collaborative working environment.

ANS was a virtual environment that replaced ADR. This new environment proved helpful in making the tasks in Advance more visible. That did not suffice, however, to attain the level of integration considered necessary. It is possible that frequent changes in the composition of the work packages and membership changes in the task teams did not allow the development of stable collaborative relationships. But it is also possible that AGA only should have been earlier in the project. Figure 4.3 shows at what stage of the Advance project the AGA team entered the scene.

The EU review report of April 2000 was positive about the ADR document classification, but the reviewers were also worried about the information overload that might result from the increasing number of users and use of the system. They were also concerned about the system's user-friendliness. And indeed, the ADR system had deficiencies, in technical as well as in social terms. The system was meant to be an instrument for sharing information, but it was not widely used for that purpose. Most information was not up to date, or was not present at all. Only WP leaders could upload documents to the ADR, in their own task section. Some did so, others did not. All in all, ADR offered poor functionality because of:

*   no appropriate synchronization;
*   no document description available along with each document;
*   no history function, showing who changed what and when;
*   no easy, platform-independent navigation facility;

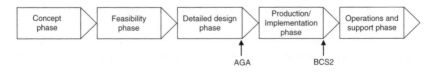

Figure 4.3   Stages in Advance project and entry of AGA

- no efficient and consistent way to manage documents access rights; and
- no simple way to add comments or ranking to documents.

As a result, ADR was partly used, and partly updated. This created confusion, and sometimes even led to work wasted. The AGA team, after being appointed as 'the integrator team', was soon to acknowledge the failures of ADR, and replaced it with a newly built system, the Advance Navigator System (ANS). ANS was meant to become a project integration tool and, unlike ADR, it was used not only as a document repository.

A major reason for introducing ANS was to improve collaboration between the many Advance tasks and teams. But it was already late in the Advance project when ANS was brought in, so it was considered necessary that this system be soon operational (within two months), if it could be of any value to the project at all. 'Operational' meant that the system had to support the AGA integration methods, support dissemination and support the concurrent, multi-site, collaborative Advance working environment.

To support the AGA integration methods, the instrument had to enable:

- the creation and management of multiple views and their inter-relationships;
- the creation of mappings on the basis of these relationships; and
- an easy navigation through the various views.

To support multi-site concurrent collaborative teamwork the instrument had to provide basic functions for data sharing and role-based access rights, but it also had to offer functions for:

- signaling the maturity – or status – of data elements;
- (semi-)automatic notification of changes; and
- tracing the change history.

And in order to support dissemination, ANS:

- had to have an intuitive user interface that allowed operation without training; and
- should be accessible from all – or most – hardware and software platforms.

In sum, ANS should be everything that ADR had failed to be. As to the system's contents, it represented the Advance project's breakdown structure and deliverables – which included descriptions of the different tasks and projects, and linkages between tasks and products. Everyone in the project was able to access ANS, provided that access to the Internet was possible (which, as mentioned earlier, was a requirement not met in some participating companies).

From a technical viewpoint, ANS had to be quite sophisticated because for virtual research projects to run it is not enough just to set up e-mail servers and an ftp site. That would have been sufficient for document storage (like the ADR system), but it would not have allowed the collaborative use of documents. This is why ANS was set up as a shared workspace that allowed partners to:

- use any Web browser to check the status of all documents;
- upload and download files, and add their own comments; and
- provide smooth integration with word processing, database and scheduling applications on partners' own workstations.

The security features and versioning enabled the editors to maintain a complete and consistent view of the whole proposal, accessible to all the partners. With the underlying clarity and security provided by ANS, ad hoc e-mails and telephone calls might have sufficed to resolve difficult points.

ANS was not very successful, however, despite all its beneficial properties. The system was introduced very late in the project, when there was not enough time left to feed it with all available, updated information – which was a prerequisite for ANS to become *the* virtual environment for information sharing and jointly creating documents. Still, ANS was evaluated positively by the management team: 'It was a success because it was the only Advance result that was presented during Forum 2 with a real live demo (while other experiments used only PowerPoint!).'

Despite this positive judgment, ANS could not save Advance from poor coordination and communication. For that, other means were necessary. The AGA team recognized that scheduled internal workshops would enhance and foster the cooperation between participants. The team also tried to use the already existing workshops to create commitment and team spirit, and to increase knowledge of the Advance project. However, these workshops were not very effective, as discussed earlier. Rather than becoming integrative experiences, they continued to be occasions on which people from the same company looked out for each other. Still, Dearmark and his team persistently tried to use the workshops as an integration device, as they did not cease to believe in the benefits of face-to-face communication: 'A workshop could be used as a pressure mechanism to intensify communication. At least, according to the literature that favors face-to-face communication over electronic communication, since it would create a warm team atmosphere.'

In total, ten workshops were organized, by different Advance members. Preparing these workshops – the contents and the agenda – required intense e-mail discussions. Every task had to prepare a presentation, to be sent to the person in charge of the organization of the workshop, and to adjust the presentation to the agenda of the workshop. Simultaneously with, or in extension of, these workshops, task meetings were organized to discuss the content and the progress of a particular task. However, just like the workshops, these task meetings were poorly attended, or attended by replacements. It even happened that members visited the task meeting for their part of the task and left immediately afterwards, as became clear from the minutes of the task meetings located in the e-mail archives, which included the attendance lists.

The work of the AGA team did not have the desired effects, for reasons inherent to the Advance project. Dearmark was hired to solve the interrelated issues of poor communication, absence of cooperation and lack of integration, but by the time he arrived these had become firmly embedded in the project's culture and practices. Still, not all communication was poor in Advance. There were teams in which cooperation was close and communication intensive. An example is the A-lab, where team members discussed (horizontally) all kinds of practical issues, such as the schedule for running tests.

The A-lab was a virtual laboratory in Advance, with various tasks (as described in the previous section). The A-lab was non-collocated; physically, two lab sub-teams were situated in Frencité, and there was an associated partner in the Netherlands. The A-lab in the Netherlands, a secondary site, consisted of a number of Advance computer systems grouped in a project zone, which made it possible to secure communication through virtual private networks (VPNs). Thus a safe communication route was established between Frencité and the Netherlands. Strict rules applied with regard to access to this secure site – which created discussion, as it meant that not all information was available to all Advance partners. The A-lab in the Netherlands was coordinated by someone who was involved in Advance from the very beginning, employed by a company for which the A-lab was part of the daily business, and was member of a WP of which his company was the WP leader. The Advance consortium also tried to run an A-lab in Italy, but this lab failed to become operational. Interviewees suggest that the Italian organization was not very committed to develop R&D activities within Advance (Italy had become involved in the BCSs only at a very late stage). However that may be, the Italian A-lab also suffered from serious technical problems: safety rules made it difficult, if not impossible, to make this A-lab run properly.

In the A-lab, communication was preferred to be ad hoc and real-time, which may explain the frequent use of the telephone. Some A-lab members would spend long hours on a normal working day on the telephone to exchange information. Interviewees tend to see this as a matter of personal preference, but they also mentioned that communication by phone was much faster than e-mail contact, which implied that the person being called would be present to answer the phone. E-mail was seen as an alternative that fits only specific purposes. An A-lab member explains: 'In discussing matters about the tests of the A-lab I would prefer the phone, but when we need to set dates for meetings or to formalize agreements, I use e-mail.'

However, for other teams in Advance the A-lab would never become an example to be followed. Perhaps its tasks were considered too far removed from the other teams' tasks. Moreover, the other teams, clearly seeing the failure to make the Italian lab functional (it delayed tests!), must have perceived the A-lab as performing less than excellently.

While this section has described the attempts to change the course of the project, we end with a further example of intentionally good communication in Advance and its results. One of the members who really liked working on the project was Mr Marsh. He encouraged others in Advance to be proactive, he liked to play with cultural differences and to make jokes, and he probably was the one who invented most of the nicknames that were given to various Advance members. Mr Marsh persistently tried to create team spirit and an informal atmosphere in order to break the ice between so many partners. He created the *Advance Bulletin*, an informal newspaper that was a mixture of project-related and social information. The bulletin circulated only within the Advance consortium and was not disseminated outside. However, the *Advance Bulletin* did not exist for long. Mr Marsh released three issues (May 2000, August 2000, February 2001) but then stopped working on it. 'It is unfair to say they stopped the bulletin. I really did that myself because of the lack of speedy support and the need to do things of a higher priority. We did have freedom of speech, but often it was politically advisable to not write all things down as the bulletin usually went to the Commission.' Thus it was easy to write about births, marriages and even workshops, but things became complicated as soon as 'tough issues' were addressed, for instance about slippage of the project, or about poor meeting outcomes. To some extent the technical messages in the bulletin were also covered in the workshop meetings, which were widely circulated by the project manager, but after Mr Marsh stopped issuing the bulletin, 'unfortunately the social side was then left to the face-to-face meetings, e-mail gossips and phone calls'.

The *Advance Bulletin* seems to have been an isolated phenomenon, which was not considered worth imitating by others members in the consortium. While Mr Marsh tried to create team spirit and a common identity among the Advancers, his attempt failed. We have already discussed the fact that the project structure prevented 'mingling' between different partners.

We argue that this old-fashioned effort (by means of a paper news bulletin) to create 'team spirit' seems inappropriate within a virtual team.

4.5 CONCLUSIONS

Collaboration is far from easy. Huxham and Vangen (2003) discuss seven important factors (referred to as 'perspectives') that together explain why so many collaborations, in spite of all advantages envisaged, result in 'collaborative inertia'. This term is used to indicate 'what happens very frequently in practice: the output from a collaborative arrangement is negligible, the rate of output is extremely slow or stories of pain and hard grind are integral to successes achieved' (Huxham and Vangen 2003: 1). The list of factors presented is compelling. The authors describe the problem of reaching agreement on common aims (perspective 1), the presence of different 'points of power', yet the inability to acknowledge these (thus 'powerful' people may act defensively and aggressively, as if they had no power) (perspective 2), the need to start collaborative work without having had the opportunity to build trust (perspective 3), partnership fatigue, resulting from lack of clarity about who is involved in the collaboration, and from the large number of collaborative partnerships entertained by some companies (perspective 4), constantly changing collaborative structures, both because of reorganizations within member organizations and because of external constraints imposed on the collaboration itself (government policy, market instability, a member organization's new strategy) (perspective 5), leadership ambiguity, as collaborative processes are often shaped by previous structures and processes rather than being controlled by members of the collaboration (perspective 6), and leadership dilemmas, most notably the dilemma of unintended effects that result from simultaneously occurring unselfish actions ('within the spirit of collaboration') and self-interested actions (perspective 7).

We will not present examples from the Advance case that may fit these perspectives. Instead, we quote a fragment from the first perspective:

> Organizations come together bringing different resources and expertise to the table, which in turn creates the potential for collaborative advantage. Yet organizations also have different reasons for being involved and their representatives seek to achieve different outputs from their involvement. Sometimes these different organizational aims lead to conflicts of interest. Furthermore, for some organizations the joint purpose for the collaboration is perceived as central to achieving organizational purposes whereas others are less interested and

perhaps only involved (reluctantly) as a result of external pressure. Tensions often arise therefore because some organizations are very interested in influencing and controlling the joint agenda and some are reluctant to commit resources to it and so on. (Huxham and Vangen 2003: 2)

This fragment nicely captures one of the main problems in Advance: not all organizations involved were equally committed to the project, willing to collaborate and determined to make the project a success.

However, unlike the Advance case study, Huxham and Vangen's account does not relate to some large-scale, international, thoroughly planned project, and it does not involve companies trying to make profit. Instead, it is largely based on a study (Eden and Huxham 2001) of face-to-face discussions about social policy involving public and not-for-profit organizations. We may gather that the problems observed in Advance reflect, at least partly, a general problem of interorganizational collaboration. Then, in the context of this study, the question is whether virtual communication and geographically dispersed teams alleviate this problem, make it worse, or make it different.

In a way they alleviate it. Virtual communication and geographically dispersed teams are likely to prevent those involved (team members and leaders alike) from noticing early that collaboration is difficult or deficient. This is only short-term alleviation, of course, but significant nonetheless in a project of limited duration. In the Advance case, the effect of this deferred perception was reinforced by the thorough division of tasks, which implied that the consequences of poor collaboration would only become visible when a task or WP leader had to integrate pieces of work produced by dispersed individuals, or when some of these individuals had to build on work delivered by others – to learn that this work was delayed and/or was not good enough. Here it must be added that the work in Advance was quite different from the negotiations studied by Huxham and Vangen (2003). In a negotiation setting one will be inclined to pay close attention to what others say and to how they say it, and try to grasp the reasons and foretell the consequences of what is being said. Such an attentive posture was unlikely in the 'work setting' of Advance (it was likely at the levels of management team or TOP team). 'Ordinary' team members had to deliver a product according to more or less detailed specifications.

If we stay with the above line of argument, we may also argue that virtual communication and geographically dispersed teams – in this specific Advance case – made the general collaboration problem even worse. Broadly speaking, it is easier to deal with beginning product inconsistencies than with fully developed but incompatible products. Reasons are the time delay produced by having to reject fully developed products, people being attached to the product they deliver (perhaps after a period of hard work), and the chore of identifying sources of incompatibility and making a verdict. During such a repair process (presumably coordinated by a task leader or WP leader), again virtual communication has to be relied upon, but now it is really difficult: individuals are involved who are not used to communicating with each other, who probably think that they just did what they were supposed to do, and who suddenly find themselves bargaining with another because the other party was incompetent or shirking or because 'the system' failed (hard to tell what has been worse).

There is a further reason why virtual communication and geographically dispersed teams may make the general collaboration problem worse. As noted earlier, the Advance project was very complex. It is highly question-able that such a project would have been ventured in the absence of elec-tronic communication media. Now that such media were widely used, however, restrictions seemed hardly to apply with regard to the number of people, companies and countries involved, or with regard to the organiza-tion of tasks. It was attractive to define detailed sub-tasks, apparently, for reasons of efficiency and monitoring. And perhaps this way of arranging tasks complied with established views in the aerospace industry on how to organize a development project. The result was a type of project organiza-tion, hardly providing for communication between task team members, that may work in collocated teams – in which there (often) is no need to encourage horizontal communication. In Advance, in contrast, it produced isolation, poor team spirit and poor collaboration. In addition, it deprived those team members who were still motivated by the possibility of repair-ing what they perceived was going wrong, while those who were adminis-tering the Advance project were unable to see what was going on (as argued above) until it was too late, i.e. when communication and collaboration practices had already become largely established.

Thus, in the stage of preparing the Advance project, the possibility of relying on CMC was taken (and rightly so) to eliminate distance as a factor that inhibits large-scale, cross-national collaboration. However, it was not sufficiently recognized that a collaboration setting was created in which many of the compensation mechanisms that help collocated teams to func-tion were eliminated as well. We may conclude that virtual communication and geographically dispersed teams may make the general collaboration problem even worse, and they certainly did so in Advance, precisely because they created a new setting in which many traditional measures and prac-tices no longer worked.

This was not one of the conclusions drawn in the 'lessons learned' report that was described in a previous section. Some lessons in that report are that 'a successful project must be built on strong foundations'. The bigger the project, the more detailed the official documents and the consortium agreement. 'The coordinator must provide templates for every kind of document at the very beginning of the project': 'all documents should be compliant to "working software standards" (in particular document templates)': and it is useful to 'circulate at the very beginning of the project the organization chart of the management team, along with a short presentation of each member'. As such suggestions may also be sound in a dispersed set-up, they will not cure the lack of communication and collaboration in Advance-like settings, nor will they contribute to team spirit or identification within a larger project. The report does acknowledge the importance of project identity and motivation, devoting a full paragraph to the subject. But most of the guidelines provided (a logo, tee-shirts and posters, an international joke book) are only useful, we think, if the more basic requirements of team and project identity are already fulfilled: knowing what to do, how, and with whom; knowing whether one's work will contribute to an end product; being able to discuss problems with other team members, and if necessary with others outside your team; and being able to assume responsibility.

In Advance, these basic requirements were not met, partly because the Advance project organization pre-empted it and, partly because several partner companies felt only loosely connected with Advance – not hesitating to withdraw or replace team members if that suited them best. These companies were also reluctant to grant other project partners access to their own development data. While such reluctance is not uncommon, generally, it hampers collaboration. Here, we may speculate that some of the companies in Advance did not even look forward to making the Advance project a success, if only because that would confirm the coordinating company's position as the leading firm in the European aerospace industry, and support this company's attempts to create European aerospace industry standards modeled after its own standards. A consortium leader with no such clear interest in a particular outcome might have been able, better than Flysky, to deal with the lack of commitment of some companies. Finally, in addition to all these comments, it surely helps virtual communication and collaboration if all have adequate Internet and e-mail facilities.

In sum, we questioned whether virtual communication alleviated the communication problems within Advance, or made them worse, or made them different. We have argued that virtual communication both alleviated the problem as well as made things worse. However, we also showed that it was not the inherent lean characteristics of the medium that influenced the course of the project.

In fact, according to media richness theory, we should have seen major differences in the richness of communication between the cooperation in face-to-face meetings and the cooperation in the virtual mode. We did not. According to Warkentin et al., (1997), asynchronous communication (e-mail communication) is widely assumed to limit the prospects of building social links or relationships between group members compared to those in face-to-face settings. However, the Advance case showed that in face-to-face meetings, no social links or relationships were established either. The communication richness, supposed by the media richness theorist, should have been high in face-to-face meetings. We concluded from our interviews and the attendance lists of diverse workshops and forums that this was only the case with teams that already had a high level of cooperation and communication using different forms of communication media.

This case showed that, despite all the reasons provided by the MRT, face-to-face communication was not able to enhance the cooperation and communication within the Advance consortium. Neither was virtual communication. This reinforced our idea that the characteristics of the medium did not set the course for communication; instead, the organizational context and the structure of the project set the course for the Advance project. The project management of the Advance consortium probably has been over-optimistic about the usage of CMC (to bridge distance between organizational members) within a context in which traditional mechanisms were dominant. Most certainly the project management did not calculate (enough) how high the complexity of the project could become and how to deal with issues such as the lack of commitment from some of the partners.

Key issues

- If objectives within project teams are unaligned, conflicts of interest may arise.
- Virtual communication and geographically dispersed teams are likely to prevent those involved (team members and leaders alike) from noticing early that collaboration is difficult or deficient.
- As virtual communication enables coordination of (large) project teams across distances, it can alleviate (but not solve) problems inherent in the organizational structure of the (large) project.
- The Advance project was very complex. It is highly questionable that such a project would have been ventured in the absence of electronic communication media. Now that such media are widely used, however, restrictions seem hardly to apply with regard to the number of people, companies and countries involved, or with regard to the organization of tasks. It is very hard to keep things simple and well structured in such an environment.

- In the stage of preparing the Advance project, the possibility of relying on CMC was taken (and rightly so) to eliminate distance as a factor that inhibits large-scale, cross-national collaboration, only it was not sufficiently recognized that a collaboration setting was created in which many of the compensation mechanisms that help collocated teams function were eliminated as well.
- Virtual communication both alleviated the problem as well as made things worse. However, we also showed that it was not the inherent lean characteristics of the medium that influenced the course of the project.

5.   The Debian case study

5.1   INTRODUCTION

4.5 Important Events
4.5.1. July 2000: Joel Klecker died

On July 11th, 2000, Joel Klecker, who was also known as Espy, passed away at 21 years of age. No one who saw 'Espy' in #mklinux, the Debian lists or channels knew that behind this nickname was a young man suffering from a form of Duchenne Muscular Dystrophy. Most people only knew him as 'the Debian glibc and powerpc guy' and had no idea of the hardships Joel fought. Though physically impaired, he shared his great mind with others.
Joel Klecker (also known as Espy) will be missed.

More than 900 volunteer package maintainers are working on over 8250 packages and improving Debian GNU/Linux. Debian is a free operating system (OS). An operating system is the set of basic programs and utilities that make your computer run. Debian uses the Linux kernel, i.e. the core of the operating system, but most of the basic OS tools come from the GNU project; hence the name GNU/Linux. Debian is being developed cooperatively by many individuals through the Internet. Joel Klecker was one of them. What is striking in the announcement above is that Joel was known through his programming skills; the person behind Joel was unknown. However, still he was still a part of the community. His gender, age, race, nationality or personality did not matter much: his contributions did. The famous citation from Charles Handy (1995): 'trust needs touch', can be replaced by the phrase: trust needs code. The Debian community is not so much built around personalities; it is built around code.

A few notable points in the message quoted above will guide us through this case study on the Debian project. Since Joel shared his great mind with others, we assume that there has been cooperation between Joel and various developers. This cooperation has been in a virtual mode, since no one really knew Joel; he was mostly known by his nickname. Nicknames are commonly used in virtual environments, especially on IRC (Internet relay chat) channels. We are interested in this virtual cooperation. How does it work? In this chapter the open source community will be examined from an

organizational perspective, mainly focusing on communicative processes
fostering collaboration processes. We want to understand the underlying
(organizational) principles of OSS (open source software) communities.
The Debian community is one of these OSS communities coordinating the
efforts of thousands of individual programmers.

There has been a growing interest in describing the OSS phenomenon,
especially since new forms of network organizations arise everywhere and
the management of these organizations has to face various challenges while
the number of employees and sites increases:

> But the real fascination with [an organization like Debian, GR] stems from the
> fact that it is *not* an organizational project. No architecture group developed the
> design; no management team approved the plan, budget, and schedule; no
> human resource group hired the programmers; no facilities assigned the office
> space. Instead volunteers from all over the world contributed code, documenta-
> tion and technical support over the Internet just because they wanted to. (Moon
> and Sproull 2000: 382)

We do not entirely agree with Moon and Sproull, and believe that there are
reasons to argue that Debian is in fact an organizational project. The real
fascination is rather that people organize themselves and do coordinated
productive work without any financial reward.

There have been various studies on the question why open source
members give their work away for free and why they cooperate in sharing
code with each other. Hertel et al., (2003) have carried out an Internet-
based survey of contributors to the Linux kernel trying to explain the
motivation of software developers in open source projects. Their study
reveals that cooperation cannot be explained just through ethics and the
altruistic ideology that free/open software makes the world a better place
to live in. Taking the study by Hertel et al., (2003) as a point of departure,
we want to identify the key preconditions that are necessary for effective
virtual cooperation and communication.

Eric Raymond (1998: 19) argues that there is more than the Internet as
an enabling condition:

> While cheap Internet was a necessary condition for the Linux model [or in our
> case the Debian model] to evolve, I think it was not by itself a sufficient condi-
> tion. Another vital factor was the development of a leadership style and set of
> cooperative customs that could allow developers to attract co-developers and get
> maximum leverage out of the medium.

Schweik and Semenov (2003) provide a kind of life cycle model of open
source projects, and hypothesize that success and cooperation will depend

on the way projects are initiated and organized over time, what rules for participation have been established and how the methods for maintaining versions of new submissions have been managed.

By analyzing the interactions in the OSS world we continue our research in an environment where virtual communication has proved to be successful. This case study will explore the Debian project from its origins and further development until 2003. We will pay special attention to the institutional design and the recruitment strategies as potential critical factors explaining the willingness of participants to collaborate. We are not so much interested in why people give away their work for free, but rather in how those virtual workers are able to cooperate in a virtual mode without planned face-to-face meetings, as it is the case in most commercial projects. As in any team or project, the open source project follows a certain life cycle. We use the model by Schweik and Semenov (2003) to describe the different stages in the Debian project. Schweik and Semenov provide a summary of the life cycle of open source programming projects based on the existing literature that is largely focused on high-profile open source projects like Linux and the Apache Web Server. Following this line of reasoning will provide answers to questions such as how projects are initiated and organized over time, what (informal) rules for participation have been established, and what other governing mechanisms are present in the Debian project. Schweik and Semenov (2003: 1) argue that 'the institutional designs and management of open source projects could be critical for ensuring participants' willingness to collaborate . . .'.

In sum, this case study examines the Debian project, i.e. a virtual organization, and how dispersed its virtual team members can collaborate without rich media. We will identify the enabling conditions or factors behind this project, with emphasis on coordination and communication processes. The ordering of the Debian material will take place in sections 5.2 to 5.4. In section 5.2 we will discuss the character of OSS organizations such as Debian which can best be understood as communities or collaborative networks. In section 5.3 we will discuss the very phenomenon of OSS and its underlying mechanisms. In open source projects we can identify three different stages of development. These stages will be described in section 5.4. The different factors related to the three stages are important for the collaboration processes and project/team formation.

In section 5.5 we will discuss the Debian project. Debian is a perfect example of a virtual project: co-developed and maintained by numerous developers. Debian has one of the most coordinated project structures but, unlike Linux, it does not depend on one leader. The open source governance model within Debian is far more detailed and developed than in any other open source project. Debian fits our need for a perfect virtual organization since all of the development processes take place over the Internet without face-to-face meetings between developers.

5.2   COMMUNITIES VERSUS TEAMS?

> . . . despite the clear potential for chaos, open source projects are often surprisingly disciplined and successful through the action of multiple, interacting governance mechanisms. (Markus et al., 2000: 14)

OSS projects are run through the Internet without face-to-face contact of the members. This collaboration can be seen as purely virtual collaboration. There are various ways to describe this type of collaboration. It is teamwork in the sense that we could compare it to the commercial virtual project teams that arise every day. Hertel et al., (2003) state that due to the high number of participants and the ease of access, OSS projects are generally better understood as a community or collaborative network (Wellman 1997) than as a team.

When people take the opportunity to gather with others on the Internet, sharing a common interest, this social aggregation could be labeled a 'virtual community' (Rheingold 1993). Kozinets (1999) points out that many virtual communities are based upon shared passion for, and knowledge of, specific consumption activities. Hemetsberger (2002) argues that occasionally, the social interactions get deepened and those enthusiastic consumers 'even actively engage in collective innovation and production processes'. In recent years an intriguing example of such joint production, the open source community, has attracted major interest, both of business practitioners (e.g. Microsoft 1998) and theorists (e.g. von Hippel and von Krogh 2003; Hemetsberger and Pieters 2001; Dalle and Jullien 2001; Lerner and Tirole 2000):

> Communities usually include a large number of people, and are open to anyone who wants to join as long as s/he obeys some general behavior rules. Collaborative networks are more restrictive in their access policy, relying on referral or reputation and develop a more specific community code including sanctions for violating this code. However, the boundaries of collaborative networks are still relatively flexible, allowing a rather frequent change of collaborators. A 'team' in contrast, refers to a relatively small group of collaborating people (about 2–20) with clear and relatively stable team boundaries, functions, roles, and norms. (Hertel et al., 2002)

Others argue along similar lines. 'A group of people who interact directly, frequently and in multi-faceted ways. People who work together are usually communities in this sense . . . connection, not affection, is the defining characteristic of a community' (Bowles and Gintis 2000: 3). A more general definition of community is provided by Michael Taylor (1982): 'A group of people (*i*) who have beliefs and values in common, (*ii*) whose relations are direct and many-sided and (*iii*) who practice generalized as well as balanced reciprocity.' The reciprocity factor – giving something to a person and retrieving something back from that person – has to be lifted to the group level in the case of the OSS community: an individual adding code (or whatever) to the group and getting something from the group in return (for instance other code or bug reports). To define the OSS community even more narrowly, the notion of community of practice might be applicable. A community of practice is, according to Wenger and Snyder (2000), a group of people that is informally bound together by shared expertise and passion for a joint enterprise. The individuals within the OSS community are bound together by shared as well as complementary expertise, which makes it possible to manage a complex project. According to Wenger (1998), identity is an important aspect of the community of practice. Identity is about the role of the individual within such a community. An individual can be connected very strongly with the group; however, this connection can increase or decrease over time, considering that most of the time an individual does not belong to only one community, but is a member of different communities. The commitment will vary: sometimes it will entail concrete actions, while occasionally it will consist (not always so visible) of thoughts or feelings.

Unlike a team, a community of practice cannot be formed by putting people together. A community is not something you create. It emerges. As Brown and Duguid (1991) put it, you can 'detect and support': when a community is detected you can try to provide support for it, but managing it goes too far, they argue. However, 'the paradox of management', as described by Wenger and Snyder (2000: 144), is that on the one hand the community of practice is free; on the other hand, it has to be managed:

> Although communities of practice are fundamentally informal and self-organizing, they benefit from cultivation . . . To get communities going – and to sustain them over time – managers should:
>
> - identify potential communities of practice that will enhance the company's strategic capabilities;
> - provide the infrastructure that will support such communities and enable them to apply their expertise effectively; and
> - use nontraditional methods to assess the value of the company's communities of practice. (Ibid.)

Although OSS projects such as Debian appear to be more like a community or a collaborative network, team-based approaches and organizational structures can also be identified. However, this distinction between a community and a team makes it difficult to compare commercial teams with these community-based teams: although team processes might be similar, their organizational embeddedness is not. In other words, commercial teams work based on financial and contractual incentives, while community-based teams work with different kinds of mechanisms, which will be explored later in this chapter. If a project in the business world, the world of neckties and contracts, fails, then this *does* matter. People get fired. Organizations go bankrupt. When a company flourishes, the stock goes up. It is a whole different ballgame in the world of nerds and geeks. It is a world on its own and it seems that 'nerds and geeks' are defeating the world of Microsoft in a battle they are not even (intentionally) playing. Thus one objective of the present study is to explore these identifying mechanisms in community-based teams and how this stimulates virtual work.

In 'What makes a virtual organization work' Markus et al., (2000) characterize this issue by identifying the working mechanisms behind OSS projects, trying to come up with recommendations for commercial teams. An answer to the question implied in the title of their article can be found in an economic enterprise that acts in many ways like a voluntary organization: the open source software movement. Markus et al., (2000) used the work by Peter Drucker (1998) to set the tone of their article:

> Managers today, Drucker tells us, must direct people as if they were unpaid volunteers, tied to the organization by commitment to its aims and purposes and often expecting to participate in its governance. They must lead workers instead of managing them. (Markus et al., 2000: 13)

Markus et al., focus their article on the motivations of people to participate in open source projects and on the governance of this participation. Answers to these questions might be helpful for commercial companies in their challenge to keep knowledge workers in all types of virtual organizations motivated. Obviously, motivation is important, but in the following we want to focus on the communication and coordination processes in OSS projects in order to see whether (or not) they differ from collaborative efforts in other contexts.

Key issues

- OSS projects use the Internet as an enabling mechanism but operate without actual face-to-face contact of members.
- OSS projects can be labeled as a 'virtual community', as people take the opportunity to gather with others on the Internet by sharing a common interest.

- OSS can best be characterized as a community of practice, i.e. undertaken by members that are informally bound together by shared expertise and passion for a joint enterprise. Unlike a team, a community of practice cannot be formed by putting people together.
- To get communities of practice going – and to sustain them over time – managers should:
  - identify potential communities of practice that will enhance the company's strategic capabilities;
  - provide the infrastructure that will support such communities and enable them to apply their expertise effectively;
  - use non-traditional methods to assess the value of the company's communities of practice.

5.3 OPEN SOURCE SOFTWARE: MAY THE SOURCE BE WITH YOU

A relatively quiet, but potentially important phenomenon related to human collaboration occurred at the end of the 20th century in the field of computer science. The phenomenon, called open source (OS) software development, has the potential to change, perhaps dramatically, the way humans work together to solve complex problems in general, and specifically in areas of public policy and management. (Schweik and Semenov, 2003: 1)

Schweik and Semenov identified Linux as probably the best-known OSS project. They outlined why OSS projects such as Linux and Debian are so interesting: (1) extremely complex software was designed, built, maintained; (2) it continues to be improved primarily by a global team of volunteers collaborating in a virtual community over the Internet; and (3) OS software is made available to the world at no cost. For our study we are mainly interested in point 2 combined with point 1: a global team of volunteers collaborating via the Internet and designing complex software. We do not intend to describe the open source history in detail; we will provide some general aspects of this phenomenon. First we will give an explanation of the term open source:

Open Source is a collective term for software licenses that not only give the user the right to read the source code of the software, but also to change it according to one's need and to publish these amendments with the original or the changed source code. Furthermore, one is not allowed to raise any license fees or other fees for the source code . . . (Osterloh et al., 2002: 3)

One of the whole ideas with free software is not so much the price thing and not having to pay cash for it, but the fact that with free software you aren't tied to any commercial vendor. You might use some commercial software on top of Linux, but you aren't forced to do that or even to run the standard Linux kernel at all if you don't want to. You can mix the different software you have to suit yourself. (FM interview with Linus Torvalds: 2)

The name open source consists of two parts. 'Source' refers to the source code of software, which is the human-readable instructions that make up the software before it is transmitted into something computer-readable (van Wendel de Joode 2002). In order to use software, source code has to be compiled. When source code is compiled, a special program (a compiler) translates the human-readable code into a machine-readable code which a computer can understand (Edwards 2001: 4). The other part, 'open', refers to the interesting part of the OSS community. It means that the source code is kept open and available to anyone with Internet access (van Wendel de Joode 2002: 2).

Kasper Edwards (2001) explains that just understanding the mechanisms between source code and license is not enough. It is a phenomenon we are chasing and trying to grasp. It is more than the software. 'It is also the community that has created the software and the emerging economy, which is based on open source software' (ibid.: 2). In the famous Halloween Documents, a confidential Microsoft memorandum on a strategy against Linux and open source which was annotated by Eric Raymond with explanations and commentary over the Halloween weekend, we can find a similar observation by Microsoft:

> Commercial software development processes are hallmarked by organization around economic goals. However, since money is often not the (primary) motivation behind Open Source Software, understanding the nature of the threat posed requires a deep understanding of the process and motivation of Open Source development teams. In other words, to understand how to compete against OSS, we must target a process rather than a company. (Halloween Documents, version 1.14:13)

The community of OSS connects many thousands of people, programmers, testers, users, translators and writers to the development of the software. These people differ in their backgrounds and nationality as well as in the amount of time they spend on programming or being part of the community. This differentiation is one of the reasons why there are so many different projects (in size, scope and duration) to be found within the OSS community. Edwards (2001) emphasizes that the nature of the activities in OSS projects is a development effort: 'It is the objective of open source projects to create some particular software' (Edwards 2001: 5). Edwards describes the basic development cycle in open source development as follows:

1. Maintainer releases software and source code;
2. Contributor downloads software and source code;
3. Contributor identifies problems or needed features;
4. Contributor implements corrections;
5. Corrections are mailed to the maintainer/mailing list for inclusion in the project;
6. Corrections are discussed on the mailing list;
7. Maintainer reviews the corrections and includes changes;
8. Maintainer releases new version software and source code; and
9. Contributor downloads software and . . . (and so forth).

We will examine this process in greater detail in our Debian case study. We can use some examples from initial maintainers' initiatives, which will make this process clearer. In sum, the development process of OSS is characterized by the following:

- OSS systems are built by potentially large numbers (i.e., hundreds or even thousands) of volunteers.
- Work is not assigned: people undertake the work they choose to undertake.
- There is no explicit system-level design, or even detailed design.
- There is no project plan, schedule or list of deliverables.

Taken together, these differences suggest an extreme case of geographically distributed development, where developers work in arbitrary locations, rarely or never meet face to face, and coordinate their activity almost exclusively by means of e-mail and bulletin boards (Mockus et al., 2000). Participation in OSS development requires a person to read or scan many e-mails, referred to as high traffic (Edwards, 2001).

Schweik and Semenov (2003) elaborate further on the cycle of OSS projects. They examine the three major stages of the open source project. They differ with Edwards (2001) as he focuses on the development stages while they concentrate on the community process. Since the team-building process is an important aspect of virtual teamwork, we will now look more closely at these three stages. After a review of Schweik and Semenov's (2003) article, we will focus on the Debian project and connect this with Edward's cycle and Schweik and Semenov's stages.

Schweik and Semenov (2003) identified three major stages in open source projects:

1. Project initiation;
2. Going 'open'; and
3. Project growth, stability or decline.

We think that these stages in the project are important, especially for the OSS environment, since membership is fluid and not contractually restricted as in commercial projects. Members can easily join a project and leave just as easily. There are no restrictions on membership. In fact, it is almost impossible to speak of members. People do not sign in to become members and people do not sign out to leave the project. And yet the diverse OSS projects have developed their own informal rules and various norms, and sometimes there are guidelines to become a specific type of member. We will focus on that issue in the Debian case, which has strict procedures for members to become developers.

Stage 1: Project Initiation

Schweik and Semenov (2003) argue that like any area of endeavor, OSS projects are initiated because one or more people realize that there is a computing-related problem or challenge left unfilled, and for one or more reasons, they decide to take it on (Godfrey and Tu 2000). Here the 'itching problem' described by E. Raymond (1999: 32) comes into play: 'every good work of software starts by scratching a developer's personal itch'. At that point it is important to reach programmers who think on the lines of this new initiative. Motivation, 'the kernel' and a modular design are three important components of this stage of an OS project, according to Schweik and Semenov (2003). The motivation issue is not widely studied, at least in the sense of what motivates the initiator to start a project. Schweik and Semenov have summarized some likely motives of initiators. According to Raymond (1998) 'from a technological standpoint, initiators are motivated to meet some personal need'; to work on the leading edge of some technology; to address some software crisis; or to provide intellectual stimulation. Socio-political motivations for project initiators include the sheer enjoyment of doing the work and an interest in taking on a technical rival (e.g. a large, dominant monopolist software company provided the motivation in the Linux case). 'Skill-building and low opportunity costs (e.g., nothing to lose by undertaking the project) are likely economic reasons for initiators to start a programming project.' Eric Raymond (1999: 46) was also interested in the success or failure of initiating a project. Therefore he used his own project as an experiment. To test his theory about the success of Linus Torvalds in initiating Linux, Raymond copied Torvalds's (global change) approach in these ways:

> I released early and often (almost never less often than every ten days, during periods of intense development, once a day). I grew my beta list by adding to it

everyone who contacted me about fetchmail. I sent chatty announcements to the
beta list whenever I released, encouraging people to participate. I listened to my
beta testers, polling them about design decisions and stroking them whenever
they sent in patches and feedback.

According to Raymond, this immediately worked. From the beginning of
the project he received bug reports of high quality. He got thoughtful criticism and even fan mail. This led to Raymond's observation: 'If you treat
your beta-testers as if they're your most valuable resource, they will
respond by becoming your most valuable resource' (Raymond 1999: 46).
Raymond's focus was on how to attract other programmers. Of course this
is part of the initial stage. We will keep his observations in mind when
reviewing the initial Debian stage.

The second component of the initial stage is not very much explored by
Schweik and Semenov (2003). They saw that the development of an initial
product for others to build upon – what we might call the project core, or
kernel – was important. For example, Torvalds developed the kernel of the
Linux operating system largely on his own and then, once he felt that it was
ready to be shared, he made the kernel source code available on the
Internet, and encouraged others to help improve it. The announcements
are very important in attracting developers. Encouragements to participate
are equally important.

A good design and the concept of modularity is the third critical component in this first stage of OS development. Modularity makes it possible
for programmers to work in parallel:

> With a modular design, multiple programmers (perhaps unknown to one
> another) can be working to build new functions into the same module.
> Modularity also allows development to continue thereby avoiding a situation
> where the impact of one person's enhancements to a module leads to problems
> with the work in some other module. (Schweik and Semenov 2003)

This modularity also enables the project leader to keep better control over
the project when the work progresses (in complexity). 'The easiest way to
get coordinated behavior from a large, semi-organized mob is to point them
at a known target' (ibid.: 5). A concrete vision and a strategy for the future
coupled with a modular structure helps to recruit others into the project.'
However, we doubt whether most of the initiators, for example Linus
Torvalds, knew where they were heading for, let alone that Torvalds could
forsee that Linux would grow so famous. In the Debian project we will find
out if this clear vision was available in the initial stage.

In sum, according to Schweik and Semenov (2003), Stage 1 of the OS life
cycle requires one or several motivated individuals who have an idea for a

project that answers a need many others have as well. The initiators have to pay significant attention to product design (e.g. modularity) and the development of an initial project kernel that shows some promise, so that other virtual members join in.

Stage 2: 'Going Open'

Stage 2 requires closer attention to team communication and approaches for participant recruitment. A point that was difficult to research according to Schweik and Semenov (2003) is the design of the project governance structure and rules outlining day-to-day operations, and collective-choice and constitutional-choice mechanisms. 'Understanding the governance structure and institutional designs of cases from publicly available online material is difficult. This could be because governance structures are not formally documented, or because they are documented in locations not in the public domain.' In the Debian case the governing mechanism and the institutional design are documented in the public mailing list. In Chapter 2 we explained that this extensive documentation (high degree of an organizational and communication structure) was one of the reasons to choose the Debian project over other OSS projects. According to Schweik et al., in this 'going open' stage, the initiator of the projects decides to follow the OSD (Open Source Definition) licensing principles and selects a particular license for the product. Five factors need to be considered at this stage:

1.   Project/product credibility;
2.   Adequate communication systems;
3.   Suitable version control systems;
4.   Effective recruitment strategies;
5.   Appropriate project governance structures and institutional designs.

Project and product credibility
Schweik and Semenov (2003) studied the work of Raymond in his Halloween Documents and identified the key criteria for a project to be credible to others:

> (1) there needs to be at least a handful of enthusiastic 'core developers' already interested in the project; (2) the project has 'plausible promise,' both technically and sociologically (i.e., the kernel can evolve into something very good with a little effort, and the people in the core developer community are enthusiastic and of high reputation); (3) the project or product is something that will attract interest and is innovative; (4) the project is important and deployable for a

(future) large number of developers; and, (5) the right amount of the problem has already been solved before it becomes 'open.'

Within Debian we will find that the initiator had done some preliminary work but left room for debate for programmers to join. If everything had been fixed beforehand this would have turned programmers off, since potential developers would be turned into 'testers' – a task many programmers find uninteresting.

Adequate communication mechanisms

> Coordination of an OSS team is extremely dependent on Internet-native forms of collaboration. Typical methods employed run the full gamut of the Internet's collaborative technologies. (Halloween Document: 1.14):
>
> - E-mail lists;
> - Newsgroups;
> - 24 × 7 monitoring by international subscribers;
> - Websites (Schweik and Semenov 2003)

This is a rather general description which we will extended even further. Since the medium is not the message, but the medium needs to be a suitable conduit for the message to have impact, we can divide the systems into systems: (a) 'Free form' discussions (for instance mailing lists, IRC channels), (b) strongly structured discussions (bug tracking systems within Debian, or more generally the trouble ticketing at helpdesks), and (c) knowledge-based discussions (Wiki platform, http://www.wiki.org).

Schweik and Semenov (2003) identified several Web systems which are available to support collaboration on OS projects. Sourceforge.net, for example, advertises itself as the 'largest open source development website' (Sourceforge.net 2002). This site provides free project hosting services, which includes version management, problem tracking, project management, backing-up facilities and various communication tools such as mailing lists and Web discussion forums. Another website having a similar mission with a different design approach is http://www.freshmeat.net/. Other sites, such as http://slashdot.org/, http://www.osdn.com/ and http://www.newsforge.com/, have emerged in recent years to enhance communication and provide news and information to the general OS community.

> And with all the development happening on the Internet, and all the tools being found there, if you have a problem with something, you have a large community to help you (and ultimately you can even e-mail the primary developers themselves, although for understandable reasons 'us developers' tend to be

pretty busy doing other things and are sometimes insensitive to a single user need).

Effective recruitment strategies

When an initiator decides to open up his or her project, he or she has to choose a platform for announcing the project and reaching as many readers as possible. Nowadays one can find central websites for project hosting. For instance, Surgeforge.net provides a 'project help wanted' option on their main menu for people to post requests for participation in non-commercial, volunteer projects.

On http://www.debian.org/devel/wnpp one can find packages or projects that need help or attention from other people in the community. In the Debian case we will see that the initial (non-official) pre-posting from initiator Ian Murdock was on a discussion list. We will go over this later in the Debian case.

Appropriate governance/institutional designs

Schweik and Semenov (2003) make clear that little attention has been paid to the governance and institutional designs of OSS projects. However, they think that those designs include critical variables for success or failure of different projects. The work by Markus et al., (2000) outlines a few different open source governance models. So et al., (2000) also discuss different governing mechanisms, for instance a mechanism to judge which part of a contribution should be accepted or rejected has to be established. So et al., (2000: 4) identify two different authority systems. 'If the benevolent dictator system is adopted, a maintainer is that person who makes final judgments on decisions of the project. If an autocratic system is adopted, a membership system has to be set up to distinguish between developers and non-developers and it may also involve a voting system for decision-making.' Markus et al., (2000) have also identified different authority systems and different dispute resolutions in different OSS projects. Markus et al., (2000) state that open source projects exhibit 'four interrelated coordination mechanisms: managed membership, rules and institutions, monitoring and sanctioning, and reputation. By means of interaction of such governance mechanisms, open source projects can stay on track despite their obvious potential for chaos' (ibid.: 21). The authors describe the differences between open source projects in managing membership. The managing of the membership of open source project works in conjunction with rules and institutions (such as how members and leaders are chosen) and with monitoring and sanctions (such as dispute-resolution processes and the ability to expel members). An interesting aspect of rules and institutions that differs per open source communities, is the procedures for discussing and voting on important issues. Also the sanctions and conflict-resolution mechanisms vary between the different communities. Markus et al., (2000) discuss four different open source governance models, referring to the Apache community, the Debian project, Perl and Mozilla. They characterize two important aspects of the governance models: the leadership aspect and dispute resolution. We will investigate the governance structures of Debian (e.g. governing body, leadership, dispute resolution, voting, sanctioning rules and institutions), and especially how this structure influences/structures/guides/enables communication and cooperation.

Stage 3: Growth or Decline

'At Stage 3, projects can grow with new membership, remain stable with about the same number of participants as they had before going open, or they can gradually die from a lack of participant interest' (Schweik and Semenov 2003: 10). The willingness of people to continue to cooperate in a particular project is related to the progress that is made, and related to the components of stage 2 – credibility, communication systems, version control, recruitment strategies and project governance:

> I really don't think you need all that much 'quid pro quo' in programming – most of the good programmers do programming not because they expect to get paid or get adulation by the public, but because it is fun to program. A lot of people enjoy just the interaction on the Internet, and the feeling of belonging to a group that does something interesting: that's how some software projects are born.

Mockus et al., (2000) found evidence that many developers will be more likely to join an open source project at the beginning (or during take-off) than at the end, as development will be more highly regarded than maintenance and the influence on the whole project can be greater if they join early on. Recruiting new members to the community is an essential part of stage 2 and of course it will be extremely important for stage 3 as well. New members will have to find motivation to stay members. The components of stage 2 are important factors that can stimulate the motivation. Hertel et al., (2001) pointed out that in their discussions within the Linux kernel community two main motive classes of OSS developers were suggested: (a) intrinsic motivation ('fun to program') and personal challenges to improve existing software for own needs, and (b) social comparison motives such as competition with other developers (either within OSS projects or between OSS projects and commercial software projects) and/or the interest in building a reputation that might be helpful for their career (see also

Hars and Ou 2001). In our case study we will try to identify factors that have stimulated or impeded membership of Debian.

5.4   DEBIAN

In the Debian case we will discuss the different stages distinguished above to examine the conditions for cooperation at every stage of the project. Special attention will be paid to leadership issues, commitment, coordination mechanisms, information sharing and technical information systems, and the usage of these systems.

Stage 1: Project Initiation/The Past

> In 1993, when Ian Murdock decided to start an Open Source distribution that would always be free, he found a group of like-minded people to work with him. The question of freedom was important to Murdock, as it will appear later from his first e-mail message about Debian. It started as a small, tightly-knit group of free software hackers, and gradually grew to become a large, well-organised community of developers and users. (Varghese 2003)

This text basically refers to the three stages, as explained earlier. Ian Murdock was the initiator at stage 1. At stage 2, after his official announcement of the Debian project, a group of people decided to cooperate in this project. Eventually, more and more people were joining Debian and it started to evolve into a real community. Let's start from the beginning.

Debian/GNU Linux is the largest Linux distributor. Debian is not a commercial entity but rather a non-commercial organization run by volunteers. There basically is no commercial advertising for Debian. With just an Internet connection you can download Debian and install it with no strings attached and that is why the term 'open software' is used, since Debian has everything to do with the freedom to modify, enhance and change the software as desired. For the history of Debian we will use the work of Lameter (2002) and the Debian website: http://www.debian.org.

According to Lameter (2002), Debian was founded by an initiative of the Free Software Foundation. Legend has it that Richard Stallmann was concerned about the rise of commercial Linux distributions and wanted to make sure that a completely 'free' (as in freedom; however, also as in 'free' speech, not in 'free' beer!). Linux distribution would come into being. He offered a grant for someone to develop a Linux distribution that would be done in the spirit of the Free Software Movement and where all software would be available under licensing of the Free Software Foundation. Ian Murdock responded to this advertisement he saw in a magazine. The project was officially founded by Ian Murdock on 16 August 1993. Murdock began developing a Linux distribution and named it Deb-ian after the first names of his wife Deborah and himself. Murdock intended Debian to be a distribution network which would be made openly, in the spirit of Linux. In the Debian Manifesto, written by Ian Murdock, one can read what Debian was to be and why it was set up:

> Debian Linux is a brand-new kind of Linux distribution. Rather than being developed by one isolated individual or group, as other distributions of Linux have been developed in the past, Debian is being developed openly in the spirit of Linux and GNU. The primary purpose of the Debian project is to finally create a distribution that lives up to the Linux name. Debian is being carefully and conscientiously put together and will be maintained and supported with similar care. It is also an attempt to create a non-commercial distribution that will be able to effectively compete in the commercial market. It will eventually be distributed by The Free Software Foundation on CD-ROM, and The Debian Linux Association will offer the distribution on floppy disk and tape along with printed manuals, technical support and other end-user essentials. All of the above will be available at little more than cost, and the excess will be put toward further development of free software for all users. Such distribution is essential to the success of the Linux operating system in the commercial market, and it must be done by organizations in a position to successfully advance and advocate free software without the pressure of profits or returns.

In his manifesto Ian Murdock further explains why he started the Debian project:

> Distributions are essential to the future of Linux. Essentially, they eliminate the need for the user to locate, download, compile, install and integrate a fairly large number of essential tools to assemble a working Linux system. Instead, the burden of system construction is placed on the distribution creator, whose work can be shared with thousands of other users. Almost all users of Linux will get their first taste of it through a distribution, and most users will continue to use a distribution for the sake of convenience even after they are familiar with the operating system. Thus, distributions play a very important role indeed. Despite their obvious importance, distributions have attracted little attention from developers. There is a simple reason for this: they are neither easy nor glamorous to construct and require a great deal of ongoing effort from the creator to keep the distribution bug-free and up-to-date. It is one thing to put together a system from scratch; it is quite another to ensure that the system is easy for others to install, is installable and usable under a wide variety of hardware configurations, contains software that others will find useful, and is updated when the components themselves are improved . . . This is a bad combination indeed, as most people who obtain Linux from these 'distributors' receive a bug-ridden and badly maintained Linux distribution. As if this wasn't bad enough, these 'distributors' have a disturbing tendency to misleadingly advertise non-functional or extremely unstable 'features' of their product. Combine this with the fact that the buyers will, of course, expect the product to live up to its advertisement and

the fact that many may believe it to be a commercial operating system (there is also a tendency not to mention that Linux is free nor that it is distributed under the GNU General Public License). To top it all off, these 'distributors' are actually making enough money from their effort to justify buying larger advertisements in more magazines; it is the classic example of unacceptable behavior being rewarded by those who simply do not know any better. Clearly something needs to be done to remedy the situation.

Ian Murdock was determined to remedy the above-sketched situation. He explains very well why he cannot cure this on his own and why he needs the help of other programmers:

> The Debian design process is open to ensure that the system is of the highest quality and that it reflects the needs of the user community. By involving others with a wide range of abilities and backgrounds, Debian is able to be developed in a modular fashion. Its components are of high quality because those with expertise in a certain area are given the opportunity to construct or maintain the individual components of Debian involving that area. Involving others also ensures that valuable suggestions for improvement can be incorporated into the distribution during its development; thus, a distribution is created based on the needs and wants of the users rather than the needs and wants of the constructor. It is very difficult for one individual or small group to anticipate these needs and wants in advance without direct input from others.

The grant ran out after a while and Ian gradually dropped out of the Debian project. The creation of Debian was sponsored for one year (November 1994 to November 1995). It is not clear whether Murdock left Debian because the grant was finished or for other reasons. One of the interviewees remarked that Ian Murdock was still a student at that time, just married and focused on having a family, so not in an ideal situation to invest a lot of time in a project without a steady source of income.

If we look at the first mailing list posting from Ian Murdock, which was posted on 16 August 1993 on a mailing list named comp.os.linux.development, we see that he is announcing a new release in the Debian-development. Ian Murdock posted his intentions to the Usenet in August of 1993 and immediately found outside interest for his idea, including that of the Free Software Foundation, the creators of much of the core software of all Linux-based systems. Murdock credits this early interest as being pivotal to the acceptance of Debian within the 'free' software programming community. Here we refer back to the three stages outlined earlier and attribute this early interest from the Free Software Foundation as an important point in the first stage of project initiation similar to Schweik and Semenov (2003).

When we read the e-mail below we find a few interesting points that relate to stage 1 of Schweik's and Semenov (2003) development cycle. Below we highlight these points and refer to them later on. We have eliminated some pieces of the message since they were too technically oriented; we want to emphasize only the factors that influenced stage 1.

> From: *Ian A Murdock*
> Subject: New release under development; suggestions requested
> This discussion contains only one message
> View: *Original Format*
> ?Discussions:*comp.os.linux.development*
> Date:1993–08–16 06:09:59 PST
>
> Fellow Linuxers,
> This is just to *announce* the imminent completion of a brand-new Linux release, which I'm calling the Debian Linux Release. This is a release that I have put together basically from scratch; in other words, I didn't simply make some changes to SLS and call it a new release. I was inspired to put together this release after running SLS and generally being *dissatisfied* with much of it, and after much altering of SLS I decided that it would be easier to start from scratch. The base system is now virtually complete (though I'm still looking around to make sure that I grabbed the most recent sources for everything), and I'd like to get some feedback before I add the 'fancy' stuff.
>
> Please note that this release is not yet completed and may not be for several more weeks; however, I thought I'd post now to perhaps *draw a few people out of the woodwork*. Specifically, I'm looking for:
>
> 1) someone who will eventually be willing to allow me to upload the release to their anonymous ftp-site. Please contact me. Be warned that it will be rather large :)
> 2) *comments, suggestions, advice, etc. from the Linux community*. This is your chance to suggest specific packages, series, or anything you'd like to see part of the final release.
>
> . . .
>
> Suggestions along that line are also welcomed.
>
> 9) Lots more, but I'll detail later . . .
>
> Anyway, I'll provide more specifics in a week or so after I receive enough replies. *Please, all replies by mail. I'll post a follow-up. If you wish to discuss this in the newsgroup*, please don't turn it into a flamewar. :)
> Until later, Ian
> Ian Murdock Internet: imurdock@shell.portal.com
> The Linux Warehouse

Murdock posted his announcement in order to try to reach a small group of motivated individuals who had ideas for the project. He made his announcement sound interesting by using some jokes in his posting and by pointing out why Debian would be such a wonderful and promising project.

> When you start community-building, what you need to be able to present is a
> plausible promise. Your program doesn't have to work particularly well. It can
> be crude, buggy, incomplete, and poorly documented. What it must not fail to
> do is convince potential co-developers that it can be evolved into something
> really neat in the foreseeable future. (Raymond 1998: 1)

'Like any area of endeavor, OS projects are initiated because one or more
people realize that there is a computing-related problem or challenge left
unfilled, and for one or more reasons, they decide to take it on' (Schweik and
Semenov 2003: 15). Ian Murdock started the Debian project from scratch
after being dissatisfied with the SLS release. Motivations, and a new Debian
release are two important parts of this first stage of an OS project. Ian
Murdock wanted to 'draw a few people out the woodwork', and had put
down a request for comments, suggestions and advice. This is another important component of the initiation stage. Ian Murdock made clear that he was
developing an initial product for others to build upon. An issue related to
stage 1 in the cycle is the modularity in the project. Ian Murdock explains:

> The nice thing about Debian in this respect is that it's modular. The package
> concept lends itself very well to modularity. That was the whole reason behind
> basing Debian on packages. I wanted others to be able to contribute to Debian,
> to participate in the development process, and breaking the system into modular
> packages seemed the best way to enable that.

Other distributions have adopted the package concept by now too, but
most of them still tend to be arranged as complete, take-it-or-leave-it
systems. Debian is more of a collection of packages that can form a complete system, custom-tailored just the way you want it. So, because of the
package concept, the resulting modularity, and the 'collection-of-packages'
approach to constructing the system, it's very easy for someone to take just
those parts of Debian that they need and build value from them.

Murdock made clear that he was working on a draft release that was virtually ready; however, he was waiting for comments about the 'fancy' stuff.
He asked people to reply by e-mail; this is why there were no other postings
on this subject. We assume the replies went to his personal e-mail address.
Murdock made clear he would post a follow-up after receiving enough
comments. This is still part of stage 1, since his follow-up was still not the
official announcement of the Debian project.

His follow-up was posted on the same mailing list on 27 August 1993. In
it he provided a status report on the Debian project. It makes clear that
Murdock received feedback from developers, and probably he received
numerous e-mails since he apologized for the fact that he could not reply to
them all. In this posting he is trying to reach the whole Linux community,

since he is not referring to specific members or groups. 'I just wanted every-one to know . . .' By apologizing (again) for the fact that he has been busy, he is creating an informal sphere around this posting. He is asking people to 'please tell me' things about technical issues. 'Please help me out.' From interviews we have learned that this approach works the best in the OSS world. When people are too demanding, the probability that others will help are almost zero. To return to Murdock's follow-up posting, he makes it clear that he wants Debian to be a cooperative distribution. He immediately downplays his role as a leader by telling everyone that he will only serve as a coordinator. Of course, acting as a dictator or simply a leader is not appreciated by everyone in the hacker culture.

In stage 2 we will see that Debian has evolved into a very democratic project in its governance structure, unlike Linux, which has Linus Torvalds, who has the final say over the kernel and is an authority above all other members. Murdock's aim to make Debian a team effort also becomes clear from his final phrase, where he asks that everyone interested in joining the team should drop him a line:

From: *Ian A Murdock*
Subject: Debian: a brief status report
View: *Complete Thread (3 articles)*
Original Format
Newsgroups: *comp.os.linux.development*
Date: 1993–08–27 08:22:14 PST

First of all, I'd like to thank everyone who dropped me a line with comments and suggestions. I'm sorry that I didn't have time to respond to them all, but there was simply no way for me to do so and make progress on the Debian release at the same time :)

I'm going to keep this brief, but I just wanted everyone to know how things were going. Sorry I've been so quiet for the last few weeks, but I've been extremely busy (to say the least). First of all, two requests:

1) I have a generic IDE controller and drive, so if there are kernel patches for your SCSI board that are not yet a part of the standard kernel then please let me know. Please tell me the *exact* name of the package and its *exact* location. I will patch the bootdisk kernel with all available SCSI patches to ensure that as few people as possible have trouble with the initial install. I don't keep up with SCSI developments so please help me out. :)

2) Would everyone prefer a distribution in 'package' format (i.e. base.tgz, bin.tgz, etc.) or 'disk' format (i.e. disk1, disk2, etc.)? The latter 'disk' format would consist of Linux disk images that would need to be either rewritten (under DOS) or added (under UNIX). I would personally prefer the latter, but if everyone else

likes the 'package' format then I will use it instead. The 'series' format, ala SLS and Slackware, will not be used. Please let me know what you would prefer.

I would like to point out here that I would like this distribution to develop in the same way as much of the rest of Linux has developed. In other words, I want everyone to *contribute* to this effort and not simply use something that one man or team has put together. This distribution will be improved by the Linux community as a whole, and I will simply serve as the coordinator of the effort.

For this reason, the first release of the Debian distribution will only be a TESTING release. It will be available to everyone who wants it (the exact location will be disclosed when an official announcement is made on c.o.l.a.), but I strongly recommend that anyone who does not want to be involved in its initial development wait until Debian has left the TESTING phase. Please remember that I started this release from scratch and that thus far only a few others have seen it. I want to get some input and make some changes before I deem the distribution suitable for the 'end-user'.

Anyway, that's all for now. Keep an eye out for an official announcement on c.o.l.a. at the beginning of next week. Please drop me a line if you're interested in 'joining the team'.

See you on c.o.l.a., Ian

Ian Murdock Internet: imurdock@shell.portal.com

The Linux Warehouse

Stage 2: Going Open: The Present

When Ian Murdock felt that Debian was ready to be shared, he made the official announcement on the Internet, and encouraged others to help improve it. On 2 September he officially announced the Debian project. This announcement was made on the same Linux newsgroup (c.o.l.a. = comp.os.linux.development newsgroup); he also posted his two earlier postings about Debian. However, in this official posting he released the name of the Debian mailing list which should be used for the project:

I'd like to announce the creation of the DEBIAN channel on the linux-activists mailing list. To join, send mail to ? with the following as the first line of the message body: X-Mn-Admin: join DEBIAN. For further instructions on using the mailing list please refer to the Linux FAQ.

Here follows Murdock's first official announcement:

What is 'Debian,' anyway?
Debian is a brand-new kind of Linux distribution. Instead of being developed by one isolated individual or group, Debian will be developed by its *users* in

the tradition of the Linux kernel and other critical components of the Linux system. In this way I hope that it will eventually develop into a powerful yet flexible product just as Linux in general has done under the same development philosophy. Although the first release of Debian is still undergoing testing and is not yet publicly available, the amount of interest that my few posts to the newsgroups has generated has been encouraging. It was suggested to me that I create a Debian channel to allow open discussion on the topic, and so I have. I invite all interested to join the channel and become a part of the Debian project. As soon as Debian is made publicly available the channel will become the center of communications for the project: bug reports, discussion concerning developing and improving the distribution and the organizational center of development in general.

For now, however, it will serve as a way of bringing everyone together, hopefully. I would like to begin organizing what I have been generally referring to as 'the Debian project'; how will the development be organized, who will be coordinating specific efforts within the project (such as someone in charge of the uucp packages, for example), what kind of features should eventually be implemented in the release, what software should be included, and so on. I have received some excellent suggestions since my initial post to c.o.l.a., and I'd like to generate some discussion based on these suggestions and more. If you contacted me earlier then you might think about joining and submitting your ideas to everyone. Any idea, suggestions, offers to contribute, etc. will be welcomed on the DEBIAN channel. Anyway, that's it for now. The first release of Debian is actually done, but I'm trying to test it as thoroughly as possible before its first public release, so hang in there everyone! Thanks, Ian

This official announcement brings us to stage 2 in the cycle of OSS projects. Stage 2 requires an understanding of the governance structure and institutional designs of Debian (see also von Hippel and von Krogh 2003). Ian Murdock decided to follow the Open Source Developers' licensing principles; he made the decision to follow the GNU/General Public License (GPL). Debian GNU/Linux is a strong supporter of free software. Since many different licenses are used on software, a set of guidelines, the Debian Free Software Guidelines (DFSG), was developed to come up with a reasonable definition of what constitutes free software. Only software that complies with the DFSG is allowed in the main distribution of Debian. The Debian developers of the Debian GNU/Linux system have also created the *Debian Social Contract*. 'The Debian Free Software Guidelines (DFSG) are part of the contract. Initially designed as a set of commitments that they agreed to abide by, they have been adopted by the free software community as the basis of the Open Source Definition.' Even more important to our case are the five additional components, described by Schweik and Semenov (2003). We will concentrate on the project governance structures and institutional designs. Our main emphasis will be on the linkage between the governance structure and the communication and collaboration patterns. In this stage 2 the communication between developers becomes important. What Murdock did – putting up a mailing list – is quite common for OS projects. Communication within the community is handled through e-mail, mailing lists and sometimes web-based discussion forums.

Face-to-face meetings are not common in the first two stages of this cycle. We had to build up an understanding of the governance structure and institutional designs of the Debian project from publicly available online material and interviews. Unlike Schweik and Semenov (2003), we had the advantage that the Debian governance structures, unlike other OS projects, have been formally documented, and are publicly accessible. The social norms had to be captured through interviews. Altogether, these formal rules and informal social norms are important components of collaboration and communication within the teams. Before describing the governing bodies and rules of the Debian project, we will describe the timeline in this second stage. The governing bodies will be linked to this time-frame, information about which was derived from http://people. Debian.org/~psg/ddg/ and the Debian website in general. We decided to use an overview of Debian releases to organize the time-frame. Table 5.1

Table 5.1   Overview of Debian releases

Version	Year	Packages	Developers	Arches?	Milestones
0.93R6	1995	250	60	2	First port to the m68k arch
1.1 (Buzz)	1996	474	90	2	ELF and Linux 2.0 kernel. The number of maintainers here is an interpolation
1.2 (Rex)	1996	848	120	2	
1.3 (Bo)	1997	974	200	2	
2.0 (Hamm)	1998	1500	400	2	GLIBC
2.1 (Slink)	1999	2250	410	4	Add Alpha/SPARC architectures. The Apt tool is included. Work on Hurd begins. The number of maintainers is an interpolation.
2.2 (Potato)	2000	3900	450	6	Add Power PC/Arm architectures
3.0 (Woody)	2002	9000	1000	11	Debconf and more architectures (S/390 IBM Mainframe)

Source: Lameter (2002: 2).

provides an overview of Debian releases. Lameter (2002) remarks about these releases:

> I just hope that you are not surprised by these numbers. Debian releases are named after characters from the movie *Toy Story*. The successor to Ian Murdock was Bruce Perens, who used to work for Pixar the company that had made the movie. 0.93R6 was released under Ian Murdock and therefore it does not have such a name. Buzz was the initial release with a 2.0 Linux Kernel.

Lameter (2002) did not include the early years of Debian in this table, presumably because 1995 was the first release year, according to Lameter. However, from http://www.debian.org/intro/free.en.html we learn that

> through fall and winter of 1993, the development of Debian proceeded through several internal releases, culminating in the public release of Debian 0.91 in January of 1994. Debian 0.91 gave its first glimpse of the Debian philosophy in action. By this time, a dozen or so people were involved in development, though Ian was still largely packaging and integrating the releases himself. After this first public release of Debian, attention was turned toward developing the package system called dpkg. A rudimentary dpkg existed in Debian 0.91, but at that time this was mostly used for manipulating packages once they were installed, rather than as a general packaging utility. By the summer of 1994, early versions of dpkg were becoming usable, and other people besides Ian began to join in the packaging and integration process by following guidelines that explained how to construct packages that were modular and integrated into the system without causing problems. By the fall of 1994, an overloaded Ian Murdock, now coordinating the efforts of dozens of people in addition to his own development work, transferred responsibility of the package system to Ian Jackson, who proceeded to make many valuable enhancements, and shaped it into the current system. After months of hard work and organization, the Debian Project finally made its first distributed release in March of 1995, Debian 0.93 Release 5. Debian 0.92 had never been released, and Release 1 through Release 4 of Debian 0.93 had been development releases made throughout the fall and winter of 1994.

> By this time, the Debian Project, as it had come to be called, had grown to include over sixty people. In the summer of 1995, Ian Murdock transferred responsibility of the base system, the core set of Debian packages, to Bruce Perens, giving Ian time to devote to the management of the growing Project. Work continued throughout the summer and fall, and a final all-out binary format release, Debian 0.93 Release 6, was made in November of 1995 before attention turned to converting the system to the ELF binary format. Ian Murdock left the Debian Project in March of 1996 to devote more time to his family and to finishing school; Bruce Perens assumed the leadership role, guiding the Project through its first ELF release, Debian 1.1, in June 1996.

At this point we can follow the table provided by Lameter (2002). We can now observe issues regarding the government structure of Debian.

5.5   MANAGERIAL ISSUES

Leadership

Debian has had several leaders since 1993. In the constitution, section 5, the role of the project leader is described. The project leader has various powers; he/she may:

1. Appoint Delegates or delegate decisions to the Technical Committee. The Leader may define an area of ongoing responsibility or a specific decision and hand it over to another Developer or to the Technical Committee. Once a particular decision has been delegated and made, the Project Leader may not withdraw that delegation; however, they may withdraw an ongoing delegation of particular area of responsibility.
2. Lend authority to other Developers. The Project Leader may make statements of support for points of view or for other members of the project, when asked or otherwise; these statements have force if and only if the Leader would be empowered to make the decision in question.
3. Make any decision which requires urgent action. This does not apply to decisions which have only become gradually urgent through lack of relevant action, unless there is a fixed deadline.
4. Make any decision for whom no one else has responsibility.
5. Propose draft General Resolutions and amendments.
6. Together with the Technical Committee, appoint new members to the Committee.
7. Use a casting vote when Developers vote. The Project Leader also has a normal vote in such ballots.
8. Vary the discussion period for Developers' votes.
9. Lead discussions amongst Developers. The Project Leader should attempt to participate in discussions amongst the Developers in a helpful way which seeks to bring the discussion to bear on the key issues at hand. The Project Leader should not use the Leadership position to promote their own personal views.
10. Together with SPI, make decisions affecting property held in trust for purposes related to Debian.

We will name all the people who ran for election to become project leader and focus a bit more on two of them. Of course, every one of them is interesting to focus on, since all had a different leadership style and all brought their unique qualities into the Debian community. From interviews we learned that Debian has been organized in many different ways. There have been experiments in leadership style. At the beginning, when only a few people were involved, Debian worked with a dictating leader. However, when it was expanding, this dictating style no longer worked, and Debian ran into managerial problems. That is why Debian arranged leadership elections. These elections also grew in time, from simple plain text mission statements on personal election platforms to election debates on IRC channels. One of the interviewees describes the role of the project leader as follows:

> The role of the project leader becomes much more formal. You have to see it as a Monarchy: you become a King through hereditary succession; you have to become the image of Debian. However, the rest of your tasks are outsourced (for example by the government). However, despite this formal role, Debian is still a herd of cats: which means there is a distribution of workload.

In the constitution, section 5.2, we can find the formal rules for the elections:

1. The Project Leader is elected by the Developers.
2. The election begins nine weeks before the leadership post becomes vacant, or (if it is too late already) immediately.
3. For the following three weeks any Developer may nominate themselves as a candidate Project Leader.
4. For three weeks after that no more candidates may be nominated; candidates should use this time for campaigning (to make their identities and positions known). If there are no candidates at the end of the nomination period then the nomination period is extended for three further weeks, repeatedly if necessary.
5. The next three weeks are the polling period during which Developers may cast their votes. Votes in leadership elections are kept secret, even after the election is finished.
6. The options on the ballot will be those candidates who have nominated themselves and have not yet withdrawn, plus None Of The Above. If None Of The Above wins the election then the election procedure is repeated, many times if necessary.
7. The decision will be made using the method specified in section §A.6 of the Standard Resolution Procedure. The quorum is the same as for a General Resolution (§4.2) and the default option is 'None Of The Above'.
8. The Project Leader serves for one year from their election.

We will highlight the leadership period of Wichert Akkerman (1999–2001) and Bdale Garbee (2001–2). Ian Murdock founded the project in 1993 and left it March 1996. Bruce Perens took over from Murdock from April 1996 until December 1997. Ian Jackson led Debian from January 1998 until December 1998. This is the point in time when the project leaders were elected. The enormous growth of the community prohibited informal ways of transferring leadership. Jackson tried, together with the community, to 'fit the governance structure' to the size of the community and to the feelings of freedom that lived in the community (structure is fine, but not more than necessary). According to one of our interviewees, Ian Jackson was very formal in most things: it is not strange that he had major influence on how Debian is structured (writing the constitution, election methods, leadership models). We will discuss these election methods after the description of the candidates.

Wichert Akkerman was the leader from January 1999 until March 2001. Akkerman had to run against three other candidates. In his election speech we read the following:

> I hereby declare my intention to run for project leader. I have been with Debian for a couple of years now (end 1995, beginning of 1996, I'm not really sure). In that time I have seen the project grow and prosper. More importantly, after seeing lots of discussions, flamewars, success stories and romances (okay, maybe not the last). I think I have gotten a good 'feel' for the project. I've learned a lot while being here and seeing things happen or fail to happen.

Akkerman also discusses the leadership qualities of former project leaders:

> I do not intend to be as dictating and vocal as Bruce was, but neither as silent as Ian was the last year. Both have done a good job, but things are not what they were. Debian has grown to be too big for Bruce's style of leadership, and Ian has laid a great foundation for a new period by giving us the constitution. This also means the role of project leader is now very different: most functions have been delegated, leaving the leader to act as a kind of benevolent overseeing person who nudges the project in a good direction.

Akkerman declares that he does not want to be an evangelist and spread the word about free software. 'But I am not a fanatic who tries to convince everyone free software is the one and only true way. There are already others who are doing a great job with that, and I do not see it as the role of project leader.' Since the project has gone through some changes, and the Debian constitution was ratified that year by vote, Akkerman did not think any organizational changes to the structure of the project were needed. 'We have just ratified the constitution and it will be interesting to see how it works out. It introduces a bit of official rules and politics, but I think it will allow us to work as a the sort of organized anarchy that we have always used while adding some much needed safety nets.'

At that time, Akkerman was a 22-year-old student. His personal information is not very detailed but it is very related to programming. A few years later, in 2001, we had an interview with Wichert Akkerman about his project leadership. The reasons why he ran in the elections are not very clear to him. 'Someone said to me that I would make a good leader, it appealed to me at that time.' He further explains:

> when Bruce Perens was a leader, he had a very clear opinion, this caused frictions and Bruce left the project. At that point the first elections were held, and

Ian Jackson was chosen, but only because no one else was running to become elected. Jackson's goal was to set some rules and guidelines for the elections. Those rules became established the next election.

That was the election that was won by Akkerman. He did not invest much time in these elections. He wrote his platform speech and that was it. Akkerman was aware that he would become the 'face' of Debian, but not to any great extent. 'I had thought about it, knowing that I would become the end-responsible for Debian. However, I never thought I would become so much involved in non-technical issues.' However, Akkerman said that he was not such a public relations person. Without being an evangelist, his idea was that when you work hard and put a great deal of effort into things, people will notice you as well. Akkerman thinks a leader can only guide people in a certain direction, but not require them to do something. The Debian project was self-regulating, according to Akkerman; therefore the task as a leader is minimal. If a project looks like failing, then a leader will interfere and ask: why doesn't that work, how can we change it, what is a solution? Of course, this will take months of discussion time.

Overall, Akkerman was very much respected within the Debian community. He was honored because of his relaxed style of leadership and his programming qualities. At his platform for the elections Akkerman referred to Debian as an 'organized anarchy'. At the time of our interview he did not remember this. 'I do not know if I have said this, but it sounds nice . . .' He continues: 'however, there are many rules which make Debian organized in a way, on the other hand there are more unwritten rules than written ones'.

In this time period something odd has happened. Although Akkerman was the formal Debian project leader, we found a discussion on the mailing list in which one of the members clearly called for a leader to guide the discussion. On the Debian development mailing list there was a discussion about the deficiencies in Debian, posted by Martin Schulze on Monday 13 September 1999. Schulze starts off: 'This mail is some major rant. I've already ranted in private and was asked several times to move this to Debian-devel. I've added some more problems I have detected. Most of the following was discussed either or with a bunch of developers and keen people at the LinuxKongress.' What follows is a major discussion about all the deficiencies within Debian. One of the conclusions from the discussion is that 'Someone needs to stand up and take responsibility for this whole thing and just dictate what we are going to do [by vote, by fiat, whatever].' The reply on this conclusion is interesting. 'Sorry; this is an ultimately dumb newbie question, but . . . who *is* in charge? I see lots of developers talking amongst themselves, but where is the central team who tells the developers what to do? Where's Ian Murdock? What happened to Ian

Jackson (who wrote many of the manuals)?' At that point in time Akkerman is the leader, but is not named in this discussion. What follows is a reply to this 'newbie' question:

> There is a Debian core who have the powers you refer to. They are VERY judicious in their use of them. That is as it should be. The people that get the real work done stay out of the limelight, so they don't get bombarded and harassed when something breaks. Even most developers don't know who the true 'power' behind Debian is. I leave it as an exercise to the reader to figure out who the true powers behind Debian are. However, because of the way things are structured, it won't do you much good to find out. The reason the leadership doesn't come to our attention much is because they make things run so smoothly. Don't fuck with that. Don't mess with them. Trying to use them as weak points to push through your own policies will only delay them in getting work done, and raise their frustration levels. It is NOT a way for you to 'get your own way' over the general consensus of the Debian project.

The reply to this message refers to a cabal, since the previous message was aiming at the true power behind Debian:

> I must have been naively blind for the last few years because i've never noticed any such Debian cabal(*). The truth is that the 'true power behind Debian' is held by those who actually get off their butts and do some work – any work that they see fit. Working code that actually exists is a lot more powerful and compelling an argument than any amount of theory or policy. (*) The truly paranoid may wish to believe that I am a member of this cabal and am merely trying to confuse the issue and deny its existence. I have only one thing to say to that: I can neither confirm nor deny such rumours. Haha! Debian today, tomorrow the world! Notice that there is no smiley on this paragraph . . . this may or may not be another deliberate attempt to confuse and hinder non-cabal members.

Within the Debian community there is a Debian private mailing list where things are discussed that are not known to outsiders. However, within this private space, rumors abound; there is also an inner core: the cabal. A cabal is a number of persons united in some close design, usually to promote their private views and interests in church or state by intrigue; a secret association composed of a few designing persons; or a junto. However, there are no clues and these are still just rumors. One of our informants, who was a member of the Debian community almost from the beginning, explains it as follows. 'The cabal is like the inner circle. However, it is used more like an inside joke. Of course, there must be some truth in it that the "old-timers" have some more privileges than the newbies in Debian, and of course some of the crucial tasks are done by a small group of people.' The next election was also won by Wichert Akkerman (see Table 5.2).

Table 5.2   Election of project leader

Date:	Jan 9, 2000
Time Line:	Nominations Close: Jan 31, 2000
	Campaigning Ends: February 21, 2000
	Voting Ends: March 16, 2000
Nominations:	Ben Collins [*bcollins@Debian.org*]
	Wichert Akkerman [*wakkerma@Debian.org*]
	Joel Klecker [*espy@Debian.org*]
	Matthew Vernon [*matthew@Debian.org*]
Quorum:	With 347 developers, Q=9.3 making a quorum of 28
Outcome:	Leadership results – 216 valid votes.
	The winner is, for a second term, Wichert Akkerman.
	Detailed election results.
	Check out the leadership debate.

New in this election were the leadership debate and speeches by the opponents. This Debian debate was held on Tuesday, 15 February 2000 at 1900 UTC, at the irc.debian.org on channel #debian-debate, which is an asynchronous chat channel, which everyone can log on to. The format of this new election was as follows. Twenty-four hours before the debate each of the candidates e-mails their 'opening speech' to the debate organizer, Jason Gunthorpe. They are then placed on this page. Everything will be added at the same time to ensure fairness. The actual debate has two parts. First, a strongly moderated traditional debate, in which the moderator asks a candidate a question. The candidate then has a reasonable period to respond. After the response, each of the other candidates responds in turn. The first candidate gets to make closing remarks on the question. The order of the candidates is rotated for each question.

The second part of the debate is more freestyle. Questions submitted by the audience and developers are put to the candidates. Each candidate gets a short period to respond. After the debate there will be a log of the debate, so the voters can read everything at their own pace. Wichert Akkerman was not so fond of this new election style, especially since not every member logs into the IRC channel and, more important, since this is a real-time dicussion medium, half of the world lives in another time zone, and cannot join in the discussion. His dislike of this new freestyle debate has probably also to do with his aversion to being a PR person. 'Welcome to my opening speech/platform/boring rant. Since I'm not a politician or a skilled PR person, I didn't really know what to put in here. So I've written a short reflection on what has happened over the last year, and what I think will/should happen next year.'

After he was elected for the second time, he did not run for another election. Enough is enough, he said. The next chosen leader was Ben Collins, from April 2001 until April 2002. Bdale Garbee was elected in April 2002 and ran for elections again in 2003. At Garbee's election platform (http://www.debian.org/vote/2003/platforms/bdale) he asks the community to re-elect him. He had also tried to become elected in earlier years. 'For those of you who are new to the project, my platform posting from two years ago is full of biographical information about me, and my platform from last year contains many ideas that are still relevant.' Bdale Garbee is in the lucky position of being able to work on Debian not only as a hobby, since he is also sponsored by his work. 'I thank my managers at HP for their strong support in the last year, which included allowing me to spend part of my work time on Debian, and supporting my travel to the many conferences where I gave Debian talks in the last year.' For Garbee it was clear that being a leader mainly meant being a facilitator. 'I approached this by spending a lot of my "Leader time" listening and reading, looking for contributors I could send words of encouragement to, making connections between contributions by introducing people to each other, and generally working to guide our collective actions towards our vision.' Being a leader also means being a promoter of Debian. Garbee invested time traveling to speak on behalf of Debian at various events around the world. We see here the differences with Wichert Akkerman. Garbee obviously likes being a spokesman for Debian. The opponents of Garbee did not have the right vision for becoming the new leader. Garbee describes what kind of leadership style Debian needs. According to Garbee his opponents

represent nearly opposite approaches. I believe the Debian community expects and deserves more involvement from the project leader than Moshe offers, while Branden proposes a much more active role for the DPL based on greater process formalism. Martin talks in his platform about the things he has worked on in Debian and the projects he would like to pursue. I am aware of, appreciate, and support these activities . . . but as he points out himself, most of them have little to do with leading the project. Many of the things he says about how he would act in the role of DPL describe the way I have tried to operate, in particular I think we have very similar ideas about how to build the sense of community within Debian. Effectively leading a volunteer project like Debian requires patience, and balanced application of many forms of motivation and encouragement. I placed a strong emphasis in my platform on communication within our community, because many concerns brought to my attention as DPL in the past year have been or could be addressed by improving communication on some level.

Garbee's speech focuses on different issues within the Debian community. One of the important points for him is communication:

One of the biggest challenges facing communities in general is communication, and Debian is no exception. Our sense of community is based on our shared values, and the activities we engage in to foster those values despite our many differences. No single change or action will solve all of our communication concerns, but if we all make an effort to better communicate our actions and progress to others, the cumulative effect will make a difference!

That Garbee has a different communication style than Akkerman becomes clear in Garbee's closing section. While Akkerman is modest in his wording and had no idea of what to write in his speech, Garbee is very straightforward:

I'm proud of what Debian has accomplished, and what we represent. I worked hard in the last year to establish good working relationships inside and outside our community, to foster activities within the project that further our vision, and to represent Debian well in public. Working on Debian continues to be my way of expressing my most strongly held beliefs about freedom, choice, quality, and utility. I ask you for the opportunity to continue serving as Debian Project Leader. Thank you for your time, and your vote!

An important aspect of leadership, according to Garbee, is a clear vision for Debian's future. For statistics on the elections, we refer to: http://www.debian.org/vote/2002/stats. Here we can find that 475 used their votes. And at http://www.debian.org/vote/2002/vote_0001, we see that Garbee won these elections.

At the time this is written, Martin Michlmayr is the leader of Debian. The Debian Project Leader Elections 2003 followed a time line of a nomination period (from 24 January until 14 February), followed by a campaigning period from 14 February until 8 March. The voting period was from 8 March to the closing date, 30 March. There were four nominations, which all had their own platform. There was a debate on 7 March 2003 22:00:00 UTC, on the IRC server irc.freenode.net. There were two relevant channels, namely, #debian-dpl-debate and #debian-dpl-discuss. The #debian-dpl-debate channel was moderated. Anybody could view the proceedings, but only the candidates, the moderators and those participating in the immediate discussion were able to post messages. The #debian-dpl-discuss channel was unmoderated, and anybody could post messages to it – the intention was for real-time, unmoderated discussion of the candidates' responses to the debate questions. The discussions on the IRC channels were logged, so everyone can read them back (#debian-dpl-debate / #debian-dpl-discuss).

We will now discuss some comments on the leadership paragraph based on responses from our interviewees. Leadership within an OSS community is not the same as within a commercial organization:

For an OSS community the leadership is not connected to status, in a commercial organization it is. There is some kind of hierarchy within the OSS projects, however this hierarchy is marginal: in one project a developer can be a core member, in a different project he could only be a peripheral member. Of course, a good reputation does help within the OSS community. Developers with an established reputation do attract other developers.

One interviewee stated that this shows a shift from the hierarchical way of thinking to a more networked way of thinking.

If you ask someone in the OSS community: who is your boss, the member will reply with: this depends on what subject you are talking about or even: what are you talking about. Everyone in the community can receive the same recognition as any one else, no matter if we are talking about leadership or craftsmanship. There is no more reason for 'wanting to be the leader' when you are not suited for that, you gain more by 'wanting to be the best in a certain area.'

Another interviewee agrees:

the leader is very important and at the same time very unimportant. The leader is a hat-rack, a walk-on. The leader could have been someone else. It is no Übermensch.

Voting

The voting process for leadership elections was automated; however, every one who voted had his or her own responsibility to check whether or not his or her vote was counted. There are specific rules on how to vote (http://www.debian. org/vote/howto_vote).

Anything else may be rejected by the automatic vote counting program. The votetaker will respond to your received ballots with an acknowledgement by mail – if you do not receive one within several days, try again. It's your responsibility to make sure your vote is registered correctly. Only one vote per person, no more than one vote per account. Addresses and votes of all voters will be published in the final voting results list.

Voting is not only used for elections; it is also used when individuals send a proposal to the community. The Debian project has a vote-tracking system which gives the status of ongoing General Resolutions and the results of previous votes. The status of ongoing General Resolutions include the proposal and list of seconders, all important dates and the necessary rules for passage. Of course, the status will also include one of the following:

- Proposal – Waiting for seconders;
- Discussion – In minimum two-week discussion period;
- Voting – Voting process taking place;
- Closed – Voting is over.

The results of previous votes (closed resolutions) include the outcome as well as a list of all the people who voted and how they voted. It also makes public the text of each vote sent. When an individual or group of people wants to change something in the Debian community they can send in a proposal. Of course, there are guidelines for this (for details see weblink at http://www.debian.org/vote/howto_proposal). Not following some of these guidelines will not disqualify a proposal: 'However, consider them to be polite in helping developers to find and understand your proposal in mailing lists that already generate huge quantities of mail.' All the guidelines are included in a template. When a proposal is completed it has to be sent to the debian-vote mailing list or directly to secretary@debian.org (who will bounce it to -vote anyway). Proposals will not be recognized by any other mailing list or e-mail address. This is to prevent the Project Secretary from missing a proposal in the huge volumes of mail generated on some of the lists and to prevent him/her from having to subscribe to each and every list created by the project. Sponsors must also be sent to the debian-vote list or to secretary@ debian.org in order to be recognized as valid. There are different rules around this voting and sending in of proposals. There are rules on what mailing list to post the message, and how to post it. All these rules contribute to organized communication, which is necessary due to the high amount of e-mail traffic. There have not been many votes within Debian. There have been five leadership elections that required a vote and four other issues (e.g. a voting about the constitution, one about the logo license, one about new logos and one about swap logos). Another proposal which was intended to be discussed and voted on was withdrawn. We come back to this proposal later in this study since it is related to the communication channels used within the community.

New Maintainer Process

Following the table provided by Lameter (2002) (our Table 5.1), we jump to the year 1999, which is an important year, since Debian entered the phase in which the community became concerned about the quality of maintainers joining the project. There was even a freeze on accepting new ones. The whole community was worried about this issue; we found a discussion on the Debian-devel mailing list that captured this problem quite well.

There are a lot of people wanting to become maintainers of some new (often little) packages, often also without a clue. Packages are buggy, partially not well maintained, also for packages taken over. Just adding them to the list of people who are allowed to upload into the main archive will just increase the distribution in size, not in quality. [No new-maintainer bashing please!] I have to acknowledge that Debian has reached the point where it has grown too much and cannot continue as before. At the moment we already have chaos all over with no proper leadership. The next release is months away, boot-floppies are not working, several goals are only slowly getting passed, still it is the bazaar of little cathedrals. Most developers are only working on their tiny five packages or are even entirely inactive nowadays. Only very few people are taking care of general management tasks. Remember this is an association of >500 people. There is still no proper management. Guess what would have happened if it were a company . . .

A process was implemented to ensure that the identity of the developers was known and that they knew about the aims and the policies of the Debian project before having access to Debian machines. Sponsors were initiating newbies into the project (Lameter 2002). The Debian new maintainer process is a series of required proceedings to become a Debian developer. There is a special webpage where prospective Debian developers can find all the details of applying, the process details, and how to track the progress of ongoing applications.

> The Debian design process is open to ensure that the system is of the highest quality and that it reflects the needs of the user community.
>
> The Debian Linux Manifesto

The current registration process of new maintainers is handled by the NM Committee, which is composed of the front desk, the application managers and the developer accounts managers. The front desk officers receive new application requests and pass them to appropriate application managers. The application manager is a Debian developer who is assigned to an applicant in order to monitor their progress through the application process. One person can be the application manager for several applicants. We will provide an example of an e-mail send by an applicant (Paul) to his application manager (in response to the initial mail from this application manager).

On Thu, Sep 21, 2000 at 12:10:41PM +0900, Fumitoshi UKAI wrote:
> I have just been appointed Application Manager for your Debian maintainership application. I have not seen your original application, so I know nothing about you or your application, I'm afraid.

Cool you were appointed to me at a moment I wasn't expecting it ;) Well, I can tell you a bit about my 'linux' history, so you know what I do. I installed RH 5.1

about 2 years ago, after having upgraded to 5.2 (real pain with RH, just reinstall) I tried to keep up with every new version that came out of the software I used, compiling everything once a week, quite a job! Then I got Debian 2.1 CDs and installed it in April 1999. I use that install until now, only I am running potato/woody hybrid. What do I do with Debian now? I maintain kernel/pcmcia packages for laptops we 'get' from the University (http://luon.net, really outdated though), I package software I use that is not in Debian (I ITP-ed gmoo and wminet lately . . . and Sean Perry is sponsoring my wminet package). I also packaged asmon, wmessage, wmnd and wmthemeinstall. I work for a linux company and for that company I have written a perl program that I Debianized also of course. I have created aptable trees on the ftp of the server I maintain with others in favour of Linux (and hopefully Debian) on the notebooks (apt-line: deb ftp://ftp.luon.net/ftp woody main).

> As a first step, have you checked out the New Maintainer corner of the website? Have a look at http://www.debian.org/devel/join/newmaint, and especially at the checklist referred to from there.

Yeah, I have been there sometimes to view the stats and queues.

> So, if you can start by letting me have the following, we should be able to progress fairly quickly: GPG key (preferably signed by a current developer or certification authority).

My key is in wwwkeys.nl.pgp.net or available by fingering 'paul@luon.net'. It is already signed by Ruud de Rooij (ruud@debian.org).

> If you can also let me know a bit about: – what you intend to do within Debian?

I want to package some more WindowMaker dockapps, some very useful ones are still missing. Furthermore can I write some manpages for packages that are undocumented and maybe I can help with some webstuff.

> – what skills do you possess in order to be able to do this sort of work that would be useful?

I am able to write a bit in groff, I am reasonably good at perl/php3/[x]html. I can read and find errors in C code, I am generally not really good in writing some C code (I like perl more). Looking forward to walking through. Greetings, Paul

Then there are the developer accounts managers (DAMs). These are the people who manage user accounts on Debian machines, and finalize the details of membership by assigning accounts to new developers. The DAMs are delegates appointed by the Debian project leader. Normally, the process is started with an application through the new maintainer application webpage interface. Then an existing Debian developer (an advocate) has to verify the application. After this an application manager is assigned for each applicant, to collect the required information for registration and to form the final report. Finally, the DAMs judge the final report from the application manager, do additional checks such as phone contact if required, and complete the process by assigning accounts to the new maintainer. The applicant has to go through different stages of becoming a developer. Here are the steps in detail for applicants to follow:

1. Initial contact;
2. Identification;
3. Philosophy and procedures;
4. Tasks and skills;
5. Evaluation and check-in.

Before the initial contact the applicant needs to read and understand the Social Contract and the Debian Free Software Guidelines and agree to abide by them in Debian-related work. Also the applicant needs to have read the documentation on the Developers' Corner (http://www.debian. org/devel/). Furthermore, the applicant's identity needs to be verified. In our section about digital identity we will explore this issue more thoroughly. There are also technical demands that applicants needs to fulfill. For instance, applicants need to be able to perform their duties as developers. This means that applicants should have experience in packaging if they want to make packages, or experience in coding if they want to code patches, or experience in documenting if they want to write documents, etc. It's recommended that applicants get a sponsor to help them achieve this. A sponsor is an existing Debian developer who acts as the mentor of an applicant: they check packages done by the applicant and help them improve the packaging. When the sponsor is satisfied with the package, they upload it on behalf of the applicant to the Debian archive. The applicant is recorded as the maintainer of such a package, despite the fact that applicants aren't yet allowed to upload packages themselves. Later on in the process, the application manager will test the applicant's knowledge of concepts described in Debian Policy, Developers' Reference, New Maintainers' Guide etc. An existing developer needs to act as advocate for the applicant. In order to persuade developers to be their advocates, applicants should get involved in Debian development – help tackle open bugs against existing packages, adopt an orphaned package, work on the installer, package useful new software, write or update documentation etc. Once the applicant has satisfied the above standards, they can submit their new maintainer application.

Step 2 in the process is that of identification. This step is described as follows:

Debian is an association or a club, much like your local LUG or Rotary, with the principal exception being that we hardly ever meet face-to-face. This poses a problem for the initial introduction process with Debian. At your LUG, everyone meets from time to time in a cosy location where everyone can shake hands and 'eyeball' the other member. As Debian lacks many opportunities for this eye/hand connection, the identification process must close the loop between hand and eye.

Therefore the applicant must provide his/her GPG (GNU Privacy Guard) public key and some kind of ID at some stage. If the applicant supplies a GPG public key which has been signed by a current member of Debian, then the identification process is complete since that member who signed his/her key must have checked some kind of ID at that time. This key-signing event is an interesting phenomenon which will be explained in more detail when discussing other governing bodies of Debian. When providing the application manager with the GPG, the 'handshake' portion of the introduction is finished. The 'eyeball' portion can be satisfied by meeting one of several possible conditions. Satisfaction of the identification requirements can happen in parallel with the other activities required of the applicant, but it must be complete before the application can be completed.

The third step in the process is about the Debian philosophy.

The applicant is expected to agree with the Debian philosophy as expressed in the Social Contract and the Debian Free Software Guidelines. The applicant needs to understand these documents well enough to express these ideas and ideals in their own words. Just exactly how this understanding is accomplished and communicated is left up to the applicant and their manager to determine.

The following fragment is an example of such a 'philosophy' check, as found in an e-mail communication between a Debian applicant and a maintainer.

Next is 'philosophy' and 'procedures'

> Debian's philosophy is described in Debian Social Contract and Debian Free Software Guidelines. You can find these documents in http://www.Debian. org/social_contract. Did you read these documents? Do you agree?

Yes, I've read it a while ago when I started packages and was getting interested in the structure of Debian and its ways to accomplishing its goal. And now, after getting to know the workings of the open source community by working with linux for two years and contributing to it by writing my own open source program, I really got to know all the facets of it.

> Could you explain why your intention to join Debian fits in with our social contract?

One way is to package free software to provide free alternatives for commercial software, as Debian developers are doing a lot now. The whole contract seems as complete logic to me, one gives and takes. The other way is to add software to Debian to provide more choice in software which leads to flexibility. That is surely beneficial for the Debian users, for whom we are doing this of course. Feedback and bugreports are the things one gets back.

> What kind of freedom is important for us?

* Freedom to modify! We should be able to modify software to make it more useful or secure for our users.* Freedom of choice! Diversity and alternatives are important.* Freedom of communication. Very important in Debian since all developers are scattered throughout the world. * Free software, the thing that drives us.

> Procedures in Debian project is described in several documents such as Debian-policy, packaging-manual, developers-references. And you should check http://www.debian.org/, especially http://bugs.debian.org/ (our bug tracking system) and http://www.debian.org/devel/ (developers corner) If you haven't see these materials, please read these.

I have read them all before packaging wminet and gmoo :) I am only familiar with the user side of the BTS of course :)
Greetings, Paul

The reason for step 3 is that Debian wants to create stability and a shared vision in its community. 'Debian does not attempt to control what the applicant thinks about these subjects, but it is important to the stability of such a large and amorphous project that all participants work within the same set of basic principles and beliefs.'

Step 4 deals with the skills of the applicant and the task he/she wants to perform in the community. Most of the current members in the Debian project maintain one or more packages for the distribution. However, there are many other jobs that need to be done that do not involve package management. The application manager will work out with the applicant just which tasks the applicant wishes to volunteer to perform. Step 4 is also about testing the applicant's skills. What is required of the applicant will depend on what task is to be done. The applicant must provide assurance that they can, in fact, do the job for which they have volunteered.

The last step in the procedure occurs when the applicant has completed the tasks and skills tests, expressed an understanding of 'The Social Contract', 'The Debian Free Software Guidelines' and Debian policies and procedures, and has been properly identified. Then the application manager can make a final report to the NM Committee.

> This report includes the completed identification information, a sample of the discussions about the Social Contract and the DFSG, and details of the performance testing. It also includes a summary of applicant's packages, the documentation that was written or updated, the work completed, or whatever task the applicant and manager have determined will adequately test the performance of the applicant. The Application Manager will include a recommendation for either acceptance of the applicant, or rejection. This recommendation should come with specific reasons for the acceptance or rejection of the applicant. The Application Manager will deliver the report to the NM-Committee for assessment, and then the same report with the additional documents should be sent to the Front Desk and the DA Manager.

An example of such a report will be provided here:

AM's Final Report for Paul van Tilburg <paul@luon.net>

Paul van Tilburg has completed the new-maintainer checklist to my satisfaction. I recommend that he be accepted as a Debian developer.

First name: Paul

Last name: van Tilburg

Current e-mail: paul@luon.net

Desired e-mail: paulvt@debian.org, forwarded to paul@luon.net

(or paulvt@debian.org)

Identification

Paul has provided the following gpg public key.

pub 1024D/50064181 1999–09–26 Paul van Tilburg <paul@donald-duck.ele.tue.nl>

sig! 50064181 1999–09–27 Paul van Tilburg <paul@donald-duck.ele.tue.nl>

sig? 4DA95DCF 1999–09–27

sig! 42CFFE4B 2000–04–30 Ruud de Rooij <ruud@debian.org>

uid Paul van Tilburg <paul@luon.net>

sig! 50064181 2000–05–10 Paul van Tilburg <paul@donald-duck.ele.tue.nl>

sub 1024g/6AE3F608 1999–09–26

sig! 50064181 1999–09–26 Paul van Tilburg <paul@donald-duck.ele.tue.nl>

His gpg public key is signed by Ruud de Rooij <ruud@debian.org> so he has passed the identification check.

Philosophy and Procedures

Paul explicitly agreed the Debian Social Contract and understands Debian Free Software Guidelines. He is already packaging some free software on his site, and has asked for sponsors or Debian-mentors. He also shows good understanding about free software licenses. So I believe he has passed philosophy and procedures check.

Tasks and Skills

I got his package from his site, and checked it. His packages are almost lintian clean, one lintian warning is W: checkservice: perl-script-uses-unknown-module./ usr/lib/checkservice/check/ldap.plugin use Net::LDAP but checkservice depends on libnet-ldap-perl which provides Net::LDAP, so this is lintian bug, not his packaging bug. I think he's good skill to package free software.

Evaluation and Check-in

I believe that Paul will be a valuable contribution to the Debian family. He would be a good package maintainer. I hereby recommend Paul be accepted as an official Debian maintainer. Thanks for your help.

Yours sincerely,

Fumitoshi UKAI

Application Manager for Paul van Tilburg

Now the NM Committee has the responsibility to determine from the manager's report whether or not all the requirements have been met. This NM Committee may make recommendations or requests for additional information or some other demonstration of skill if the report does not seem complete. Finally the developer accounts manager (DAM) receives the report on the applicant and when the DAM is satisfied with the complete application, they will create the necessary accounts for the applicant and subscribe the applicant to the essential mailing lists. Once all the final details of membership have been completed by the DAMs, the applicant and the rest of the NM Committee will be notified and the applicant will be welcomed as a developer. Introduction of a formalized new maintainer process was a necessary action because Debian was growing too fast. Without this maintainer process, just everyone could put something in the archives, and this would turn into chaos. The point is to become a registered maintainer. So far there has not been much criticism of this system. Only two people were rejected; one of them left and the other is still trying to pass the test. According to our informant, Debian has a few applications per week: this means that Debian is still growing fast. 'Of course, this system is a barrier to the project and of course there are people who are leaving for this reason. This is a pity, however necessary.'

Web of Trust/Digital Identity

The identification check in the new maintainers' process brings us to another important aspect of the Debian governance system. Although an identification check is often associated with 'secret' communication, in the Debian context is has to do with security issues. When uploading a package, a maintainer sends along his/her signature, which guarantees that this uploaded package is really from the maintainer and approved by the maintainer to be uploaded. Working with these signatures makes it difficult to corrupt the distribution with 'backdoors' (Trojan horses) or viruses. The concept of the digital identity as well as traceability and accountability are important issues in the identification check.

> A Digital Identity is the representation of a human identity that is used in a distributed network interaction with other machines or people. The purpose of the Digital Identity is to restore the ease and security human transactions once had, when we all knew each other and did business face-to-face, to a machine environment where we are often meeting each other for the first time as we enter into transactions over vast distances. (From an interview with W. Akkerman)

Interestingly, the mutual recognition of digital identities involves some form of face-to-face communication, as outlined below. The purpose of this face-to-face communication, however, is not to get to know each other better, to exchange views on complex problems or to facilitate cooperation in other ways, but simply to establish the true identities of people participating in the network. The face-to-face meeting happens mostly at key-signing parties or at open source conferences. Key-signing is based on a security principle: when I show you my PGP (Pretty Good Privacy) key together with my passport, you can trust that this is my key and that you can use it for safe communication with me, without being afraid of forgery. However, since you cannot check everyone on his or her key and passport, you can trust on the keys that were signed by someone else, whose passport you have checked. This way everyone builds their own web around them, of course trusting their own key the most, and the ones from their direct environment.

'A key-signing party is a get-together of people who use the Pretty Good Privacy (PGP) encryption system with the purpose of allowing those people to sign each others keys.' Key-signing parties serve to extend the web of trust to a great degree. Key-signing is the act of digitally signing a public key and a user-ID packet which is attached to that key. Key-signing is done to verify that a given user ID and public key really do belong to the entity that appears to own the key and who is represented by the user-ID packet. In a sense, key signatures validate public keys. They are an endorsement of validity of a public key and associated packet by a third party. This is the way in which key-signing builds the web of trust. A web of trust is a term used to describe the trust relationships between a group of keys. A key signature is a link, or strand if you will, in the web of trust. These links are called 'trust paths'. Trust paths can be bidirectional or only one-way. The ideal web of trust is one in which everyone is connected bidirectionally to everyone else. In effect, everyone trusts that every key does in fact belong to its owner. The web of trust can be thought of as the sum of all the trust paths, or links, between all key-holding parties.

Confirm that his key belongs to a person with the name mentioned in the UserID field.

This statement can be done, if Joe Smith:

1. shows his picture ID;
2. gives you his key properties;
3. proves that he can decrypt a message encrypted with this public key.

By decrypting the encrypted message, Joe Smith proves that he has access to the secret key which belongs to the given public key.

A PGP key has three important properties:

- fingerprint, for example AD 23 A1 90 B1 2B AF BA 44 49 16 7E 3D A0 F3 C3;
- key length, for example 2048 Bits;
- KeyID, for example DD934139.

If you sign a key, you need these three key properties together with the user ID. In the user ID you find the name of the person who generated this key. The key fingerprint is a kind of a checksum. It is calculated from the key.

The probability of two keys having the same checksum (e.g. fingerprint) is negligible. The Debian key-signing coordination page is intended as a service to people who wish to get involved with the Debian project, and to Debian members who are not yet connected to the web of trust. Key-signing is also important for the new maintainer process, as explained earlier. Having your GPG key signed by a Debian member is the preferred way of establishing your identity in the second step of the new maintainer process. There are different ways to find a Debian member who can sign your key:

> Check the *list of key-signing offers* for a Debian member near you (http:// nm.debian.org/gpg_offer.php). If you cannot find a Debian member among the key-signing offers, please *register your key-signing request*.

> As a last resort, you can send e-mail to gpg-coord@nm.debian.org telling us where you live exactly (plus naming some big cities close to you), then we can check in the developer database for developers who are near you.

We have already mentioned that besides the key-signing parties, developers meet at trade shows or conferences. They have become a nice way to get other people to sign one's GnuPG key and improve the web of trust. Especially for people who are new to the project, key-signing and meeting other developers is very interesting. According to an interviewee, key-signing events are often informal social gatherings; however, sometimes people only go there for the signing and not for the social talk. If you attend many conferences, the list of keys you have becomes very long. Again, it should be noted that these few occasions where people physically meet each other are not considered a necessary condition to stimulate cooperation by exchanging social cues (as would have been argued by the media richness theory), but they are deemed necessary in order to exchange keys and verify identities.

(In)adequate Communication Channels

Debian is developed through distributed development all around the world. Therefore e-mail is the preferred (or only) way to discuss various items with so many dispersed members. Much of the conversation between Debian developers and users is managed through several mailing lists. There are many world-open mailing lists, meaning anyone can read everything that is posted, and participate in the discussions. 'There are also a few lists which are only open to official Debian developers; please don't interpret this as closed development, it sometimes doesn't make much sense discussing internal topics with non-developers.'

From the Debian homepage we learned that all original Debian mailing lists are run on a special server, using an automatic mail processing software called SmartList. This server is called lists.Debian.org. All submission, subscription and unsubscription messages have to be sent to a particular address at this host. At the Debian-devel mailing list one can discuss the primary processes of the Debian project. Sometimes, a very specialist discussion will be guided to another list. According to one interviewee, the Debian (mailing) system has evolved over the years. 'The language on the list is very high tech programming language, a work-do-not-chat-mentality. Many people work behind the scenes and you do not often see them at the mailing lists. However, when they are there, they speak with great authority.' There are list indices for the following types of mailing lists: Users; Developers; Internationalization and Translations; Ports; Miscellaneous Debian; Linux Standard Base; Software in the Public Interest.

The possibility of creating meaningful interaction is enhanced by the fact that communication is exclusively based on text. The permanent transcript of the communication gives developers the possibility to read and re-read sections, thus supporting reflection. Reinhardt (2003) explains that participants can copy and paste segments of messages into their own drafts, hence building on ideas that are generated and elaborated throughout the whole communication. Nevertheless, the benefit of using others' text fragments in one's own utterances is ambiguous. On the one hand positive effects can be observed. Misguidance is avoided by establishing clear links of reference between utterances. The lack of need for reproduction of utterances in an ongoing discourse eliminates the danger of changed meaning by reinterpretation. Furthermore, communication gets more efficient, as there is no need to recapitulate or repeat previous utterances. On the other hand, copy/pasting others' text might give a false sense of achieved understanding. Using someone else's words does not automatically imply that the same meaning is attributed to them. According to Reinhardt (2003), another important characteristic of mailing lists is that the interactivity is asynchronous. It would obviously be impossible for Debian developers – who are located all over the globe and have jobs and lives besides their work for Debian – to find periods in which they all could gather at the same time in a synchronous tool, like e.g. IRC (Internet relay chat). Besides, so many people in IRC would exceed the capacity of that tool from a communicative perspective anyway, and probably from a technological perspective as well. Reinhardt (2003) argues that from a knowledge creation perspective this asynchronous communication provides a valuable additional benefit. Engaging in face-to-face communication only allows reflection-in-action: one has to think and talk simultaneously. There is usually no time to reflect on one's own utterance after having made it, because in synchronous interactive communication the communication partner takes a turn immediately and thus requires attention. As a result unconscious mental models are hardly ever questioned. Furthermore, the time to reflect on others' utterances is usually quite limited in synchronous communication. In contrast, asynchronous communication provides the necessary time for deep reflection.

> Another important feature of mailing list communication is that it is push technology. Thus all participants are actively involved in the entire communication process and have the possibility to contribute while it is still in progress. This is an important feature if the whole group wants to gain from the continuous participation of each single developer. (Reinhardt 2003: 95)

Not all mailing lists are in English. One of our informants is the coordinator of the Dutch mailing list. 'This involves a lot of work, and the work is divided over different teams and tasks.' There is discussion about those non-English mailing lists. You can see two different camps here: those who believe that everyone knows the English language and should use it and those who prefer to work in their own native language. For one interviewee, working on the Dutch mailing lists was a matter of 'scratching a personal itch.' In the leadership election of 2003 the issue was high on the agenda. For instance, election runner Garbee stated:

> we can and should deliver a better initial experience for users who are not native speakers of English. The native language support added to the Debian 3.0 installer was a big step in the right direction, but after watching an installation demonstration in Mexico last December, I realized just how frustrating it still must be for a new user who does not speak English.

However, one of Garbee's opponents had a different opinion.

> As some of you may know, I am not a native English speaker, and I come from a country where English is not an official language. However, I feel that it is important for all Debian developers to be able to communicate. Therefore, I feel that Debian development should continue to be conducted in English. I fear that attempting to cater to different languages inside the Debian development process would lead to fragmentation and miscommunication. That said, I support translation efforts. Users of Debian should not have to learn English just to use it. In addition, if translators wish to have a bug report translation service, they are most welcome too.

Both candidates for the elections of 2003, therefore, were supportive of translation activities, although from a different angle, as is made clear. Debian has different ways of structuring communication, for instance all those different mailing lists.

Sometimes there is more structure than people make use of. There are for instance specific lists for specific discussions, however during a discussion the subject may change and this discussion is not appropriate on that list anymore. So, sometimes the discussion takes place on the wrong list or simultaneously on different lists, and since not everyone always wants to join such a discussion, this can be annoying. Debian has the facilities to structure the discussions, however not everyone is using this structure properly. Sometimes there are people who re-direct the discussion by telling that this or that list is not the proper mailing list to discuss the subject. However, you can always throw the mails you do not want to read away.

Another important tool used in the Debian project is the Concurrent Versions System (CVS) (see Figure 5.1). 'CVS is one of the software configuration management systems, which store multiple versions of the source code and enables members to download and store the code' (Yamauchi et al., 2000). Yamauchi et al., (2000) provide an excellent explanation of the working of the CVS and its important role in the open source projects. The CVS is used as an important coordination tool to support articulation work in making members' involvement public.

The CVS works in the following way. First, developers copy entire source code from the central repository. After modifying the code, they update their local code by comparing it with the central code. If the central source code is changed while they are modifying their local copy, conflicts occur. If these parallel changes have no relation to each other (e.g. in different files or in different parts in the same file), the conflict can be automatically resolved by CVS. Otherwise, developers need to resolve it manually. The primary role of the CVS is to centralize the source code so that developers can always refer to the latest code. This centralization gives consistency in development organizations. Yamauchi et al., (2000) provided an example of an open source project, not using CVS. One of their interviewees stated that 'many made patches without any policy and sent them to the mailing list. Because there was no person who managed a source repository, patches couldn't be organized.' In order to keep consistency across organizational boundaries, especially in large-scale software projects, it is crucial to maintain the source so that it works at any time. In this sense, CVS repositories are 'boundary objects', artifacts that are shared across boundaries and provide shared context even if individuals focus on distinct aspects of the objects. Another advantage of the CVS is that developers can always keep the whole code in their local workspace. All members can compile, test and use the program at the same time. Therefore, Yamauchi et al., (2000) argue, the CVS is a good balance between centralization and spontaneous work, since developers need coordination by locking files before starting work and therefore work can occur

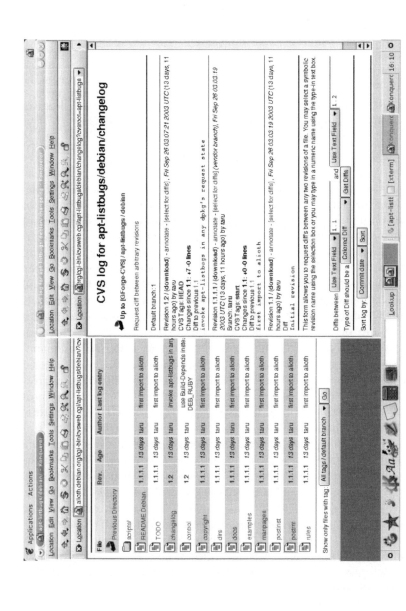

Figure 5.1   Screenshot from Debian CVS

133

spontaneously. Debian project's complexity could be kept at a level that does not obstruct progress.

> This is realized through efficient and effective communication using the CVS. It is not only a valuable tool that supports simultaneous work on same files, but also helping developers in understanding each other's work. The notifications on changes attached to every version and the database supported retrieval of changes in the source code direct developers to the work done by someone else and helps to reflect-on-action. Furthermore, messages directly written in the source code facilitate understanding. How thoroughly a developer needs to understand the others' work predominantly depends on his own work. It makes a difference if one just needs to know what features another developer is adding, or how those added features are coded in detail and implemented in existing code. As a result, it is up to everyone himself what modules one examines and how detailed this occurs. (Reinhardt 2003: 91)

Another communication tool that is frequently used is the 'reportbug' tool. Debian has a bug tracking system (BTS) which files details of bugs reported by users and developers. Each bug is given a number, and is kept on file until it is marked as having been dealt with. Reportbug is primarily designed to report bugs in the Debian distribution; by default, it creates an e-mail to the Debian bug tracking system at submit@ bugs.debian.org with information about the bug that has been found, and makes a carbon copy of the report as well for the author of the package. Normally, the only people that are allowed to close a bug report are the submitter of the bug and the maintainer(s) of the package against which the bug is filed. On http://www.debian.org/Bugs/Reporting.en.html members can find out how to report a bug. Reportbug is a tool designed to make the reporting of bugs in Debian and derived distributions relatively painless. The most important usage of the BTS, and the most popular, is to search for bugs which are relevant to problems newly experienced by other users.

A session with reportbug shows how a problem with a piece of software automatically becomes directly sent to the involved package manager in the format of a standard e-mail where the problem's priority will be decided (on the basis of objective criteria). The user will be guided through the reportbug session, so that his/her message will be automatically generated in a useful and standardized format, complete with the most relevant information about his/her system. The system will help the user to find out whether the bug has already been identified or not. Once the message from the sender is reported in the reportbug system, all the people involved in this bug will be notified.

In sum, the reportbug is process-supporting software: it facilitates the cooperation and the communication of programmers, but the programmers stay in control. The system makes some requirements and demands, but there is always enough room for the human factor. Using reportbug requires a few steps in the process:

1. It helps to find out which package one is talking about. If a member says: the problem was in this package, or the problem is in this configuration file, the reportbug will trace to which package the file belongs.
2. The reportbugs scans whether the member has installed the most updated version (see also Figure 5.2).
3. Reportbug shows a summary of all outstanding bug reports on a certain package.
4. Reportbug finds the maintainer who is responsible for the package and how he/she can be reached. It also searches for any other packages that the package is using, since a bug can exist because a certain version of a package does not cooperate well with other versions. Version-information as such is relevant for fixing a bug.
5. Reportbug asks for a short description of the problem (one sentence).
6. Reportbug will guide the members in choosing a priority level for the bug.
7. Reportbug archives all information and asks the sender to formulate a more extensive description of the problem. This is all archived.
8. All further communication is automatically updated.
9. Finally the bug report will be closed when the bug is fixed.

The Debian community is constantly trying to improve the communication channels. The announcement of Alioth on the debian-devel-announce@lists.debian.org mailing list on 29 March 2003 gave the Debian community the opportunity to get to know this new service. 'Hi everyone, This message announces the birth of a new service: Alioth is a Sourceforge installation dedicated to Debian.'

Alioth offers the same range of services as Sourceforge but only to projects that meet certain criteria. Alioth has big advantages since creating a project is easy and it offers full control over many services. It is open to non-Debian developers and it is easy to grant rights (for example CVS write access) to external contributors. The initiators of Alioth hope that this service will show that the Debian community is a very active part of the free software community. The initiators hope that Alioth will help them to allow more people to contribute to Debian without going through the complete new maintainer system. It should also help collaborative package maintenance, thus increasing the general quality of Debian. Apparently, the community has found a way to involve people within Debian without those people having to become official maintainers.

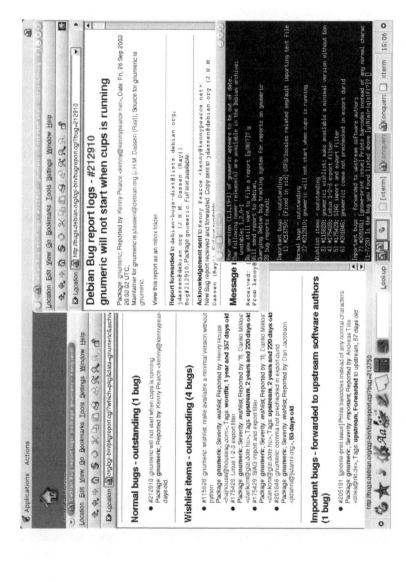

Figure 5.2   Screenshot from reportbug

Openness

Anyone is able to subscribe/unsubscribe on their own to any mailing list if the subscription policy for a particular list is 'open'. This 'openness' sometimes creates discussions in the OSS world. The opinions are very varied, and depend mostly on people's first experience with a project. On slashdot.org we found a discussion regarding this matter. An 'Anonymous Coward' asks:

> I'm a highly competent and occasionally respected software engineer, who has worked on several Open Source/Free Software projects; some of my code is in the Linux kernel. *Within the OSS community, we maintain that the main point of publicly announcing OSS projects is to invite programmers to join the project and collaborate to make better software.* But in about 90 percent of cases, I've found that publicly announced projects in development are not actually open to new members – the project leaders will ignore unsolicited code, won't respond to e-mailed queries or suggestions, and in many cases the projects in question remain in an early stage of development forever. What projects do you know of that don't make an issue out of incorporating user submitted patches and design changes, and what projects put forth huge restrictions on such submissions, even to the point of not accepting them at all? *This happens even when the project has explicitly asked for collaboration, and it happens when the project leaders are big names in the OSS community as well as when they're relative unknowns. So my question is, who actually collaborates? Which projects make unsolicited development effort worthwhile by making it part of something bigger??*

The response on this question was enormous. We have browsed through all the postings and selected a few of them in order to demonstrate different opinions. We will highlight some key issues and discuss them afterwards.

> I think (Score:2)
> by *Ravenscall (12240)* on Saturday September 15, @09:29AM (#*2302726*)
> And do not flame me for it, but I think it is one part *maintaining the public image (Jump on board!)* to one part of just not *having the resources/Manpower* to deal with every piece of submitted code. If all OSS projects had the type of man power that say, the Linux Kernel project had, Open Source would be dominating every market, but, as I do not run any of these, I really do not know.

> Good projects have to do it. (Score:1)
> by *ugen (93902)* on Saturday September 15, @09:34AM (#*2302738*)
> Look at FreeBSD – they are fairly open, in that anyone with GOOD idea will be eventually admitted. However you can't just come in with a bunch of code that does not conform to their *guidelines* and does not do something within a current plan and hope they will take it. If you are sure that your code is good and that project will benefit from it – and they don't 'let you in' – just take their work, put your changes in it and distribute it to the world. If what you do is useful or necessary – the people will make the right choice.

Join MY project – It NEEDS developers – All Welcome (Score:1)
by *cculianu (183926)* on Saturday September 15, @10:06AM (*#2302814*)
(http://www.ajvar.org/~calin)
Well, if you haven't found an open project, you haven't looked hard enough.
Typically the larger projects are the ones that already have so many people
involved, *in the interests of sanity, code must be rejected* and some questions in
mailing lists ignored. However, smaller projects are EXTREMELY rewarding
and really collaborative on a truly cool level.

The ego of the maintainer (Score:3, Insightful)
by *proton (56759)* on Saturday September 15, @10:08AM (*#2302817*)
(http://www.energymech.net/users/proton/)
A lot of the submission-friendliness depends on the *ego of the maintainer*. If it's
a person who wants to head up the project just for the fame of it, you'll probably find it hard to submit good high quality code. Such maintainers are probably more likely to take the ideas from your code and implement it themselves, for
better or worse . . .

I am a maintainer of a project myself, and I know that any submissions that
comes to me will be scrutinized quite harshly for quality. If they're not up to my
own standards then I won't accept them. . . . I think. If all else fails, you can
always look into forking the project. If you are unhappy with the current maintainer, maybe there are other people who are as well? *Can you do a better job? If
so, don't be afraid of forking, that's what free software is for I think. Letting the
best man do the job.*

My experience with Wine (Score:3, Insightful)
by *knitfoo (165390)* on Saturday September 15, @10:13AM (*#2302828*)
I think this is a very interesting question, and one that is rarely honestly discussed.
I've watched the wine-devel list closely for the past 3 or so years, and I've observed
the following: Most OSS Developers are *extremely helpful*. I can't begin to tell you
how impressed I have been by the responsiveness of developers on both wine-
devel and on wine-users. *Some OSS Developers can be very rude to newbies* who
annoy them (yes, Andreas, I mean you, but you're getting better *g*).

Some queries to the list are simply ignored. And not just ones where the author
failed to RTFM; there are often cases where someone asks a question, and
it *doesn't push anyone's hot button*, and no one replies. Lists can actually be prob-
lematic this way. Have you noticed that if you send two people an e-mail, your
response rate is lower if you send the same e-mail individually to each person?

Most new posters want to swing for the fences, not pick up the litter. This is a real
problem, IMO??, with all OSS projects. For example, Wine is hard. However,
there's lots of good work a newbie could do (testing, doco, simple test cases, small
projects that Francois does an excellent job of collating). Most new posters want
to make a real impact with their work, not start in the mailroom, as it were. Hence
the enormous number of OSS projects (why spend your personal time cleaning
the litter of Wine when you can be the lead developer on BobsCoolWidget?)

*Most OSS projects see a lot of newbies come . . . and go. They respond best to new
people who stick around for the long haul. I guess it's like Minnesotans. They're*

not very friendly for the first 10 years you're their neighbor, but after that, you're like family . . .

a few guidelines (Score:5, Interesting)
by Kuroyi (211) <rick@kuroyi. n e t> on Saturday September 15, @10:21AM (#2302854)
(http://www.kuroyi.net/)
Here's a couple guidelines off the top of my head:
1) *Follow the goals* of the project. Usually a project leader will have in mind where he wants the project headed. Follow it. Ask him about it if you can't find any information about this on the webpage or mailing list. (Sometimes a project is organic however).

2) *Follow the existing design* unless it's broken. Don't change the design unless you can articulate good reasons for it. This forces people who already know the existing design to take time to learn a new one.

3) Coding style. *Follow the style of the rest of the code.* Some people will reformat it for you if it's good enough, but don't bet on it.

4) *Keep it manageable.* It's difficult to read and verify large patches. Send separate functional pieces if possible. It takes me much longer to merge big patches than smaller ones.

5) Use cvs diff. Unless keeping it manageable prevents it, use 'cvs diff -u'. This generally makes things easier for you and whomever is applying your changes. Especially if you've never made a diff before.

6) *Tell the project leader what you're doing.* Even if you're not going to be done anytime soon, let someone know what you're doing. I had two people come up with independent Debian packages for a project because one of them didn't mention it to anyone.

7) *Put it on a webpage somewhere.* If your patch doesn't get merged put it on a webpage. Send the url to the mailing lists and keep it up to date. Maybe provide a prepatched .tar.gz. If you're going to be doing it anyway let others benefit. That's all I can think of at the moment. I try to reply to all patch e-mails even if I reject them but some people don't have the time. Don't feel bad if nobody replies, just manage the patches yourself if you find them that useful.

Code of Conduct

As we said earlier, this discussion thread was enormously long. In our interviews we also obtained different opinions regarding this issue of openness. One point that has become fairly clear is that a mailing list in an open source community is a world on its own, with rules, norms and codes of conduct. For new people on the list (newbies) this might be a bit overwhelming. While posting a message to the list you might get rude answers or a reply like: RTFM. (And of course being a newbie you will not know what RTFM means.) Since some of the mailing lists are so large in volume, with many messages a day, the OSS community users wants to structure the posting as much as possible in order to avoid having to read everything. Questions that are asked on such a mailing list that could have been answered by reading the manual are overload and noise to the members of the open source community. Probably the phrase 'think before you write' is appropriate here. E-mail communication is highly valued for this: one can take the time to think about an e-mail. However, when discussions get heated on a mailing list, it almost looks like an asynchronous chat channel. The time-lapse that normally occurs in e-mail discussions is a good thing, since one can think before posting something.

> This is something typical, the progress seems to go very slow. However, this is also the power of Debian. Debian is so complex, that it is difficult to coordinate everything, some projects and choices that are made influence the whole project and that is why people need time to think things through. For simple projects one could use for instance videoconferencing to discuss matters, however in complex problems like these you need experienced people who think things over and over again, and that is why e-mail is a more suited medium. Also because every word and every idea is archived, you do not have to respond immediately. Furthermore, since e-mail is said to be less personal, you can not be distracted by someone's voice or looks.

Another example of the advantage of a mailing list discussion was provided by another interviewee:

> Let's assume you have a driver for a USB card and you want to adjust some parts, this will influence everyone who is using a USB card. If you would discuss this in a face-to-face setting with only the members from the kernel, you would restrict yourself in ideas. If you would keep this discussion on the mailing list you would reach many more individuals with more ideas. You have to throw something that complex in the community and retrieve different levels of feedback and input.

Let's return to the discussion in which we highlighted some interesting points. The main problem with busy mailing lists is that although those lists want to maintain the public image of being open for everyone, the people involved just do not have enough resources to reply to everyone. Sometimes the ego of the maintainer is one of the problems. Most OSS members are very friendly and supportive, but of course they are all human! When a maintainer is acting in a non-friendly way, there is always an option to 'fork' with that list/project and set up your own list – 'letting-the-best-man-do-the-job idea'. Since mailing lists are open most of the time, anyone can enter, lurk around, post messages; however, one can leave just as quickly without any trace. The die-hards on those lists prefer the newbies that stick around longer. Only in that way can people build a community. Our interviewees said that they were trying to help users and newbies as much as possible; however, it also depends on how many times someone asks something. 'And of course the attitude of the person who is asking something is important. If someone keeps nagging me, he can expect a snappy answer.' A maintainer can also answer with: 'If you want a polite answer, pay me! Since users know that we are all doing voluntary work, they ought to know it is a give and take situation.' Another issue that comes into play is the fact that although in open source development more people are involved than in traditional organizational forms, the data show the existence of a relatively small 'inner circle' of programmers responsible for most of the output. Those programmers are also more active participants in the discussions pertaining to the project, although all programmers show a higher than average activity in the mailing lists compared to other participants. There is only a small number of programmers working together on a file, indicating a high degree of modularity.

From the Apache case study by Mockus et al., (2000) it may seem that the core developers are the most powerful class in the structure, but all the classes of people in this social structure are interdependent and a stable balance of power can be achieved. Users, who seem to depend on the developer community for bug fix and implementation of new features, are actually very important to the developers, since they point out bugs or non-user-friendly software. Therefore, Eric Raymond's (1998) advice on respecting users is sensible in this social structure.

Following the guidelines, reading the manual and the FAQs, and communicating in the style of the mailing list are important conditions when communicating via a list. 'If you want to reply to a message on a mailing list, you should learn about a number of rules to make the message as readable as possible.' The essence of a message is clear communication. 'A poorly constructed message is not only harder to read for the direct recipient but also for other people that would like to join the discussion. A well quoted message will show question and response in the natural reading direction, which will make the message much easier to read.' Following quoting rules while writing e-mail will probably result in more replies. The fact is that people tend to ignore sloppy messages and are attracted to well-written ones.

> The only argument I have to encourage decent quoting is readability. You won't make many friends by driving too fast on the highway nor by playing music very loud in the middle of the night. The essence of usenet is cooperation and not originality and frivolity in the way you present your messages. I agree this is not the highway and you won't keep anybody awake by doing it your way. You just lose your audience.

Not only the quoting rules apply to the Debian mailing list, but so does the intrinsic Debian code of conduct. When using the Debian mailing lists, please follow these rules:

> Do not send *spam*. Send all of your e-mails in English. Only use other languages on mailing lists where that is explicitly allowed (e.g. French on debian-user-french). Make sure that you are using the proper list. In particular, don't send user-related questions to developer-related mailing lists. Wrap your lines at 80 characters or less for ordinary discussion. Lines longer than 80 characters are acceptable for computer-generated output (e.g., ls -l). Do not send automated 'out-of-office' or 'vacation' messages. Do not send subscription or unsubscription requests to the list address itself; use the respective -request address instead. Never send your messages in HTML; use plain text instead. Avoid sending large attachments. When replying to messages on the mailing list, do not send a carbon copy (CC) to the original poster unless they explicitly request to be copied. Do not use foul language; besides, some people receive the lists via packet radio, where swearing is illegal. Try not to *flame*; it is not polite.

Flaming

We have seen the word flaming a few times in this chapter. Since it is a communication behavior, we need to pay some attention to it. Flaming means:

> > To rant, to speak or write incessantly and/or rabidly on some relatively uninteresting subject or with a patently ridiculous attitude or with hostility towards a particular person or group of people. 'Flame' is used as a verb ('Don't flame me for this, but . . .'), a flame is a single flaming message, and 'flamage' /flay'm*j/ the content. Flamage may occur in any medium (e.g. spoken, electronic mail, Usenet news, World-Wide Web). Sometimes a flame will be delimited in text by marks such as '<flame on> . . . <flame off>'. (From the Debiansite Jargonfile)

Since Debian is a community of developers interacting only through the Internet, it is rare that Debian developers meet and have a face-to-face encounter for project-related interaction. Community members do meet at conferences and key-signing events, but those meetings are not task-related. Communication is happening mostly through mailing lists, IRC (Internet relay chat) and websites.

> With that online communication comes the lack of personal encounters. This means that the emotional component of communication must be imagined. This can often lead to misunderstanding and conflicts that otherwise would not develop. One area of concern has always been the amount of 'flaming' on the mailing lists and on the IRC channels. Debian developers are known to have strong convictions and it is easy to get into some old argument when the buttons of one group or another are pressed.

We're never going to put out the flame wars. The best we can do is hope that people will learn to devote their energies to more productive things, like making the software better, and not let the flame wars get in the way of making progress. Flame wars are an unfortunate byproduct of the passion that people put into free software. When people are willing to spend hours and hours arguing about things, sometimes arcane things, that means they care very much about them. Can you imagine people arguing endlessly about the merits of a particular toaster or microwave oven? People in this community care very much about their software, and that's a big part of the reason why Linux, and free software in general, have come so far in such a short amount of time. People are willing to pour everything they've got into this. Given that kind of passion, it's inevitable that we're going to have flame wars.

With a large group of developers it is more and more difficult to maintain personal contacts. Cliques develop that deal with some aspects of the project. Decisions are frequently made in those small groups rather than as a whole project. That is unavoidable given the nature of the project but it often leads to complaints because another group or person was not consulted or not aware of coming changes. Sometimes you find 'trolls' on the mailing lists, people who are deliberately aiming at starting a flame. One of our informants says about these trolls: 'We can handle those trolls, we will shut them up.' Since all the communication goes over the Internet, the question that pops up is whether you can really get to know the other person. While discussing these issues with the interviewees we received a counter-question: 'Is it necessary to know the other person?' However, after interacting with each other you will start to recognize each other by the language that is used, the tone of the mail and the content. This way e-mails have a personal touch.

Discussions on the Mailing Lists

According to the interviewees, most discussions go 'underground', and what appears on the mailing list is only the tip of the iceberg. We cannot check this statement and we assume that it is true for a small inner-circle group of friends. Our interviewees stated that communication via a mailing list has some delay, which is a property of the medium. One can think before writing a mail, and propose new ideas. However, before proposing something, work this proposal through by yourself and discuss it within a small group of people. This works much more effectively than posting a proposal that has not really been thought through. This way you will not waste other people's time on the mailing lists. Most discussions on the mailing lists are technical ones. Discussions via mailing lists are more formal than via the IRC channels. On the IRC channels (which are asynchronous chat channels) one can talk about personal issues or about a television program.

Mails sent to the mailing lists mostly follow the same structure and content, probably, pointing out a bug or mistake in the code. In that mail you do not introduce yourself and you do not talk about informal things. The mail is just about that specific subject, nothing more and nothing less. Within Debian you can personally address the maintainer of the project, and tell him or her about the bug you have found. This is totally different when you discover a mistake in a Microsoft program; you can try to send a mail about it, but mostly it will wait on someone's desk for a long time. In Debian you can immediately address the responsible person, if he or she is still active on that project. Debian makes use of a bug-tracking system, which keeps an eye on the workload. It works on the basis of a mail system and deals with technical issues. For instance, when two packages are interfering with each other, which can happen since the interdependence between packages is high, coordination between maintainers is necessary. The maintainers mostly send each other a direct mail; however, when it is something really difficult, it is impossible to use the policy mailing list.

On the Debian-devel mailing lists we found a discussion about the status of various communication channels within Debian. The discussion had to do with a proposal that was written and called for a vote. Following the proposal rules, a proposer came up with a proposal and with sponsors to back him up. The proposer also gave a discussion time and the voting period. The proposer asks for a vote about the recognition of the Debian IRC channel as a formal communication channel (as, for instance, the mailing lists are).

Proposer: Raphaël Hertzog <?>

Time Line: Proposal Submission: October 31st, 2001
Discussion period: November 1st, 2001 to November 14th, 2001
Voting period: November 15th, 2001 to November 29th, 2001

Sponsors: Guillaume Morin <?> Michael D. Ivey <?> Stephen Stafford <?> Gergely Nagy <?> Jérôme Marant <?>

PROPOSED GENERAL RESOLUTION
IRC AS A DEBIAN COMMUNICATION CHANNEL

1. Context
A #Debian-devel operator regularly kicks (sometimes bans) people from the channel if they are not Debian developers. He does so even if they have been introduced by developers as valuable Debian contributors and behave correctly in the channel.

2. Problems
* The IRC channels #debian-* are not officially recognized as part of Debian's communication channels. * Debian can't treat valuable contributors like it's done actually on IRC. Kicking a person who naturally has his place within the developer's community (because of his interest and his work) is not reasonable.

(*Personal note: this kind of behavior gives Debian its bad image of a closed community preaching openness*)
 * Debian's philosophy concerning the development has always been to open the communication channels. There's a mismatch here.

3. Proposed changes
We should acknowledge the fact the IRC channels are used to communicate within Debian. They are only an alternate way to discuss things. They are not the main communication channels (the mailing lists are). This should be documented in Debian Developers Reference and wherever it's applicable. By acknowledging their existence, we also have to apply the usual Debian policies – all #Debian-* channels on Open Projects should be open to everyone except #Debian-private which is for registered Debian developers only (the actual 'key protection' may be replaced by a better identification mechanism at any time) – the 'netiquette' (RFC 1855, section 4.1.2) applies, channels' subjects should be respected.

4. Item proposed to vote (after the discussion period)
 [ ] I accept the ratification of IRC channels as a communication medium and as such they have to follow the usual Debian policies (adapted for IRC habits).
Outcome: Withdrawn by the proposer on 14 November 2001.

The Debian project secretary posted an announcement on two mailing lists: debian-project@lists.debian.org, debian-vote@lists.debian.org. This is the formal way to send in proposals, as we have discussed earlier. The secretary wrote that 'With these 5 sponsors, the minimum of K sponsors is met, and this is hereby acknowledged as a General Resolution. I would prefer that this discussion, now that we are in the formal discussion period, be moved over to debian-vote@lists.debian.org, which was designed to serve such a purpose.' However, after many e-mails of discussion, the initiator decided to withdraw his proposal. He decided not to follow through on the procedure of proposals and voting. 'First I'd like to thank the few people who have been constructive and tried to help instead of denigrating and nitpicking on minor points. I've decided to withdraw the general resolution proposed 2 weeks ago about IRC as communication channel.' The discussion did continue over the mailing list. From 3 November until 7 November we found 62 e-mails on this subject. On 14 November the proposal was withdrawn but until 17 November we were able to find another 22 postings regarding this subject. However, from an interviewee we obtained the following information. According to this source the discussion was initiated by a person who wanted to have stricter control and organization at Debian.

Mostly since IRC by nature is very anarchistic. Discussing whether or not IRC should become the official communication channel, and if so, what consequences should that have for the sharing of private information, is difficult to discuss. (#Debian-devel is in principle free for everyone, and that is why it is not the proper place to discuss matters regarding the debian-private list).

This proposal was withdrawn; however, now and then new policies and documentation are created through discussion on the mailing list. For instance, the Debian constitution was also discussed on the Internet.

Disputes between Developers

On one occasion, a proposal that was intended to solve disputes between developers in fact *caused* a dispute between developers. In this real mailing list example we can see a bit more discussion and flaming in action. Moreover, this section shows that the work within Debian is not only task-related, but can also be socially oriented, discussed through e-mail communication. Ian Jackson wrote a draft proposal in order to solve disputes between members. He motivates this draft by writing the following: 'Since Debian is a very large project, we will inevitably disagree, and occasionally get annoyed with each other. To allow us to work well together a bit of give and take is needed, and we must be willing to present coherent reasons for our views, and to listen to and engage with counterarguments.' His document gives advice about friendly interaction and what you can do when friendly interaction does not work. According to Jackson it is important to distinguish problems in working constructively due to an interpersonal dispute ('not getting along') from technical disagreements about how software should work, or procedural disagreements about whether some particular thing should or should not be done.

> For Debian to be able to construct good software, we must be able to disagree with the way something is done or proposed in a constructive and useful way. The best designs result when all the issues have been considered. Useful technical discussions can become derailed by flamage. To help avoid this, please phrase your technical disagreements moderately. If you receive a heated complaint about some technical matter please try to respond to the technical, not emotional content!

He continued with some more tips and tricks for 'friendly' communication. How could this attempted proposal end in a flame war, you might wonder? We will outline the beginning of the conflict, which was between two developers and caused consternation in the community. Brandon Robinson sent an e-mail to the community about Jackson's behavior; i.e. his unwillingness to discuss his proposal with Robinson. The first e-mail interaction between Jackson and Robinson was private e-mail; however, when

they got into a dispute, Jackson granted permission to post his part of private e-mails. Of course, Robinson published his part as well. Both wanted to hear the response from the community about this dispute, which can be found at: http://people.debian.org/~branden/iwj_disputes_draft_dispute.
What follows is Robinson's first message to the list about this dispute.

Hi folks, Just a brief note to those of you who have been following the 'disputes resolution' document threads. Ian Jackson sent me an unsolicited private mail a few days ago complaining that he was perceiving an abrasive tone in my messages regarding his draft. After a few private exchanges, he asked me to stop mailing him privately on the subject. He also gave me notice that he would not be paying any further attention to my contributions in the public discussion, and suggested that I would need to find a spokesperson through whom to relay my feedback on the document. (On the lighter side of things, almost as ironic as an unresolvable dispute over a document about resolving disputes is being asked by a person who sends you unsolicited private mails to stop replying to those same mails!)

I personally remain ready to discuss just about anything with Ian in what I regard as a calm and professional manner (look ma, no screaming capital letters, exclamation points, or ad hominem attacks). However, my effort to keep the discussion strictly on a logical and, admittedly, fairly formalized yet candid manner appears to be more than Mr. Jackson is willing to cope with . . .

. . . But the main point I want to make in posting this exchange publicly is to contrast Mr. Jackson's apparent approach to arguments with mine. I think it is important – *especially* when writing formal documents like joint resolutions – that one works very hard not to read between the lines when interpreting the communications of those who disagree. While it is not reasonable to expect *machine-like, perfect rationality from ourselves every waking moment*, I think it is an ideal to which we should aspire when undertaking the weighty role of a representative for many voices, as Ian is doing in this proposed document . . .

Before diving into the open discussion, we will show the private e-mail from Jackson to Robinson, telling him to stop mailing.

I'm afraid I'm finding interaction with you too stressful because I'm still finding you putting the most uncharitable, negative and generally unhelpful interpretation possible on everything I do. I've tried hard to have a constructive and friendly conversation, but all I'm getting from you is hostility and it's not good for me. So I'm going to protect my sanity (I mean that quite literally) by trying to ignore you. I'm afraid I can't promise to produce constructive and helpful responses any more. Please do not send me any more private e-mail on this topic. If you feel strongly that I'm going down some bad route, I can only suggest that you find someone willing to try to mediate. I'm happy to listen to arguments, but whether it's deliberate or not on your part, I can't sensibly cope with the way you're expressing yourself. Alternatively you can wait for me to do whatever it is

I feel is best and then try to get the Project Leader to override me. Also, note that I do not consider this e-mail exchange confidential. If you wish to publish it, please do so – on the understanding that I'd also have permission to publish your side of the exchange. If you want to publish it, it would be best to publish the whole thing perhaps. Personally I think the last thing the project needs is another petty squabble argued about in a massive flamewar.

Twenty-one developers got involved in this dispute. However, they were not involved to the same extent and volume. Around 89 e-mails were sent regarding this issue in a period of nearly two weeks. The discussion went along different lines, which we will not follow in detail. Generally, one line discussed whether or not Jackson was flaming Robinson or vice versa. Then there were people who disagreed with Jackson in his proposal and the way he brought this proposal into the community. Also some of the members were not happy with the fact they were drawn into this dispute. Jackson feels that Robinson is flaming him.

But, if I read between the lines of your messages, there seem often to be insinuations of dishonesty or lack of good faith on my part, and where you disagree with me you do so in a very snide way.

Robinson replies:

Well, try just reading what's there. Everybody knows what it sounds (and looks) like when I flame someone. I leave absolutely no doubt as to the nature and vehemence of my disagreement. If you regard calm messages from me as having the same emotional content as the flames, then you leave me with no means to express disagreement. I feel confident that you would not deliberately construct such an interpretive mechanism for justifying a complete disregard of another's opinions no matter the circumstances.

Robinson replies some messages later with the following and is more or less addressing the power status of Jackson since he is one of the inner circle people:

In the instant case, maybe people are fearful of going up against the legendary Ian Jackson, the Author of Our Package Management System and Constitution, and Chairman of the Technical Committee. This fear may be compounded by an unwillingness to be decried in public as someone that 'Ian Jackson won't listen to', as you've just done with me. It might be possible for you to achieve your ends through intimidation – even inadvertently! – that would not be achieved via an electoral process. All of this is why I think it's a bad idea to refuse to talk to people when you're trying to do something important. I am willing to talk on points about issues of substance to your proposal, and you're refusing to listen.

We will end this discussion by giving the last word to Jackson. From this dispute we can learn a few things and that is why we have quoted so many fragments of e-mails.

> So, without following up anything in particular, I'd just like to say that I'm quite frustrated by what's been going on here. Branden and Manoj have been telling us at length how high-handed and undemocratic and otherwise evil I am, when in fact all I've done so far is post a document for review and comment, and defend it against some criticisms. Branden and Manoj can complain until they're blue in the face that obviously I'm being arrogant and cabalish and what have you by disagreeing with them on some points, and declining to change my working draft (and even, in Branden's case, declining to deal with any more of his dysfunctional flamage). Shock horror, I even admit to being swayed by private e-mail! But, it's not their decision. It's currently my draft, and I'll put what I like in it. BUT, I think the way the discussion so far has been proceeding has been profoundly pointless – even harmful. Very little has been said about the actual substantive content of the document at all. We've had a few exchanges, but nothing like the vigorous discussion that there ought to be if there are real differences over what should be in it. The bulk of the conversation has turned into a meta-flamewar, which just leads to the participants getting angry.

Jackson did put up different new versions of his proposal, again leading to many discussions. However, we could not find a closing message – except one from Robinson on another draft recommendation from Jackson:

> A *DRAFT* recommendation, which Ian Jackson hopes will be approved in some form by the Technical Committee and the Project Leader.
>
> THIS DOCUMENT IS NOT YET APPROVED BY ANYONE. IT IS A FIGMENT OF YOUR IMAGINATION. IF YOU POSSIBLY SUSPECT THAT ANYONE EXCEPT IAN JACKSON AGREES WITH IT THEN PLEASE GO WASH YOUR BRAIN OUT WITH FLAMES.

Some interesting issues have been raised within this discussion. Now we all know what flaming really is, we have seen some power games and a reference to the cabal. Although our interviewees claimed that status is not important in the Debian community, this thread of discussion sometimes proved otherwise. We also saw that only a small part of the members were involved in the discussion and that they all had different reactions to it. Some of them did not want to be bothered with the discussion, others tried to be constructive, and others just ignored the discussion on a social level and tried to follow rules and guidelines to solve the dispute. However, one thing in particular is useful to our case study. E-mail communication seems to be able to raise strong emotions in people. Even in plain text people read between the lines to find emotions and meanings. Within Debian we can find both ends of communication from very technical and to the point to meta-flaming. Through e-mail behavior people get real faces even though we cannot see them. The often-heard argument that e-mail is a very lean form of communication does not apply in the Debian case. Social cues do exist in e-mail communication, but not of course in the same way as in face-to-face communication. But the outcome is probably the same. The argument that e-mail gives the receiver and sender time to reflect on the message to be sent, in order to avoid heated discussion, was not valid here. One can wonder how this discussion might have looked when being disputed over an IRC channel, which is said to be more responsive to flame wars. In one of the e-mails, Robinson refers to Jackson as intimidating; it is interesting that plain text can be used to intimidate another person, especially since gestures, social position, tone of voice and reputation are less visible in e-mail communication than in face-to-face meetings. This brings us to a section on social cues.

Different Modes of Communication

The issue of social cues and the possibility for rich communication through e-mail was discussed with different members of the Debian community. We learned a few things. Mostly, the Debian members do not think that social talk in e-mail is necessary since rich communication is seen as overload, and will only distract them from their work. They do not have the urge to meet other Debian members while cooperating in the same project or package. While the mailing lists are used mostly for work-related e-mails, on the IRC channels one can find more socially oriented talk. We have learned that the different communication media in the Debian community serve different functions. For 'free form' discussions the mailing lists and IRC channels are used; however, there are differences between mailing list discussions and IRC discussions. The major difference is that the mailing list system is an asynchronous medium, while the IRC channel is a synchronous medium. However, sometimes the discussion on the mailing list seems to be in 'real time' as well, especially when the discussion is of great interest and importance for many developers. For strongly structured discussions the bug tracking systems are used, and for knowledge-based discussions one uses different communication platforms, such as the Wiki platform. The Wiki platform will be used as an example to explain the working of such platforms. The Wiki website explains what Wiki is about: 'The simplest online database that could possibly work.' Wiki is a piece of server software that allows users to freely create and edit Web page content using any Web browser. Wiki is unusual among group communication mechanisms in that it allows the organization of contributions to be edited in addition to the content itself. Like many simple concepts, 'open editing' has some profound and subtle effects on Wiki usage. Allowing everyday users to create and edit any page in a website is exciting in that it encourages democratic use of the Web and promotes content composition by nontechnical users (http://www.wiki.org/).

Of course, Debian people meet occasionally while showing up at conferences or at key-signing events. And Debian members within the same country sometimes get together for drinks, but not all of them. As we have seen in the meta-flaming discussion, talk is not always about codes; however, the discussions all deal with aspects of the Debian community. In technical discussions it is more difficult to see someone's personality. The domain of the interaction is restrained to the technical field. You cannot see the personal interests of people, so it is very one-dimensional. Of course, one can find some clues about a person's character in the e-mails: you can see for instance if someone is intelligent or not; you can tell by their argumentation structure. However, probably you could learn more from a person by looking him/her in the eyes. Still, it is not necessary to know the other person when cooperating with him/her, according to the interviewees.

> You might know how a person can carry out his ideas through IRC, or e-mail. You can work effectively together with someone you don't know his gender or race. And sometimes I do not even want to know: it is not even relevant in this mode of communication. It is only important what that person does for Debian.

Still, a person can be a talker or a non-talker, and this stays the same whether you see him/her in a virtual mode or in a real-life setting. Without wanting to talk in stereotypes, one of our interviewees stated: 'Probably we are socially not very capable. This goes for most software developers. Of course, I can hang out with people, but I'm not very socially active.' In that case, e-mail communication can be a relief for inhibited people. 'When e-mail is the only channel to interact with, then you have to interact according to that mode. You build your world around it. The context in which the e-mail interacting takes place is predefined. It is a technical community.'

Trust is important, but knowing that someone is a developer is most of the time enough to cooperate and communicate. Through the new maintainers process you know more about the other person, since you know he or she has passed the identity check, that he or she agrees with the social contract and that he or she has read the constitution. 'The most important thing about other community members is that they perform well. If a maintainer is very good at his job but has an attitude, you are more willing to forgive this attitude flaw.'

To make this paragraph more concrete we will use the story of a mini-Debian project. One interviewee (J.P.) worked for a free software project named Posadis. He has never met the primary author of the project, although they live in the same country and distance would not be a problem. They have only communicated through e-mail since they started working together in August 2001. 'I have the feeling that we are both satisfied about our cooperation. However, this cooperation has a different character than the more traditional work-cooperation character. Our cooperation form is more like a communication form consisting of: motivation, inspiration, socialization, coordination and delegation'. For the coordination part of the project J.P. and the primary author have set up two different mailing lists. One is the mailing list for announcing new versions of software and the other one is the Devel mailing list, which is a mailing list for developers. J.P. intends to put up a mailing list for users as well, so users can interact with each other. The Posadis project is run by only two people. J.P. was looking for a name server (a phone book that translates names to IP addresses). He found one, but was not satisfied with parts of it. J.P. mailed the owner of the server, without the intention of becoming part of the project. 'I mailed M. and told him that his server was missing some items. He replied and asked me to join him.' This way J.P. became a maintainer. M. already saw that J.P. had done some more things for the community and that was for M. a reason to trust J.P. M. and J.P. have never met each other and they do not discuss social issues or social backgrounds. 'Everything goes in a virtual mode, to that extent M. could be a robot just as well.' Within the Posadis project there are no explicit rules. 'If I do not like working on a particular bit, then I will not do it. But of course, most of times it is fun to program, since it makes the software better.' J.P. thinks of M. and himself as a real team. 'We understand each other, we have the same ideas about free software, and that is already a good base to start with.' Before posting e-mails to the Posadis mailing list, J.P. often discusses the content first with M., like a brainstorming event. J.P. thinks that before you post anything for a broader audience you have to make sure you have thought things through; otherwise you will bother the community with a draft version of your work. J.P. thinks this happens in all OSS projects; there are always people who know each other and form little teams for internal feedback before going online. It is a form of peer review. For J.P. e-mail communication is a form of personal communication: 'we do not have anything else.' J.P. has never phoned M. 'We don't even have each other's numbers, however we should phone each other once, it is different than e-mail.' However, J.P. thinks it is much easier to e-mail, it is a less direct form of communication. Using the IRC channels is much more direct, you receive more feedback. Through phone calls you receive even more feedback and information about the person at the other end of the line; however, that way you have less time to reflect on the content of the ideas. 'This is the force of e-mail and at the same time also a weakness.' J.P. has no concrete image of M. besides his programming qualities. 'When our project gets very famous and when we have to present it at a conference, than we would go out for a beer, probably. But not now. There is no need for it. I know him, and I don't. I know his e-mail name and his software ideas. But it works.'

Organized Anarchy?

One interviewee told us about Debian in a historical perspective, because he was there from the beginning and saw Debian grow to the Debian it is today. For him it is clear that within Debian you do not need to make things more formal than necessary. The more informal Debian stays, the better it is for the community. Of course, Debian needs an infrastructure on a technical basis. And there has to be consensus on how to present Debian to the outer world, and on who decides what, how much authority everyone has, and when to vote on important issues. The social contract of Debian is like a mission statement to our informant. His Debian colleague sees it more like a constitution. The social contract provided the community with some rules, and in practice they will see how these rules work out. Explaining how it works with these rules is a bit difficult. In a traditional organization, you have rules that are invented by the superiors and that have to be followed by the employees. In an organization like Debian, those 'rules' are more the commonly decided rules of the game in order to cooperate in an effective manner. If someone in the Debian community has the feeling that one of the rules no longer applies he or she can propose adjustments. On the technical level one often talks of a 'meritocracy': the one who is most qualified in a certain area has the most say in that area. However, when he or she becomes less qualified this immediately impacts his or her position. Therefore, the organization within Debian can be called fluid: it permanently (implicitly) adjusts itself to the circumstances, without having a formal leader telling Debian what to do. Of course, Debian has been growing fast and this caused problems in the past, but Debian now has an organization that can cope with future growth.

In a legal sense Debian does not even exist. For commercial companies Debian is an amorphous understanding. Debian exists, but one cannot grasp it. 'We do not make fancy boxes, like other Linux distributions. For instance, Redhat has measurable objectives: amount of employees, a profit margin, and those fancy boxes lying in the shops.' Debian is not aimed at those marketing issues; Debian is only interested in making a system that works for the community. However, despite the boxes, Debian has its own identity. 'We sell

Debian t-shirts and of course we wear those T-shirts ourselves.' Our interviewee talks about 'we' when he talks about Debian. He explains:

> I have been with Debian since 1994, and when you are so much involved
> with something, it becomes like a baby to you. I have seen Debian grow from
> 13 people to 850; well actually I do not keep track of those numbers anymore.
> I feel connected with especially the Dutch part of the community, since we
> meet at conferences. However, I do not feel connected with all of those 850
> members.

The amazing thing about Debian, whether you call it an organization or not, is the fact that it exists through the Internet. All the rules that exist within Debian were formed through e-mail discussion, and all those rules had to do with communication and coordination in order to make this virtual community work. We can try to identify all the mechanisms and see how these compare with the commercial companies. However, as mentioned in our preface: 'You are free to ignore any or all of them if you don't like them.' The Debian community is free to ignore 'babbling idiots', but also free to ignore any structure at all.

Stage 3: Project Growth or Decline – The Future

> Overall, we had a very good year. Making a major release always brings attention to the project . . . it excites users, broadens the deployment of real improvements in our software, and motivates the press and others to take a fresh look at us. As a volunteer organization, all of these activities provide us with feedback and encouragement that motivate us to greater accomplishments.

Debian grew from only a few developers to a large community. During this growth the community found ways to cope with this expansion, mainly by streamlining and coordinating the communication. Their communication processes are streamlined in many ways, for instance by having different mailing lists and different procedures and rules for this communication. Structured communication is needed in such a complex environment. Debian has to deal with many packages coming out every day, and these have to be coordinated through a huge body of policies and procedures. Not only is the package management a complex issue; the management of the community also requires some effort. Of course, most of the effective work happens in small groups; however, it is important to keep the feeling with the community as a whole. As Lameter (2002: 13) puts it, 'Being one among 1000 developers also makes the individual rather anonymous. The attraction in the past for many developers was the personal relationships that develop in the project. We need to reorganize the project into smaller groups where these significant relationships can develop.' In our interviews this issue did not appear as a major problem. Of course one agrees that the communication becomes more complex, but still the Debian members feel connected to parts of the community, mostly in their own working area. Another issue that is often brought up is the slow release cycle of Debian. Debian often has to defend itself on this matter. Debian is proud of the fact that they won't release buggy software, and will release only when the software is stable. For a commercial company this would be hard to understand. A release means money. However, in the Debian community, work is done by volunteers, mostly in their spare time. Their rule is: 'We release when it is ready!' There are no deadlines. 'Of course, it takes us a long time before we release, however, when we release, our users know they can trust the software.' As Ian Murdock puts it in an interview:

> I agree that the slow release cycle is a problem. The Debian folks recognize it as a problem too and are taking steps to address it. Release management is very hard, especially when you're dealing with hundreds and hundreds of people, many of whom have never met and most of whom work on the thing purely as a hobby. It's far easier when you have a company and people are all in the same place and getting paid. So, this is a common problem among free software projects, and Debian is having to deal with it on a scale larger than most projects have had to deal with it. And they're getting there.

5.6 DISCUSSION AND CONCLUSIONS

We were interested in the Debian project because the whole structure is built on virtual communication. According to the MRT, this virtual communication should have imposed limitations (Yamauchi et al., 2000) due to the lack of rich communication, e.g. face-to-face communication:

1. Team members are limited to written (lean) communication and lack spontaneous discussions.
2. Team members have little real-time knowledge about each other (social presence is weakened in the environment).
3. Complex and ambiguous messages cannot be shared because of the limited interaction. E-mail communication is supposed to be rigid and less able to convey information.
4. Lean media reduce the social context cues, therefore not much is known about the other team members.
5. Lean media can create problems, so that it is supposed to be difficult to achieve agreement among members.

6. Communicating through lean media makes it difficult to built personal relationships, and discuss human and social topics.
7. E-mail communication increases the amount of flaming within conversations.
8. Furthermore, e-mail communication is expected to be formal and cannot initiate informal communication.

However, open source projects are competing with software developed by conventional commercial software companies, despite the fact that open source developers rarely meet. How can this be explained? One way to explain this paradox is by arguing for minimizing the need for collaboration, for minimizing the complexity of the OSS projects and to argue that the work done in these projects is routine and unambiguous, since, of course, in the eyes of the MRT, only in the case of routine work can lean communication be used for collaboration. This case study on the Debian has proven otherwise, as managing and leading software development have been challenging and complex issues. Software development is traditionally a coordination-intensive process. Often, ad hoc and situated coordination is required in the face of uncertainty. 'Problems that emerge unpredictably in the course of actions have to be resolved through flexible coordination' (Yamauchi 2000: 3). Coordinating the processes over the Internet makes the process even more intense, as one can imagine. How can the successful cooperation in OSS projects be explained?

The Debian case study has shown that organizational culture and coordination processes can enable rich communication while only using lean media. Debian showed that the organization of the community, more than the technology used, can challenge the limitations traditionally associated with 'lean' media. We learned that the organizational reaction to lean media is enough to support cooperation and that it is therefore not necessary to add more technologically advanced features to the community.

This case study has not only confirmed the conclusions of our first case study (Delta); it has enabled us to identify factors as a source of explanation for the richness in e-mail (CMC) communication. This case study has highlighted the impact of organizational factors as a positive answer to the question whether virtual teams can work at a distance when tasks are complex and information is sometimes ambiguous. We have discussed the strengths and weaknesses of the Debian organization, with a special focus on its governance structures, the project's IT maturity, the leadership style and the community culture.

In this section we will focus on explanations for the rich communication to be found in OSS projects:

- Rational culture;
- Think-before-you-act culture;
- Effective media use.

Rational Culture

During our case study on the Debian project, we were surprised that most members mentioned social talk as overload to the project. Probably this 'aversion' to too much talk that distracts from the real work could be described as a rational culture. Yamauchi et al., (2000) argue that a rational culture implies that members try to make their behavior logically plausible and that technologically superior options are always chosen in decision-making. This rational culture is necessary since communication through computers makes agreements and discussion difficult. Rationality is the only criterion by which everyone can agree to decisions. The criterion by which everyone can agree on a decision is whether the code is technologically good or bad (or whether the code is 'sexy' or not).

Still, the Debian project has shown that it is able to reach consensus over non-technical issues as well, for instance in relation to project management when discussing leadership issues or the new maintainer process. The organization of the Debian project fosters rational decision-making, even on social issues. We argue that while social cues are reduced by using lean media, this equalizes the participation.

Furthermore, the asynchronous nature of electronic media gives members time to reflect on messages they write and render the messages logical before sending them (Yamauchi et al., 2000). 'In this process, they prepare plausible reasoning, ponder on alternatives and remove superfluous information.' Again, this removes too much information (social) overload. The way communication is organized in the community, the informal rules for communication, makes communication more rationally structured. Programmers refer to their resources as code files, Webpages, research papers and others' messages to make the idea clear and reliable. By reflecting before sending messages, members not only make their messages plausible but also learn and improve their skill and knowledge by *ad hoc* learning. Written communication by electronic mail also helps break down vague ideas and serves as a reliable organizational memory. In the correspondence with diverse Debian members we observed that the e-mails received from Debian members were perfectly written (formatted and styled according the e-mail rules of clear communication). Every message was clearly structured and members made reference to the source of their information, terms used in OSS projects were explained using dictionaries.

Think-before-you-act Culture

Different mechanisms are used to deal with the enormous flow of information within the Debian community. To reduce the information overload on the mailing lists, new members in particular are asked to read the FAQs (frequently asked questions) and the manuals first, before asking a question on the mailing list. In order to keep the mailing list traffic as light and pure as possible, programmers should think twice before posting a message. When 'newbies' post unnecessary messages (questions about the project which could have been answered by reading the FAQs) on the mailing list, they can expect nasty answers from some of the members of the community. Ignorance trashes the flow of communication. While Yamauchi et al., (2000) claim that open source programmers are biased towards action rather than coordination; 'they tend to act without first declaring the commitment', we argue that the opposite is more true. While it seems that everyone can just post anything on the Net, we think that members think before they act. We have seen that when programmers have new ideas, they do not *just* put them on the mailing list. They first discuss their ideas in a group of peers, let's say in the informal circuit, before using the formal communication channels such as the mailing lists. This think-before-you-act culture seems to foster innovation: hidden experiments within peer groups (e.g. the testing of ideas) enable programmers to pre-discuss their ideas when the expected outcome is uncertain, which would have discouraged the member from 'just' posting the message on the mailing list. As we have seen, the Debian members do not want to hassle the community with ideas that are not well designed. We realize that this idea is quite the opposite from Yamauchi et al., (2000), who have argued that the bias for action lowers the threshold for submitting ideas: since members do not have to declare anything before joining projects, they can submit their ideas to the mailing list. We think that the threshold for new members to submit ideas is high, especially when they are not yet involved in a peer group, for discussing their ideas. Posting ideas that are unstructured and vague will make them lose the respect of the community. The idea of think-before-you-act concludes with the rational culture of the community. Only after discussion of ideas within the peer group can we speak of a bias for action. In this we agree with Yamauchi et al., (2000), who have stated that there are examples enough (also in face-to-face settings) where too much discussion inhibits development. When an idea is posted on the mailing list (after a round of peer review) there is not much discussion need from the community as a whole, and therefore the members can take action and work with the ideas posted.

Effective Media Use

While it is often stated that maintaining a project through computer-mediated communication is difficult or even impossible, the Debian project study proved otherwise. In combination with the rational culture as well as the think-before-you-act culture, effective usage of different media structures the project and fosters communication and collaboration.

We have already mentioned the advantages of using the CVS, which provides the balance between centralization and spontaneous work. Moreover, since software becomes repeatedly refined with the involvement of many co-workers, this iterative development ensures the quality of the work. The mailing lists also foster cooperation and transparent communication, because all project members usually post all messages to the mailing lists. This transparency provides a level of awareness about what others are doing. 'This is similar to "overhearing" a conversation between others or people "talking out loud" about their own work' (Yamauchi et al., 2000: 9). Through overhearing, members can perceive what is going on. Although mailing lists are becoming swamped with e-mail, information overload does not pose a problem. We have already mentioned that members avoid social overload e-mails, and when they do send an e-mail, the content of these e-mails is well prepared, without unnecessary information. It is also customary to read the FAQs before sending a message with a question, in order to minimize traffic. The receivers, in turn, just look through or overhear messages and read only messages about their interests carefully. Moreover, some members use technology to filter certain e-mail messages, with help from mail scripts, mail can be automatically deleted. This deletion is sometimes based on topic, and sometimes on the sender.

The effective use of media (the Internet) is also connected to another specific point, as discussed by von Hippel and von Krogh (2003). Their line of reasoning starts with the question of what exactly is unique about the knowledge and information sharing in the field of OSS. Unique is that in the OSS field the users carry out the entire innovation process by themselves – no manufacturer is required. Open source projects as such encompass the entire innovation process, from design to distribution to field support and product improvement. Von Hippel and von Krogh (2003: 219) argue that 'such "full-function" user innovation and production communities are possible only when self-manufacture and/or distribution of innovative products directly by users can compete with commercial production and distribution.' The strength of OSS lies in the usage of the Web. Innovations can be produced and distributed essentially for free on the Web, software being information rather than a physical product.

We discussed three factors that were important to the effective communication and coordination within the Debian project. It is important to note that Debian also developed a quite complex governance structure to deal with problems of leadership, coordination and decision-making. From the initial start-up phase until the current stage of the project, we have described the different stages in the Debian project. These stages provided us with answers about how Debian projects are initiated and organized over time, what (informal) rules for participation have been established, and what other governing mechanisms are present in the Debian project. The governance structure built around the communication of open source projects was critical in ensuring participants' willingness to collaborate. One of the interviewees has argued that because of a strong motivation, a technologically inclined (sub)culture and a common vision with a well-defined 'univers de discourse', the Debian project works as it does. The fact that Debian is scattered across the four corners of the earth is not the result of a conscious choice but a fact of life, and the organization has subsequently evolved has been born out of necessity in response to this state of affairs.

This is altogether different from a brick-and-mortar organization which elects to go virtual as an added option. The road from brick-and-mortar to brick-and-click has become notorious as one laden with resistance, thresholds, mine fields and dead ends, only to be circumvented by a weighed analysis of the particular organization's strengths and weaknesses, communicative style and company culture, just to name a few factors.

Key issues

- OSS projects need to create stability in the community – after the going open stage by developing new channels of communication, management techniques and organizational structures.
- OSS projects flourish best in an informal sphere; however, there has to be some consensus on formal structures (e.g. decision-making, authority, representation).
- All formal rules guiding OSS can be formed solely on e-mail communication, personal face-to-face communication seems unnecessary and is sometimes considered as hindering project work.
- Growth within OSS has been facilitated mainly by streamlining communication within the community.

At the beginning of our case study we were surprised by the fact that Joel Klecker was known through his programming skills, but that the person behind Joel was unknown. However, he was still a part of the community.

How can a community be a community when no one knows each other? Is this community cold and based on code alone? one might ask. No, it is not.

This is the first public announcement of this intention. Some may notice two new files in our archive (or on mirrors) and on the new Test Cycle 3 CDs. This is a dedication of this release to a recently departed member of our Project, Joel Klecker, who died unexpectedly at age 21. The dedication can be found (and is attached here for completeness) at:

ftp://ftp.debian.org/debian/doc/dedication-2.2.txt

You will also find a file with it called dedication-2.2.sigs.tar.gz, which contains close to 200 PGP signatures from our Developers for the dedication.txt.

Dedicated to Joel 'Espy' Klecker

On July 11, 2000, the Debian Project, and the Free Software Community as a whole, lost a very dear friend and developer. For most of Joel's life he had been fighting a disease known as Duchenne Muscular Dystrophy. Since July of 1997, Joel has been a Debian developer, and for most of that time was bed-ridden because of this disease. Joel was 21 when he died, far from the ripe age we imagine most people in our field will reach. His great dedication to the project is an inspiration to us all, and will never be forgotten. He was known by most of us as 'Espy', his IRC nickname, and also as the outspoken voice we heard on the mailing lists, never afraid to speak his mind in a way that only Joel could do, with humor and directness. He maintained a level of excellence in many important packages for Debian. His expertise and knowledge was never questioned. Those of us who have the honor of carrying on the work that he has done for us will try to maintain it to his degree of technical perfection. Most of us had no idea the trials that Joel endured every day of his life. Not until near the end did any of us know he even had this disease. Only now are we realizing his dedication, and the friendship that he bestowed upon us. So as a show of our appreciation, and in memory of his inspirational life, this release of Debian is for him.

* The 'Joel "Espy" Klecker' release – The Debian developers'

6. Conclusions and managerial implications

Internet users correspond without visible cues about the other group members, the influence of physical appearance – including but not limited to gender, age, physical attractiveness, and race – is not in operation. Feelings of liking, friendship and attraction between group members must have bases other than physical cues, such as similarity, values and interests, and conversational style, which have also been shown to be powerful determinants of friendship and attraction. Thus, liaisons may form on the Internet that would not have formed in the face-to-face world. (McKenna and Green, 2002: 120)

6.1 INTRODUCTION

This study investigated the role of CMC in (semi-)dispersed teams. In particular, we focused on the communication processes within three different case studies. Although increasingly popular, virtual teams are still a relatively under-researched organizational form. Several authors have tried to provide guidelines for the effective functioning of such teams. Such guidelines are needed because these new organizational forms can present a myriad of managerial challenges. However, none of the guidelines proposed were embedded in a consistent theory-based understanding of virtual teams.

The MRT approach has long been regarded as the main theory in the analyses of computer-mediated communication (CMC) (Daft and Lengel 1986; Rice 1984; Rice and Love 1987; Spears and Lea 1992). In our study we have challenged the conventional perspective as described by MRT which argues that CMC provides a reduced-cues environment, unable to foster emotional, expressive or complex communication. Modern communication technologies have qualities not found in traditional communication media, which allow richer communication than was previously possible (Markus 1994; Sproull and Kiesler 1991; Yu, 1997).

In our research, we have tried to fill the voids in the CMC literature, arguing that an improved understanding of the implications and use of CMC can only be gained by considering the context in which the communication takes place.

6.2   KEY MANAGERIAL CHALLENGES AND ISSUES

Today, distant cooperation is possible in a way that was hardly conceivable 20 years ago, when there were no possibilities for asynchronous rapid communication. CMC has made it possible to work together without face-to-face communication. In spite of these developments, there is still a large degree of consensus in the literature that face to face is the preferred communication medium.

Initially our research was guided by the following three research questions, which we will try to answer in this section.

1. *Do the characteristics of CMC impose strict limitations on the functioning of a virtual team?*

Whereas, according to MRT, the characteristics of CMC inhibit the success of virtual teams, we argue that CMC can actually enhance team performance in a number of respects:

- In contrast to the MRT claim that effective teamwork can only be achieved in the presence of face-to-face contacts, we found that, for example, the Debian community showed a very high degree of efficiency even in the absence of face-to-face contacts. Overall, the organization of the community seemed to be a more important factor in determining the efficiency of a team than the technology factor. In particular, organizational culture and coordination processes have been shown to actually enrich communication, in spite of the use of lean media only.
- In spite of the argument, deeply rooted in the MRT tradition, that virtual teamwork can only be effective in the case of routine and non-ambiguous tasks (Rice and Shook 1990; Markus 1994), we have been able to show that unstructured and non-routine tasks, such as software development in the Debian case as well as the unstructured task of creating a research proposal in the Delta case, can actually be carried out successfully even without face-to-face interaction.
- Whereas MRT stresses the formal and technical nature of CMC, we showed that informal communication is actually possible without face-to-face interaction. We were able to show clear patterns of informal communication between members of the Debian community, and patterns of informal communication were also found between members of the Delta project. This is in line with the suggestions of Walther and Burgoon (1992), who proposed that hyper-personal

(warm and complex communication) could be possible by means of CMC, even in the absence of face-to-face contacts, and it is in striking contrast to the assumption of MRT that CMC does not allow informal communication between team members.

- In spite of MRT's assumption that CMC does not allow for the same level of social presence and awareness as face-to-face communication, we found that both Delta and Debian team members have been able to use instruments (e.g. IRC – Internet relay chat) to increase awareness and social pressure even in the absence of face-to-face contacts. This is in line with Pantelli's (2002) finding that social cues are indeed present within CMC communication.
- A longstanding argument in the MRT literature is that the amount of 'flames' within conversations is likely to increase through means of CMC. We found, however, that the use of CMC did not account for large differences in the number and intensity of flames as compared to face-to-face meetings. Furthermore, we found that the community was able to develop norms and rules in order to deal with these flames in such a way that they did not disturb the collaboration process.

In summary, the studies described in Chapter 1, as well as findings from our case studies, allow us to reject most of the claims made by (or derived from) the MRT. Thus the present study disconfirms the idea that CMC can only allow lean communication.

2. Under what circumstances (if any) is face-to-face communication necessary for the functioning of a team?

The Debian case study proved that we can identify situations in which face-to-face communication is not necessary and can be replaced by CMC. The culture, organizational structure, technology structure and work organization of the Debian community has for example been particularly effective for efficient communication among members of the Debian community. The Advance case study, however, provides us with some other outcomes (less effective virtual cooperation) as a result of a different configuration of the four factors. Looking at the overall findings of our case studies, we can argue that some contextual factors have influenced virtual cooperation in a positive way, while other factors have prevented virtual cooperation. Contextual factors interact and can come together in many different configurations. Sometimes the negative influence of some factors may be compensated for by other factors. For instance, a team in which the predominant culture is greatly supportive of the use of CMC may be able to overcome shortcomings in the technical infrastructure more easily than a team that is already inclined to think negatively of CMC.

We have shown that face-to-face communication is not an absolute pre-condition for collaboration, but that there are specific contextual factors (technological, organizational or motivational) that can severely influence the functioning of a team in a virtual environment.

3. What are the characteristics of communication processes when face-to-face communication is replaced by CMC?

So far, the actual factors that shape the communication processes in virtual teams have been ill understood. Therefore, our research has aimed to explore characteristics of communication patterns under three different virtual team settings. We came up with two major findings.

First, we found that communication patterns do not differ that much from each other and, in situations in which face-to-face communication and CMC are combined, we can even speak of seamless transitions.

The Delta case description provided us with an example of the team's communication processes – patterns and developments in the use of electronic mail; the changeover between electronic and face-to-face communication – which has shown us that these processes were *almost* seamless in many respects. CMC communication incorporated e-mail strategies that for instance delayed decision-making.

Second, we found that CMC provides opportunities that are almost unavailable in face-to-face communication. These opportunities of CMC can be found for instance in the area of structured documentation, think-before-you-act (write) possibilities and the asynchronicity of the medium.

We found that team collaboration processes have developed differently (and had different dynamics) in a virtual environment than in a collocated setting, and this relates mainly to the cases in which various modes and features of communication have been observed that could not be found in face-to-face environments. In our case studies new patterns of communication have emerged by changing the structure of the organization as well as by the use of advanced technologies (FAQs, chat sessions and the use of blackboards).

In a similar vein Pantelli (2002: 76) has come up with a few advantages of CMC usage. CMC aids in changing the way people seek out information and the way they interact with their colleagues and supervisors. E-mail is fast, sent from all over the world and reaches its destination almost instantly. E-mail can reach multiple recipients, and therefore enhances the opportunity for the simultaneous sharing of data. CMC is likely to reduce the need for face-to-face communication and increases the likelihood of vertical and horizontal transformation of organizational processes and structures.

As is shown above, CMC has distinctive characteristics that make it different from face-to-face communication, and these specific characteristics explain the increasing use of CMC within organizations. Whenever these characteristics are considered attractive, CMC will be preferred.

Key issues

- Modern communication technologies have qualities not found in traditional communication media, which allow richer communication than was previously possible (Markus 1994; Sproull 1991; Yu 1997).
- Organizational culture and coordination processes have been shown to actually enrich communication, in spite of the use of lean media only.
- Unstructured and non-routine tasks, such as software development in the Debian case as well as the unstructured task of creating a research proposal in the Delta case, can actually be carried out successfully even without face-to-face interaction.
- Hyper-personal (warm and complex communication) could be possible by means of CMC, even in the absence of face-to-face contacts.
- Social cues are indeed present within CMC communication.
- The use of CMC did not account for large differences in the number and intensity of flames as compared to face-to-face meetings.

6.3   THE INTERACTION OF CONTEXT AND COMMUNICATIONS TECHNOLOGY

As we near the end of our research we think our initial questions discussed in the previous section are still useful, with the remark that the answers to these questions will not be found in the richness of the medium, as we were able to refute most of the MRT claims. The technical features of the medium do not appear to determine the richness of the communication. But what does? What are the factors that stimulate the usage of CMC or discourage its usage? On the one hand, it has become clear that contextual factors influence both the desire and the need for communication; on the other hand, it has also become clear that the possibilities for communication offered by computer-supported systems will not be realized automatically.

Many factors appear to determine simultaneously the richness of communication. Within the Delta project we were concerned with one specific question: is the MRT correct in stating that e-mail is not an adequate medium to promote rich communication? We tried to answer this question by studying a virtual project in a real-life setting and we did not find the large difference between communication patterns in a face-to-face setting versus the virtual setting that was predicted by MRT. Even on the contrary, we saw that the face-to-face meetings did not bring any other or faster solutions to the problems of the team as compared to using e-mail.

In our next case study we shifted our focus away from this single question to the contextual factors that contribute to the richness of the communication. Evidence for the importance of contextual factors had emerged from the Delta study, where we had observed that, for instance, the factor of leadership determined to some extent the richness of the communication. The Advance case showed us that it is not possible to organize a virtual project team as if it were just another collocated project team. The Debian case study provided evidence for the idea that virtual collaboration is a viable option, especially when the project is organized explicitly as a virtual one. We refer for instance to the rational/think-before-you-act culture, the effective usage of CMC and the effective governance structure of the Debian project.

Various additional questions came up in the course of our case study research and we therefore extended its scope. We moved beyond the idea that face-to-face communication and CMC should be compared, to argue that CMC can be looked at as a kind of communication in its own right. In this respect we want to emphasize the importance of organizational arrangements in which contextual factors and technological features interact.

4. *What are the conditions for effective communication in a virtual team? How do they differ from effective communication in a non-virtual team?*

The existing literature is quite inconclusive and unclear about the specific conditions for effective communication in a virtual team because so much emphasis is put on the technology that constrains or enables communication, while little attention is paid to other constraining or enabling factors such as the organizational and institutional context of cooperation and communication. MRT has influenced the nature of the discussion with its emphasis on the technical characteristics of the means of communication. In addition to that, the lack of attention to non-technical factors probably also originated from the fact that much of the previous research was very experimental, creating virtual teams for study purposes, but ignoring real-life situations. In our study a broader point of view has been taken through examining 'real-life' teams in different organizational and institutional contexts. We explored how social, organizational and institutional factors interact with technological factors in the development of CMC in teams. We examined the conditions that enable or constrain the (virtual) collaboration process. Unlike MRT and most of the other theoretical perspectives in this field, we emphasize that the technical characteristics of communication technologies cannot be translated in a linear way into an inherent capacity to convey rich, complex or equivocal information (for a general discussion of the 'situatedness' of technology characteristics, see Fleck and Howells 2001).

We have already identified contextual aspects that enable/stimulate virtual cooperation or conditions that inhibit the success of virtual teams. These factors are also important in non-virtual environments: coordination (for instance the importance of clear agreements about the division of tasks), communication (using the new possibilities of CMC), commitment (motivation is important for the success of a project) and other enabling conditions (leadership style, division of roles within the project, team formation issues).

Next to the conditions that apply in both kinds of team, extra attention has to be paid in a virtual team to the development of a structure (technological, but also in terms of work organization) that promotes an increase in overall communication through the proper use of the medium (such as mailing lists). Besides tangible aspects such as structure, communication rules and a stimulating leadership style, some other issues are important in the virtual context: norms and guidelines for regular information and communication. Such norms may differ from project to project and norms may also develop over time within a given context. From the case studies it became clear that it is not the individual aspects (structure, culture, leadership etc.) as such that are important, but the ability to bring a coherent and efficient configuration of these aspects together in the best possible way for specific circumstances and conditions.

5. *Are there any special problems and risks involved in the management and organization of teams that mix virtual and face-to-face modes of communication?*

One of the findings in the literature part of our study was that face-to-face communication is too often seen as ideal for cooperation. We also found that, regardless of whether researchers were optimistic or pessimistic about CMC, their judgment was often based upon expectations derived from the MRT paradigm. In reality, face-to-face communication and CMC are seldom mutually exclusive. People in collocated teams send each other e-mail to confirm meetings, and people in CMC settings sometimes meet in a face-to-face setting. In both cases the comparison between 'pure face-to-face communication' and 'pure CMC' is becoming less relevant, since these forms of communication are intertwined. 'Since co-location and electronic communication are better suited for particular types of communication . . .

both communication channels are necessary. Moreover, given that the different types of knowledge dissemination depend on each other, both communication channels will strengthen each other as well' (Song et al., 2004: 28). It is also important to note that there are forms of cooperation that would not exist without CMC, and cannot be compared with face-to-face settings. Every organization has different features and characteristics that influence the way a virtual team works, and it is necessary to understand the underlying organizational principles of virtual organizations. We expect that while using adequate (adjusted to the specific project and context) communication media, having agreements and norms about the way of communicating, and taking into account many more contextual aspects (as identified in the case studies in this study), effective communication will occur in the absence of face-to-face communication.

Within the Delta case study we saw that the use of one medium called for a response using another medium. Peaks in electronic communication happened just before and straight after the face-to-face meetings. Within the Advance team these patterns of communication were also found. Periods of high e-mail interaction were found around the dates of a meeting. Just as in the Delta case there were periods of long virtual silence at times when no meeting was planned. In that respect both modes of communication appeared to complement each other. The use of CMC versus face-to-face was less an issue of using either CMC or face-to-face and more an issue of using them in an effective way. Most often both types of communication were used. It is possible, but not necessarily true, that a strong emphasis on either CMC or face-to-face communication turns out to be the most effective approach, because it may make alignment with other organizational (contextual) factors less complicated. Future research should focus on the ways in which traditional media can be combined with new forms of communication in order to improve (virtual) teamwork.

Again, the effective mix of virtual and face-to-face communication can only be achieved in the presence of adequate (adjusted to the specific project and context) communication media, the incorporation of agreements and norms about the way of communicating and the willingness of members to adopt new technologies.

6.4 MANAGEMENT IMPLICATIONS AND FUTURE RESEARCH

Virtual teams are often composed of experts who have no shared history of collaboration, and are sometimes even from previously competing companies. Working in a virtual team therefore has some possible pitfalls and dangers. That is why people hope to find a blueprint for the working of a virtual (dream) team.

Thus far many guidelines about (virtual) teamwork have been proposed, e.g. about managing problems, virtual team leadership, training of ICT skills, making decisions, or handling conflict, and procedures have been suggested concerning teambuilding events, choice of communication media and the organization of tasks (Nohria and Eccles 1992; Townsend et al., 1998; Lipnack and Stamps 2000). These subjects have been identified as important issues in our own case studies as well; however, we could not resolve these issues merely by reading and implementing the numerous rules, as proposed in the 'how to' and 'virtual team guideline books' (e.g. Lipnack and Stamps 2000). Such rules and guidelines are not very credible, if only because they are seldom clear and unambiguous. Moreover, they are not based on in-depth research or on theoretical understanding of virtual teamwork.

On the basis of our own research, we would argue that the management of virtual teams requires:

- A technical infrastructure that is available and user-friendly (high level of IT maturity in relation to the adoption of this technology by its users). A practical solution in order to fulfill some of the background conditions that are necessary for virtual cooperation is, for instance, universal CMC access for everyone within the team. Furthermore we argue that virtual cooperation requires a high degree of explicit transparency, for instance e-mail archives, the division of mailing lists per topic, transparent decision-making mechanisms, but also guidelines (or internalized norms) to prevent e-mail overload, for instance by peer review before posting e-mails to a mailing list, as we saw in the Debian case. We also think, in line with Townsend et al., (1998) that training for team members who lack CMC skills and experience would be helpful to increase virtual cooperation. However, no one has ever discussed what kind of training would be sufficient, and for whom. Furthermore it is questionable whether the level of IT maturity within an organization will be increased by individual training solutions. We suggest therefore that more attention should be paid to questions of how to organize and implement training for virtual team members.
- A project structure and work organization that enhances the overall operational structure of the project. Again we refer to the Debian project, which is of course a project in a specific sense (it is part of the OSS community). The clear structure made the project well organized. The Advance management tried to reduce the complexity,

but this attempt resulted in reduced possibilities for cooperation and in a very complex sequence of deliverables.

- A structure that stimulates overall communication: this does not mean as much as possible communication in an organization, but a communication style that fits the organizational needs and is structured (and supported by CMC) in different ways that support all communication needs. The Debian case showed us that the members used different means of communication that were appropriate for different communication modes. The structure of the Advance project reduced the overall horizontal communication, as we discussed in Chapter 4, probably because the project management underestimated the need for such communication.

- A leadership style that stimulates the sharing of ideas and cooperation. Within the Debian community we observed that leadership within the project depended on competence rather than position. Probably this can be explained by the impact of CMC within the network. 'The introduction of new, organization-wide media, and particularly the introduction of CMC that can reach across unit, departmental, and organizational boundaries, can change structural dynamics among people, creating central figures who supply new types of information while displacing others, and forming new social networks while dissolving others' (Haythornthwaite 2001: 10).

- Guidelines and norms (netiquette) for communication between members that stimulate and coordinate interaction between dispersed members. Norms are the widely accepted ways of behaving that reflect the attitudes and values of a community or society at large. Social norms are people's beliefs about behaviors that are normal, acceptable, or even expected in a particular social context. Norms, including rules of etiquette, are learned through experience in a community (Preece 2002). Every community has its own standards and ways of behaving. The Delta team has also tried to increase cooperation through developing rules for communicational behaviors. The Advance team developed ground rules for interaction, but these rules were developed at the beginning (and not during the course) of the project and at that point in time it was not yet clear what kind of communication problems would occur. In a study of Toyota, Dyer and Nobeoka (2000) started a line of research to explore 'coordinating principles' that facilitate cooperation among team members in a network. They examined a fundamental dilemma with respect to knowledge-sharing by devising methods to motivate members to participate and openly share valuable knowledge (while preventing undesirable spillovers to competitors). Toyota has introduced a number of network-level knowledge-sharing processes that, over time, helped created a strong (identity for the) network. Some of these network knowledge processes bear some resemblance to the OSS community principles; i.e. voluntary small group learning teams, a network-level forum for creating a shared social community, inculcating network norms, and sharing knowledge. Furthermore there is a process of interfirm employee transfers (some job rotations occur at the network level). These coordinating principles have worked in the Toyota culture and it would be interesting to apply some of those principles to the effective coordination of virtual teamwork.

Furthermore, we would like to stress that it is a widespread management assumption that time is an important aspect of the development of cooperative processes within teams. In our case studies we have tried to capture the group dynamics, whereas previous research has merely studied group statics, e.g. snapshots taken instead of focusing on a longitudinal perspective (see also Cohen and Bailey 1997). Whereas 'time' is sometimes given as a solution for every team to develop (given enough time a team will develop effective ways to cooperate), we have seen that in the Delta case, for example, this was not so. Moreover, we argue that what starts wrong is difficult to put right. Much emphasis and care has to be given to the start-up phase of the project. The inevitable question is how. Many books on teambuilding refer to teambuilding events and kick-off meetings, which can provide us with some meaningful but only very general insights. As we have argued before, it is difficult to provide guidelines other than general ones, without exploring the exact context of the project which defines the communication needs.

We have argued that managers should not leave it to technical solutions only to enhance effective virtual collaboration. In every collaborative context one should pay attention to the contextual factors that may affect cooperation. Information-sharing and communication within a team may not be taken for granted or as the result of 'wiring' all the members to a network. Our case studies also identified some of the problems within virtual encounters, for example, cultural and linguistic differences, the time-zone difference (even within Europe), the unequal distribution of team members per university or any other organization, the unequal dispersion of knowledge and skills for the usage of CMC, the unequal access to CMC, the opportunity for some team members to work collocatedly whereas other team members lack this opportunity, the different background (expertise, knowledge areas) conditions, the difference in (individual and organizational) commitment towards the project, and the differences of opinion about the openness of the project.

In addition to the above guidelines we present some thoughts for future research.

1. While we have not made explicit reference to the different types of teams and different types of complexity reduction we have studied, we certainly have found evidence that the type of team matters for the effectiveness of virtual cooperation. For future research it is therefore deemed necessary to distinguish between different types of teams: teams can be formal or informal, ongoing or *ad hoc*, emerging or established; they can be cross-functional, self-managing teams, or categorized, as for instance new product development teams, work teams, parallel teams, project teams, technical and professional teams, manufacturing and service teams, management and executive teams or virtual teams (Katzenbach and Smith 1993; Cohen and Bailey 1997). The Debian case study has provided us with empirical evidence about self-organizing teams. Additional research could focus on the role of self-organizing teams in a commercial environment.

    In our study an interesting question for future research emerged while exploring the Debian community. How does the Debian situation relate to (and to what extent is the Debian example useful for) 'real' virtual teams, composed of members from 'real' organizations? The key to development in the open source strategy was creating something together and taking pride in the peer recognition that resulted from each other's additions to the program. The open source tradition also reflects the kind of environment that presumably is characteristic of an academic environment (Mark-Herbert 2004).

    Interesting subjects that can be derived from Debian are, for instance, the composition of a team, the allocation of tasks, and the way cooperation is facilitated. We think it will be interesting to develop a scale of the level of 'teamness' and a scale of 'level of virtual collaboration', and relate each scale to the other. These scales will have to be supported by literature about teams, cooperation, different tasks (e.g. McGrath's task circumflex), and team leadership facilitation.

    We started this research with the question about whether face-to-face communication could be replaced with virtual communication in order to cooperate effectively, thus ignoring team differences as well as different modes and goals of cooperation. The articulation of different types of teams was not the direction we chose to follow within our research. This is an area of research that can to be taken up in future.

2. In this study we wanted to bridge the gap between the literature stemming from the MRT tradition and the studies that are beginning to pay attention to the contextual issues surrounding and influencing the

effectiveness of virtual teams. We criticized the (uniform) technologically oriented way of thinking, proposing instead a more context-oriented perspective taking into account different contingencies that were needed to explain interaction processes within virtual teams. We arrived at the conclusion that studying teams in context means taking into account 'the whole context' of the team. Teams are embedded in larger social systems that influence the way they behave and perform. 'Performance at one level may not be related and may even conflict with performance at another level' (Cohen and Bailey 1997: 42). For example, team managers may make decisions that contribute to the organizational unit's effectiveness, but diminish a project team's effectiveness (for example, by removing key personnel from one project and placing them on another more important project). We suggest that future research should focus at multiple levels on collaboration processes in virtual teams and eventually develop a theory to explain effectiveness of virtual teams in relation to these multiple levels.

Starting from the critique of the MRT we have moved towards a framework in which contextual factors define communication needs. By doing this we moved beyond the traditional argument of MRT that inherent technical characteristics define the richness of media. Our in-depth analysis of three main case studies has shown that communication richness ultimately depends on the interplay of context and media characteristics. Furthermore, our findings allow us to argue that media richness in itself is not the main determinant of successful virtual team collaboration but rather the overall degree of communication richness. This study has tried to deal with the traditional and deeply rooted misconception that CMC provides a reduced-cues environment, unable to foster emotional, expressive or complex communication. In fact we have shown that modern communication technologies allow for rich communication as long as particular attention is paid to the specific context in which the communication takes place, and to the interplay of this specific context with media characteristics. Finally, we showed that management must fine-tune its particular management techniques to the specific requirements of working in a CMC environment.

References

Ackhoff, R.L. and M. Halbert (1958), An operations research study of the scientific activity of chemists, Cleveland, OH: Case Institute of Technology, Operations Research Group.

Allen, T.J. (1970), Communication networks in R&D laboratories, *R&D Management*, **1**(1), 14–21.

Atkinson, P. and M. Hammersley (1994), Ethnography and participant observation. In: N. Denzin and Y. Lincoln (eds), *Handbook of Qualitative Research*, Thousand Oaks, CA: Sage.

Barlow, C.M. (2001), Insight or ideas: Escaping the idea centered 'box' defining creativity, *Proceedings of the 34th Annual Hawaii International Conference on Systems Sciences*, HICSS-34, pp. 2877–85, Los Alamitos, CA, USA, IEEE Computer Society.

Baron, N.S. (1998), Letters by phone or speech by other means: the linguistics of e-mail, *Language & Communication*, **18**(2), 133–70.

Beuschel, W. and R. King (1992), How coordination processes influence CIM development, in P. Brödner and W. Karwowski (eds), *Ergonomics of Hybrid Automation Systems-III: Proceedings of the 3rd International Conference on Human Aspects of Advanced Manufacturing and Hybrid Automation*, Gelsenkirchen: Germany.

Bishop, A.P. (1994), The role of computer networks in aerospace engineering, *Library Trends*, **42**(4), 694–729.

Black, J.T. (1991), *The Design of the Factory of the Future*, New York and London: McGraw-Hill.

Blecherman, B. (1999), Adopting automated negotiation, *Technology in Society*, **21**(2), pp. 167–74.

Bowers, D.K. (1999), FAQs on online research, *Marketing Research*, **10**(4), 45–8.

Bowles, S. and H. Gintis (2000), Social capital and community governance, 21 November 2001. http://www.santafe.edu/sfi/publications/Working-Papers/01-01-003.pdf

Brown, J.S. and P. Duguid (1991), Organizational learning and communities of practice: toward a unified view of working, learning, and innovation, *Organization Science*, **2**(1), pp. 40–57, Also in: E.L. Lesser et al., (2000). *Knowledge and Communities*, Boston: Butterworth Heinemann, pp. 99–121.

Cavarero, R. and J. Schroter (2002), From dream to reality – How to ensure the achievement of significant results in a product development management system deployment, Working Paper PDT Europe.

Cohen, S.G. and D.E. Bailey (1997), What makes teams work: Group effectiveness research from the shop floor to the executive suite, *Journal of Management*, **23**(3), 239–90.

Dafermos, G.N. (2001), Management and virtual decentralised networks: the Linux project. *First Monday*, **6**(11). http://firstmonday.org/issues /issue6_11/dafermos/ index.html

Daft, R.L. and R.H. Lengel (1984), Information richness: a new approach to managerial behavior and organization design. In: L.L. Cumming and B.M. Staw (eds), *Research in Organizational Behavior*, Greenwich, CT: Jai, Vol. 6, pp. 191–233.

Daft, R.L. and R.H. Lengel (1986), Organizational information requirements, media richness and structural design, *Management Science*, **32**(5), 554–71.

Daft, R.L., R.H. Lengel and L.K. Trevino (1987), Message equivocality, media selection and manager performance: implications for information systems, *MIS Quarterly*, **11**, 355–66.

Dalle J.M. and N. Jullien (2001), Open-Source vs. Proprietary software, invited conference presented at the '01 ESSID Summer School (Cargèse, France), also presented at the EARIE Conference (Madrid, Spain, September 2002).

Dennis, A.R., S.T. Kinney and Y.-T.C. Hung (1999), Gender differences in the effects of media richness, *Small Group Research*, **30**(4), 405–37.

Drucker, P.F. (1998), The discipline of innovation, *Harvard Business Review*, **76**(6), 149–58.

Duxbury, L. and D. Neufeld (1999), The impacts of telecommuting on intra-organizational communication, *Journal of Engineering and Technology management*, **16**(1), 1–28.

Dyer, J.H. and K. Nobeoka (2000), Creating and managing a high-performance knowledge-sharing network: the Toyota case, *Strategic Management Journal*, **21**, 345–67.

Eden, C. and C. Huxham (2001), The negotiation of purpose in multi-organizational, collaborative groups, *Journal of Management Studies*, **38**(3), 373–91.

Edwards, K. (2001), Epistemic communities, situated learning and Open Source Software development, http://www.its.dtu.dk/ansat/ke/ec_sl_oss. pdf

El-Shinnawy, M. and M.L. Markus (1997), The poverty of media richness theory: explaining people's choice of electronic mail vs. voice mail, *International Journal of Human-Computer Studies*, **46**(4), 443–67.

Fleck, J. and J. Howells (2001), Technology, the technology complex and the paradox of technological determinism, *Technology Analysis and Strategic Management*, **13**(4), 523–31.

FM interview with Linus Torvalds (1998), *First New Monday*, http://www. firstmonday.dk/issues/issue3_3/torvalds/index.html

Frost, P.A. and R. Whitley (1971), Communication patterns in a research laboratory, *R&D Management*, **1**(2), 71–9.

Fulk, J. and L. Collins-Jarvis (2001), Wired meetings: technological mediation of organizational gatherings. In: F. Jablin and L. Putnam (eds), *The New Handbook of Organizational Communication*, Newbury Park, CA: Sage.

Fulk, J., J. Schmitz and C.W. Steinfield (1990), A social influence model of technology use. In: J. Fulk and C.W. Steinfield (eds), *Organizations and Communication Technology*, Newbury Park, CA: Sage, pp. 117–40.

Gallivan, M.J. (2001), Striking a balance between trust and control in a virtual organization: a content analysis of open source software case studies, *Information Systems Journal*, **11**(4), 277–304.

Gersick, C.J.G. (1988), 'Time and transition in work teams: toward a new model of group development', *Academy of Management Journal*, **31**, 9–41.

Godfrey, M.W. and Q. Tu (2000), Evolution in Open Source Software: a case study, *Proceedings of the 2000 International Conference on Software Maintenance* (ICSM-00), San Jose, CA, October. http://plg.uwaterloo. ca/~migod/papers/ icsm00.pdf

Griffith, T.L. (eds), *Research on Managing Groups and Teams: Technology*, Stamford, CT: JAI Press, Vol. 3, pp. 1–27.

Gutwin, C., M. Roseman and S. Greenberg (1996), A usability study of awareness widgets in a shared workspace groupware system, *Proceedings of the ACM Conference on Computer Supported Cooperative Work* (CSCW '96), pp. 258–67.

Hall, K. (1990), Information technology application: a British aerospace military aircraft Ltd view. In North Atlantic Treaty Organization, Advisory group for aerospace research & development, *Electronic Transfer of Information and its Impact on Aerospace and Defence Research and Development*. AGARD conference Proceedings. No. 446. (pp. 16.1–16.16) [s.l.]: AGARD.

Halloween documents. Version 1.14. http://www.opensource.org/ halloween/halloween1.html

Handy, C.B. (1995), Trust and the virtual organization, *Harvard Business Review*, **73**(3), 40–50.

Hars, A. and S. Ou (2001), Working for free? Motivations for participating in Open Source projects. In: R.H. Sprague (ed.), *Proceedings of the 34th*

IEEE Annual Hawaii International Conference on System Sciences (HICSS-34), held 3–6 January 2001, Maui, Hawaii, Vol. 7.

Häusler, J., H. Hohn and S. Lütz (1995), Contingencies of innovative networks: A case study of successful interfirm R&D collaboration, *Engineering Management Review*, **23**, 42–55.

Haythornthwaite, C. (2002), Strong, weak and latent ties and the impact of new media, *The Information Society*, **18**, 1–17.

Hemetsberger, A. (2002), Fostering cooperation on the Internet: social exchange processes in innovative virtual consumer communities. In: Susan M. Broniarczyk and Kent Nakamoto (eds), *Advances in Consumer Research*, Vol. 29, 354–356.

Hemetsberger, A. and R. Pieters (2001), When Consumers Produce on the Internet: An Inquiry into Motivational Sources of Contribution to Joint-Innovation, paper presented at the La Londe Conference.

Hertel, G., S. Niedner and S. Herrmann (2001), Motivation of software developers in Open Source projects: an internet-based survey of contributors to the Linux kernel, *Research Policy*, **32**, 1159–77, http://opensource.mit.edu/papers/rp-hertelniednerherrmann.pdf

Hertrich, R. (2000), A new giant is born – EADS, interview with Rainer Hertrich, Co-CEO of the European Aeronautic Defence and Space Company (EADS), *Air & Space Europe*, **2**(1), 5–7.

Hippel, E. von and G. von Krogh (2003), Open Source software and the 'Private-Collective' innovation model: Issues for organization science, *Organization Science*, **14**(2), 209–23.

Hollingshead, A.B., J.E. McGrath and K.M. O'Connor (1993), Group task performance and communication technology: a longitudinal study of computer-mediated versus face to face work groups, *Small Group Research*, **24**, 307–33.

Huxham, C. and S. Vangen (2003), Doing things collaboratively – Realizing the advantage or succumbing to inertia? University of Strathclyde, Working Paper Series 2003–11.

Jones, S. (1999), *Doing Internet Research: Critical Issues and Methods for Examining the Net*, Thousand Oaks, CA: Sage.

Katzenbach, J.R. and D.K. Smith (1993), The discipline of teams, *Harvard Business Review*, **71**(2), 111–20.

Kinder, T. (2003), Go with the flow; a conceptual framework for supply relations in the era of the extended enterprise, *Research Policy*, **32**, 503–23.

Klandermans, B. and D. Oegema (1987), Potentials, networks, motivations, and barriers: steps towards participation in social movements, *American Sociological Review*, **52**, 519–31.

Kock, N. (1998), Can communication medium limitations foster better group outcomes? An action research study, *Information & Management*, **34**(5), 295–305.

Kozinets, R.V. (1999), E-Tribalized Marketing?: The Strategic Implications of Virtual Communities of Consumption, *European Management Journal*, **17**(3), 252–64.

Kraut, R.E. and L.A. Streeter (1995), Coordination in software development, *Communications of the ACM*, **38**(3), 69–81.

Kraut, R., S. Kiesler, B. Boneva, J.N. Cummings, V. Helgeson and A.M. Crawford (2002), Internet paradox revisited, *Journal of Social Issues*, **58**(1), 49–74.

Kumari, S. (1999), Implementing Web-based surveys. [Web presentation] University of Houston, http://www.coe.uh.edu/~skumari/betty/index. htm

Lameter, C. (2002), Debian GNU/Linux: The Past, the Present and the Future, This material was presented at the Free Software Symposium 2002 on 22 October 2002, 15:30 at the Japan Education Center. http://u-os.org/tokyo/

Lea, M., T. O'Shea, P. Fung and R. Spears (1992), Flaming in computer-mediated communication: observations, explanations, implications. In: M. Lea (ed.), *Contexts of Computer-mediated Communication*, London: Harvester Wheatsheaf, pp. 89–112.

Lerner, J. and J. Tirole (2000), The simple economics of Open Source, NBER Working Paper 7600, http://ldb.wiwi.uni-frankfurt.de/ literature/ OpenSource/TheSimpleEconomicsofOpenSource.pdf

Lewicki, R.J., D.J. Mcallister and R.J. Bies (1998), Trust and distrust: New relationships and realities, *Academy of Management Review*, **23**(3), 438–58.

LiPera, S.D. (1996), The impact of new media: a model for the use of desktop videoconferencing in negotiations, http://is.gseis.ucla.edu/ impact/f96/Projects/slipera/

Lipnack, J. and J. Stamps (1997), *Virtual Teams: Reaching Across Space, Time, and Organisations with Technology*, New York: John Wiley & Sons Inc.

Lipnack, J. and J. Stamps (2000), *Virtual Teams: People Working Across Boundaries with Technology*, New York: John Wiley & Sons, Inc.

Mabry, E.A. (1997), Framing flames: the structure of argumentative messages on the net, *Journal of Computer Mediated Communication*, **2**(4) http://www.ascusc. org/jcmc/vol2/issue4/mabry.html

Mark-Herbert, C. (2004), Innovation of a new product category – functional foods, *Technovation*, **24**(9), 713–19.

Markus, M.L. (1994), Electronic mail as the medium of managerial choice, *Organization Science*, **5**(4), 502–27.

Markus, M.L., M. Brook and C. Agres (2000), What makes a virtual organization work: lessons from the Open Source world, *Sloan Management Review*, **42**(1), 13–26.

Markus, M.L., A. Majchzak and L. Gasser (2002), A design theory for systems that support emergent knowledge processes, *MIS Quarterly*, **26**(3), 179–212.

McKenna, K.Y.A. and A.S. Green (2002), Virtual group dynamics, *Group Dynamics: Theory, Research and Practice*, **6**(1), 116–27.

Mockus, A., T. Fielding and J. Herbsleb (2000), A case study of Open Source Software development: the Apache server, *Proceedings of the 22nd International Conference on Software Engineering* (ICSE 2000), pp. 263–72. http://opensource. mit.edu/papers/mockusapache.pdf

Moon, J.Y. and L. Sproull (2000), Essence of distributed work: the case of the Linux kernel, *First Monday*, **5**(11), http://www.firstmonday.dk/issues/ issue5_11/ moon/

Ngwenyama, O.K. and A.S. Lee (1997), Communication richness in electronic mail: critical social theory and the contextuality of meaning, *MIS Quarterly*, **21**(2), 145–67, Online version with corrections: http://www.people.vcu.edu/~aslee/ ngwlee97.htm

Nohria, N. and R. Eccles (1992), Face-to-face: Making network organisations work. In: N. Nohria and R. Eccles (eds), *Networks and Organisations: Structure, Form and Action*, Boston: Harvard Business School Press.

Olson, G.M. and J.S. Olson (2000), Distance matters, *Human Computer Interaction*, **15**, 139–79, Lawrence Erlbaum Associates.

Olson, J.S., S.D. Teasley, L. Covi and G.M.S. Olson (2002), The (currently) unique advantages of collocated work. In: P. Hinds and S. Kiesler (eds), *Distributed Work*, Cambridge, MA: MIT Press.

Orlikowski, W.J. and J. Yates (1994), Genre repertoire: the structuring of communicative practices in organizations, *Administrative Science Quarterly*, **39**(4), pp. 541–74.

Osterloh, M., S. Rota and B. Kuster (2002), Trust and Commerce in Open Source: a Contradiction? 22 November, http://www.sses.com/public/ events/euram/complete_tracks/trust_within_organizations/rota_von-wartburg_osterloh.pdf

O'Sullivan, A. (2003), Dispersed collaboration in a multi-firm, multi-team product-development project, *Journal of Engineering and Technology Management*, **20**, 93–116.

Pantelli, N. (2002), Richness, power cues and email text, *Information and Management*, **40**(2), 75–86.

Pelz, D.C. and F.M. Andrews (1976), *Scientists in Organizations* (revised edn.), Ann Arbor, MI: Institute for Social Research.

Poole, M.S. and R.Y. Hirokawa (1996), Introduction: Communication and Group Decision Making, *Communication and Group Decision Making*, London: Sage Publications.

Preece, J. (ed.) (2002), Supporting Community and Building Social Capital, Special edition of *Communications of the ACM*, **45**(4), 37–9.

Rafaeli, S. and F. Sudweeks (1997), Networked interactivity, *Journal of Computer Mediated Communication*, **2**(4). http://www.ascusc.org/jcmc/vol2/issue4/rafaeli.sudweeks.html

Rasters, G., G. Vissers and B. Dankbaar (2002), An inside look: Rich communication through lean media in a virtual research team. *Small Group Research*, **33**(6) 718–54.

Raymond, E.S. (1998), The Cathedral and the Bazaar, *First Monday*, **3**(3), Reprinted in: *The Cathedral and the Bazaar: Musings on Linux and Open Source by an Accidental Revolutionary*. Beijing: O'Reilly, 1999. http://www.firstmonday. dk/issues/issue3_3/raymond/

Raymond, E.S. (1999), *The Cathedral and the Bazaar: Musings on Linux and Open Source by an Accidental Revolutionary*. Beijing: O'Reilly.

Reinhardt, C. (2003), Collaborative knowledge creation in virtual communities of practice. A research on KDE software development processes. http://kde. klevahhehd.com/

Rice, R.E. (1984), *The New Media: Communication, Research and Technology*. Beverly Hills, CA: Sage.

Rice, R.E. and G. Love (1987), Electronic emotion: Socio-emotional content in a computer-mediated communication network. *Communication Research*, **14**, 85–108.

Rice, R.E. and U. Gattiker (2001), New media and organizational structuring. In F. Jablin and L. Putnam (eds), *New Handbook of Organizational Communication*. Newbury Park, CA: Sage, pp. 544–81.

Rice, R. and D. Shook (1990), Relationships of Job Categories and Organizational Level to Use of Communications Channels, Including Electronic Mail: A Meta-Analysis and Extension, *Journal of Management Studies*, **27**(2), 195–223.

Riley, M.W. (1963), *Sociological Research, Volume I: a case approach*. New York, NY: Harcourt, Brace & World.

Robey, D. and M.C. Boudreau (1999), Accounting for the contradictory organizational consequences of information technology: Theoretical directions and methodological implications. *Information Systems Research*, **10**, 167–85.

Rogers, P. (2002), Group decision making via CMC. Commorg literature review, topic 4. Internal document. www.commorg.net

Rose, J. (2000), New structure, new programmes, bright future. *Air & Space Europe*, **2**(6), 4–5.

Sanderson, D. (1994), Mediated collaborative research? Claims, evidence, and a case study of a distributed science group. *Computer Supported Cooperative Work*, **2**(1–2), 41–66.

Schweik, C.M. and A. Semenov (2003), The institutional design of Open Source programming: implications for addressing complex public policy and management problems, *First Monday*, **8**(1), http://firstmonday.org/issues/issue8_1/schweik/index.html

Sharma, S. V. Sugumaran and B. Rajagopalan (2002), A framework for creating hybrid-open source software communities. *Information Systems Journal*, **12**(1), 7–25.

Sia, C.L., B.C.Y. Tan and K.K. Wei (1999), Can a Group Support System Stimulate Group Polarization? An Empirical Study, *IEEE Transactions on Systems, Man, and Cybernetics*, **29**(2), 227–37.

Siegel, J., V. Dubrovsky, S. Kiesler and T. McGuire (1986), Group processes in computer-mediated communication. *Organizational Behavior and Human Decision Processes*, **37**, 157–87.

So, H., N. Thomas and H. Zadeh (2000), The keys to success in building a Free/Open Source Community for software development. http://www.businessit.bf.rmit.edu.au/haggen/TaiwanOS.pdf

Song, L., E. Singleton, J. Hill and M. Hwa Koh (2004), Improving online learning: student perceptions of useful and challenging characteristics, *Internet and Higher Education*, **7**, 59–70.

Soukup, C. (2000), Building a theory of multimedia CMC, *New Media and Society*, **2**(4), 407–25.

Spears, R. and Lea, M. (1992), Social influence and the influence of the 'social' in computer-mediated communication. In: M. Lea (ed.), *Contexts of Computer-mediated Communication*, Hemel Hempstead: Harvester-Wheatsheaf, pp. 30–65.

Sproull, L. and S. Kiesler (1986), Reducing social context cues: electronic mail in organizational communication. *Management Science*, **32**(11), 1492–12.

Stroebe, W. and M. Diehl (1994), Why groups are less effective then their members: on productivity losses in idea-generating groups. In. W. Stroebe and M. Hewstone (eds), *European Review of Social Psychology*, Wiley: Chichester.

Sudweeks, F. and M. Allbritton (1996), Working together apart: communication and collaboration in a networked group. In: C.D. Keen, C. Urquhart and J. Lamp (eds), *Proceedings of the 7th Australasian Conference of Information Systems* (ACIS96), Vol. 2, pp. 701–12. Hobart, Tasmania: University of Tasmania, Department of Computer Science.

Susman, G.I. and A. Majchrzak (2003), Research issues in knowledge management and virtual collaboration in new product development: an intro-ductory essay. Editorial, *Journal of Engineering and Technology Management*, **20**, 5.

Tan, B.C.Y., K.K. Wei, C.L. Sia and K.S. Raman (1999), A Partial Test of the Task-Medium Fit Proposition in a Group Support System Environ-ment, *ACM Transactions on Computer–Human Interaction*, **6**(1), 47–66.

Taylor, M. (1982), *Community, Anarchy and Liberty*, Cambridge: Cambridge University Press.

Thacker-Kumar, L. and J. Campbell (1999), Fostering inter-European cooperation: Technological collaboration among nations of the European Union. *The Social Science Journal*, **36**(1), 103–16.

Townsend, A.M., S. DeMarie and A.R. Hendrickson (1998), Virtual teams: technology and the workplace of the future. *Academy of Management Executive*, **35**(3), 17–29.

Trevino, L., R. Lengel and R. Daft (1987), Media Symbolism, Media Richness, and Media Choice in Organizations: A Symbolic Interactionist Perspective, *Communication Research*, **14**(5), 553–74.

Tuckman, B.W. (1965), Developmental sequence in small groups. *Psychological Bulletin*, **63**, 384–99.

Tuckman, B.W. and M.A.C. Jensen (1977), Stages of small group develop-ment. *Group and Organizational Studies*, **2**, 419–27.

Tuomi, T. (2000), Internet, innovation, and Open Source: actors in the network, *First Monday*, **6**(1), http://www.firstmonday.dk/issues/issue6_1/tuomi/

Van den Besselaar, L. Ekkel and R. Spears (2001), Literature review: impact of e-mail in organizations. Internal document Commorg project. http://www.commorg.net

Varghese, S. (2003), Living up to the Linux name. http://www.theage.com.au/ articles/2003/01/08/1041989994382.html

Vennix, J.A.M. (1999), Group model-building: tackling messy problems. *System Dynamics Review*, **15**(4), 379–401.

Walther, B. (1996), Computer-mediated communication: impersonal, inter-personal and hyperpersonal information, *Communication Research*, **23**(1).

Walther, J.B. and J.K. Burgoon (1992), Relational communication in computer-mediated interaction. *Human Communication Research*, **19**(1), 50–88.

Warkentin, M.E., L. Sayeed and R. Hightower (1997), Virtual teams versus face-to-face teams: an exploratory study of a web-based conference system. *Decision Sciences*, **28**(4), 975–996. Also in: K.E. Kendall (ed.) (1999), *Emerging Information Techniques*, Thousand Oaks, CA: Sage, Chapter 10, pp. 241–62.

Weber, K. and M. Hallerberg (2001), Explaining variation in institutional integration in the European Union: why firms may prefer European solutions. *Journal of European Public Policy*, **8**(2), 171–91.

Weick, K.E. (1979), *The Social Psychology of Organizing*. Reading, MA: Addison-Wesley.

Weisband, S. (2002), Maintaining awareness in distributed team collaboration: implications for leadership and performance. In: P. Hinds and S. Kiesler (eds), *Distributed Work*, Cambridge, MA: MIT Press, pp. 311–33.

Wellman, B. (1997), An electronic group is virtually a social network. In: S. Kiesler (ed.), *Culture of the Internet*. Mahwah, NJ: Lawrence Erlbaum.

Wendel de Joode, R. van (2002), Coordination and collaboration in open source communities, In: E.F. Ten Heuvelhoff (2002), *Proceedings of the First International Doctoral Consortium on Technology, Policy and Management*. http://www.tbm.tudelft.nl/webstaf/rubenw/paper%20doctoral%20consortium_Ruben.pdf

Wenger, E. (1998), Communties of practice: learning as a social system, *Systems Thinker*, http://www.co-i-l.com/coil/knowledge-garden/cop/lss.shtml.

Wenger, E. and W. Snyder (2000), Communities of practice: the organizational frontier, *Harvard Business Review*, **78**(1), 139–46.

Williams, F., E.R. Rice and E.M. Rogers (1979), *Research Methods and the New Media*, New York: The Free Press.

Yamauchi, Y., M. Yokozawa, T. Shinohara and T. Ishida (2000), Collaboration with Lean Media: How Open-Source Software Succeeds. ACM Conference on Computer Supported Cooperative Work (CSCW 2000), Philadelphia, PA, December.

Yin, R.K. (1994), *Case Study Research: Design and Methods*, Beverly Hills, CA: Sage, (Applied Social Research Methods Series; 5). 3rd upd. and exp. edn, 2003.

Yu, R. (1997), Information technology and media choice of CFO. http://members.optushome.com.au/raymondyu/pub/thesis/content.htm

Index

feedback (Debian) 152–3
firewalls 70, 71
'flagship tasks' (Advance) 53, 55, 69
flaming 3, 164, 166
    Debian 103, 112, 137, 142–3, 146,
        148, 149, 156
    Delta 28–9, 31, 32
Fleck, J. 168
Flysky 42, 45, 64, 67–8, 69–70, 82
forums (Advance) 54, 63, 73, 76, 83
FreeBSD 137
free-rider problem 40
Free Software Foundation 100–101,
    102
Free Software Guidelines, Debian
    (DFSG) 107, 122, 123, 124–5,
    126
Free Software Movement 100, 161
Frencité 47, 58, 59, 73, 77
frequently asked questions (FAQs) 141,
    158, 159, 165
freshmeat.net/ 97
Front Desk (Debian) 120, 125
Fulk, J. 2
Fumitoshi UKAI 120, 126

Gallivan, M.J. 5
Garbee, Bdale 111, 116–17, 131
Gattiker, U. 6
General Resolutions (Debian) 110,
    118, 144–6
Gersick, C.J.G. 29, 30
Gintis, H. 89
GLIBC 108
GNU project 85, 91, 100, 101
    General Public License 102, 107
    Privacy Guard 121, 123, 125–6, 129
goals 3, 29
Godfrey, M.W. 94
'going open' 93, 96–9, 106–9
governance model (Debian) 87, 88, 96,
    98–9, 105, 107–8, 111, 160, 167
Green, A.S. 162
ground rules (Advance) 58–9
Group for Aeronautical Research and
    Technology in Europe 41
group formation stages/processes 29,
    31
groupthink 6
guidelines 171

Debian Free Software 107, 122, 123,
    124–5, 126
Gunthorpe, Jason 115

Hall, K. 40
Hallerberg, M. 41
Halloween Documents 92, 96–7
Hammersley, M. 12
Handy, C.B. 6, 85
hard rules (Advance) 57
Hars, A. 100
Häusler, J. 40
Haythornthwaite, C. 171
Hemetsberger, A. 88
Hertel, G. 5, 86, 88, 99
Hertrich, R. 42
Hertzog, Raphaël 144
Hirokawa, R.Y. 17
Hollingshead, A.B. 25
Howells, J. 168
Huxham, C. 79–80

industrial consolidation 41, 42
information and communication
    technology (ICT) 18, 50–51
information richness theory 2
information sharing 50, 74, 159, 172
information technology 9, 50–52, 62,
    67
innovation process 43, 159
inspiration 152
institutional designs (Debian) 98–9
integration work package (Advance)
    50–51, 55–6
'integrator' (Advance) 72–3, 75, 76–7
internal documents 10, 57
internal reviews 53, 54
international management groups 44–5
Internet
    Advance 9, 14, 76, 82
    Debian 85–6, 88, 90–91, 97–8, 100,
        143, 159
    Delta 9
Internet relay chat (IRC) channels
    Debian 85, 97, 111, 115, 117, 130,
        142–5, 150–52, 164
    Delta 164
interviews 10, 13, 15, 16, 61–5
intra-team communication processes
    34–6